CHINESE GEOMANCY

CHINESE GEOMANCY

Dr J J M de Groot's seminal study of *Feng Shui*
together with detailed commentaries by the Western
world's leading authority on the subject.

DEREK WALTERS

ELEMENT BOOKS

First published 1989 by
Element Books Limited
Longmead, Shaftesbury, Dorset

Printed and bound in Great Britain by Billings Ltd,
Hylton Road, Worcester

Designed by David Porteous

Cover design by Max Fairbrother

British Library Cataloguing in Publication Data
Groot, J. J. M. de (Jan Jacob Maria de)
Chinese geomancy.
1. Feng-shui   I. Title
II. Walters, Derek *1936–*   III. Groot, J. J. M.
de (Jan Jacob Maria de). Religious system of China
133.3'33
ISBN 1–85230–058–2

Contents

Introduction

Feng Shui is a philosophy, of Chinese origin, which maintains that the configurations of the earth shape the affairs of the people that live among them.

Though many of its precepts are based on sound practical sense, others seem to be merely a matter of convention, while much of the canon of *Feng Shui* lies beyond any rational explanation.

In its present form, its documented history dates from the fifth century, but archaeological evidence described later in this book shows that the underlying tenets can be traced to the very roots of Chinese culture. Its impact on Chinese society is immeasurable; whether tangible, as in the planning of cities, the siting of temples, and the routing of railways, or intangible, in the way in which a belief in *Feng Shui* affects the organization of daily life.

The subject is becoming known in the west mainly through such well-publicized events as the construction of vast modern office buildings in accordance with *Feng Shui* principles, and, on a smaller scale, in the growing interest in the application of *Feng Shui* to the design and interior lay-out of homes and commercial premises. Indeed, scarcely a month passes without a mention in the western press that some new building project or development in the Far East has been helped, or hampered, by the exigencies of *Feng Shui*. 'Dead fish herald lucky launch for Hong Kong lingerie' (a headline which was no less ludicrous for having appeared in the London *Times* of July 15th, 1988) is a typical example.

Feng Shui is sometimes – and philologically quite correctly – called 'Chinese Geomancy', though somewhat confusingly, the term 'geomancy' is less accurately applied to an entirely different form of divination using patterns of dots marked on paper or sand, and generally familiar as 'Napoleon's Book of Fate'. As a translation of *Feng Shui* however, geomancy is accurate in that it proposes the concept of divination by portents revealed by the earth itself. This is exactly how the Chinese interpret it, for it is believed that hills and streams, through their position and orientation, are no less able to reveal future events than are the stars and planets as they progress through the heavens. *Feng Shui* is therefore the terrestial counterpart to astrology.

Feng Shui, however, is not merely a system of divination. For while it is impossible to stop the planets in their tracks, and so change the course of the destiny they portend, it is possible to alter the shape of the surrounding skyline, either by cutting down offending heights, increasing them with ornamental follies, or simply by moving to another location.

Fundamentally, there are two schools of *Feng Shui*, the 'Form' or Kuangsi School, and the 'Compass' or Fukien School; the Form School, originating in Kuangsi, South-West China, interpreting the auspices to be found in the relief of a landscape, and the Compass school, founded in Fukien, South-East China, giving attention to the precise orientation according to the magnetic compass.

To these two main systematic approaches to *Feng Shui* must be added a large corpus of miscellaneous oral traditions, for the main part little more than a heterogenous collection of unrelated superstitions and portents, seemingly expanded from time to time as the whims of various practitioners and the contingencies of expediency dictate. In this category would be included the bizarre example of the dead fish presaging good fortune for a Chinese lingerie business, but despite the fact that this would be popularly imagined to be an example of *Feng Shui*, auspices such as this, having nothing to do with the configurations of topography, the orientation of buildings, nor the use of space, cannot be considered geomantic, and thus belong more properly to the realms of omen-lore.

In China, *Feng Shui* has a much wider application than the evaluation of the auspiciousness of everyday affairs. It has an integral role in the religious and social system, particularly with respect to mourning customs and rites. More specifically, the siting and orientation of graves is decided according to the rules of *Feng Shui*, as this is held to assure the well-being of the dead in the after-life, and consequently, bring benefit to the descendants, both those living and those as yet unborn.

This identifies two main functions of *Feng Shui*: one pertaining to premises occupied by the living, known as *Yang* dwellings, and the other concerned with the abodes of the dead, known as *Yin* dwellings. When evaluating the *Feng Shui* of a *Yang* dwelling, the theories of both the Kuangsi and Fukien Schools of *Feng Shui* will be supplemented by adages and observations drawn from omen-lore, but when calculating the ideal situation for a grave site, it is more likely that only the most revered authentic texts will be followed. In brief, for a true appraisal of Chinese geomancy, the methods employed by *Feng Shui* practitioners advising on the siting of graves and tombs will be found to be a much more reliable source than the popular traditions which might be proposed by *Feng Shui* consultants, employed to advise on the design of homes and business premises.

Prefatory Notes

The Source of the Present Work

But as might be supposed, since the *Feng Shui* of *Yin* dwellings is much more of an academic discipline, its practice is generally confined to a few professionals specialising in this field, and it also follows that texts on *Feng Shui* for the *Yin* dwelling are scarce. In the eastern hemisphere, self-help books on the ever-popular subject of how the *Feng Shui* of shops and houses might be modified in order to increase prosperity and good fortune greatly outnumber the manuals on *Yin Feng Shui*. To an extent, this might be accounted for by the fact that with the shortage of land available for burial purposes in Hong Kong or Singapore, for example, interest in the subject has been considerably diminished.

A hundred years ago, however, the case was quite different. The Belgian Missionary, Dr J. J. M. de Groot, in his *The Religious System of China* compiled one of the earliest, and certainly one of the most detailed observations of the study of *Feng Shui* ever undertaken by a Western scholar. This work, long recognised as a valuable source of reference, is frequently quoted in later literature, but because of the book's scarcity, seldom at first-hand.

The Religious System of China, despite its all-embracing title, is in fact for the greater part devoted to a study of funeral rites and customs. In this respect, the work is undoubtedly one of the most exhaustive anthropological studies ever undertaken, and some idea of the size and scope of this work might be gleaned from a brief glance at this abridged table of contents:

Volume I: Book I: Disposal of the Dead
  Part (I) Funeral Rites (9 chapters)
  Part (II) Ideas of Resurrection (7 chapters)

Volume II: Book I (cont.)
  Part (III) The Grave (Chapters *I – IX*)

Volume III: Book I (cont.)
  Part (III) The Grave (Chapters *X – XV*)
  (The twelfth chapter being the one devoted to *Feng Shui*)

Volume IV: Book II: The Soul and Ancestral Worship
  Part (I) The Soul in Philosophy and Folk-Conception (16 chapters)

Volume V: Book II (cont.)
  Part (ii) Demonology (15 chapters)
  Part (iii) Sorcery (5 chapters)

Volume VI: Book (II) cont.)
  Part (iv) The War against Spectres (22 chapters)
  Part (v) The Priesthood of Animism (6 chapters)

It would be surprising if, as a Christian missionary, the author had adopted a tone that was other than scathing, not merely of *Feng Shui,* but of all the indigenous practices connected with the religious beliefs of the Chinese. An impartial observer might draw a parallel between, say, the respect accorded to the Eight Immortals (legendary figures whom later generations had decreed immortal) and the Christian veneration of various saints (such as George) of dubious historical authenticity. Naturally, it would be virtually incumbent on him to present *Feng Shui* as a curious heathen practice, perhaps only slightly less remarkable than human sacrifice. Yet despite this outward scepticism, instead of dismissing the subject as unworthy of attention, de Groot fortunately went to considerable lengths to record as much detail as he could assemble. If at times the writing is ponderous, it is always informative, and indeed, often amusing, since he frequently illustrates the highly complex subject with anecdotes, drawn from different periods of history. The later accounts, even allowing for the author's particular prejudices, throw light on some of the social conditions which prevailed during the closing decades of Imperial China.

Feng Shui Today

Many of de Groot's castigations of the *Feng Shui* professors remain as true today as they did a hundred years ago. Despite the meticulous mathematical calculations which are a feature of the Compass School of Fukien, or the trained aesthetic appraisal needed by the geomancers of the Form School of Kuangsi, there are undoubtedly a great number of geomancers who practise plain charlatanism, and while deficient in the genuine traditions and techniques of *Feng Shui,* impress gullible clients by supplementing their ignorance with an assembly of complex and expensive props. Certainly, the apparatus of the *Feng Shui* professor is extremely costly, whether it consists of the revered traditional antiques, worn with age and frequent use, treasured by a family firm established over several generations, or the high-precision surveyor's instruments used by the aspiring modern consultant. These, incidentally, are often surprisingly expensive, the price bearing little relation to the intrinsic value of the instrument. As an example, the cost of a small, brass-plate 'Heaven Pool' compass is virtually a hundred times more than an ordinary magnetic compass which might be bought in a toy shop, though the functions of the two instruments are identical. But the successful geomancer would no doubt consider such expense entirely justified, in view of the high fees which can be commanded. The scale of charges is frequently based on the area of the premises under inspection, and those for commercial enterprises can match, for example, the fees which might be charged by design consultants. Of course, whether the geomancers employ the benefits of advanced technology to further the accuracy of the geomantic measurements, or use them merely as theatrical window dressing, depends entirely on the integrity of the individual geomancer.

In this respect, and being fully aware of the widespread charlatanism which abounds in the world of mystics and psychics in both the eastern and western hemispheres, I have been extremely fortunate to have met and made friends with *Feng Shui* professionals who were experts in their fields, conversant not only with the oral traditions, but well-versed in the Compass and Form School philosophies.

I must acknowledge firstly the help given to me by Mr Richard Tsui, of the diviners fraternity at the temple of Wong Tai Sin in Kowloon, Hong Kong, who kindly invited me to join him on a professional visit to inspect a site, carefully examining me on my opinions, and pointing out for me all the relevant matters which had escaped my attention.

Mr Kim Sung, of Ipoh, Malaysia, was of valuable assistance in escorting and introducing me to members of the Chinese community who had employed professional *Feng Shui* consultants, enabling me to have first-hand experience of both sides of the *Feng Shui* process.

The help which I received while researching in Taiwan was inestimable. I can only record my debt of gratitude to Messrs Chen Jung Chin, Lee Chü Kao, and Lin Tseng Feng, but particularly to Mr Kan Cheng-Hung, of the Kuo Tai Lien Pang Co., Taiwan, not only for his valued comments, but also for his kind permission to reproduce his copyright designs of the modern examples of *Lo P' an.*

Preface

De Groot's text frequently refers to passages in *The Religious System of China* which do not appear in the *Feng Shui* chapter. When these are related to the subject of *Feng Shui*, or of interest for some other reason, they have either been integrated tacitly into the text, added as footnotes or supplementary paragraphs, or, in the case of lengthier passages, included as appendices.

In addition, further commentary has been made when it was considered to be useful to expand on the original text. The availability of later scholarship has made it possible to clarify points over which de Groot was in doubt, and to rectify the few statements which may have been erroneous or misleading.

The photographs which originally accompanied the *Feng Shui* chapter of *The Religious System of China* were not so historically important that their inferior quality warranted their being recopied. Instead, I chose to use the opportunity to replace de Groot's faded plates with new photographs which would perhaps illustrate the points made in the text with greater clarity, and with this in mind, I travelled to the Republic of China to assemble appropriate material. It must be stressed that the new photographs are not re-takes of the originals, but of entirely different subjects; indeed, they include photographs which are possibly of historic importance, since they actually portray professional geomancers at work on site.

Romanisation of Chinese Words

It is difficult to be consistent regarding the Romanisation of Chinese words and names. Until recently, the system with which most western readers would have been familiar is the one known as the Wade-Giles system, but as an international standard this has been superseded by the Mainland China's approval of the Pinyin system. As de Groot was writing even before the Wade-Giles system came into use, it might be thought logical to transfer all Chinese Romanisations into the Pinyin system, but unfortunately, this has the disadvantage of rendering otherwise familiar names into a form that is not always readily recognisable. (In the Pinyin system, for example, Peking appears as Beijing, Hong Kong as Xianggang, and Canton as Guangdong.) Because of this, in de Groot's text I have left all Romanisations as they appear; elsewhere I have preferred to use the Wade-Giles transliterations, as these are the forms used in existing Western writings on *Feng Shui* which readers may wish to consult.

Li Shan,
July, 1988

Plate 1.   A party of present-day Feng Shui professionals on a field trip

FUNG-SHUI

FUNG-SHUI

1. Introductory Notice

We have several times had to refer in this work to a custom of the Chinese of placing the graves in such a situation as they think will bring the occupants thereof happiness and comfort, and at the same time secure the prosperity of their ownselves, both in this world and in the world to come. In connection herewith we have mentioned certain theories, popularly styled Fung-shui [1] or Wind and Water. We will now consider this custom in detail, and try to answer the question: What is Fung-shui?

The answer is suggested by the word itself. Fung 風 means the wind, and shui 水 the water from the clouds which the wind distributes over the world; thus, the two words combined indicate the climate, regulated as it is in China, in the first instance, by the winds, which bring dry or rainy weather, according as they blow from the North in winter, or from the South or South-west in summer. Fung-shui consequently denotes the atmospherical influences, which bear absolute sway over the fate of man, as none of the principal requirements of life can be produced without favourable weather and rains. In a hyperbolical sense, however, Fung-shui means *a quasi-scientific system, supposed to teach men where and how to build graves, temples and dwellings, in order that the dead, the gods and the living may be located therein exclusively, or as far as possible, under the auspicious influences of Nature.*

This system is by no means a creation of modern times. It originated in ancient ages, from the then prevailing conceptions, easily traceable in the books, that the inhabitants of this world all live under the absolute sway of the influences of heaven and earth, and that every one desirous of insuring his own felicity

---

[1] 風水

must live in perfect harmony with those influences. If — such was the reasoning — human acts disagree with the almighty Tao[1] or »Path", the unalterable Course of Nature, conflicts will ensue, in which man, being the weaker party, must inevitably give way and become the sufferer. This reverential awe of the mysterious influences of Nature is the fundamental principle of an ancient religious system usually styled by foreigners Tao-ism. Popular opinion in China, as well as the expounders of the Fung-shui theories, are unanimous in considering Fung-shui to be almost as ancient as China itself.

It follows from the above that building graves, houses, villages and towns in accordance with the Fung-shui theories is looked upon by the nation as an absolute necessity, as indispensable because it is impossible to withdraw one's self from the sway of the powers of Nature. No wonder then that Fung-shui holds the nation in its grip and reigns supreme in the Empire, through its whole length and breadth. It derives prestige and sanctity from antiquity, which gave birth to the principal dogmas and conceptions upon which it is based. The leading ideas being the same as those of Chinese philosophy in general, it commands the sympathy of every one as a system which embraces whatever combined human wisdom and sagacity have, during a long series of ages, suggested as prac- tically useful. It is considered in China the greatest benefactor of mankind, though in reality, as we shall see anon, it is one of their greatest scourges.

The hiao, the pious reverence which every Chinaman accords to his deceased parents and nearest relations, naturally constrains him to place their graves in such a situation that they may find themselves under the same good influences of Nature which he would desire to concentrate upon his own dwelling. In this way he not only insures their rest and comfort, but also renders them well disposed towards himself, arousing in them feelings of gratitude which must necessarily bear fruits in the shape of various blessings to be showered down upon the offspring. Besides, the heavens are Nature's great source of life, for it is they who distribute warmth, light and rain; and life and vigour are naturally imparted to those souls which dwell in graves placed under the full influence of the heavens: then they are enabled to work vigorously as pro- tectors of their offspring, and to distribute among them liberally

---

[1] 道.

that vitality which they themselves borrow from the heavens, thus promoting the birth of sons, the most coveted of all blessings in China. This conviction is confirmed by the consideration that it is not only the living who profit hereby, but also the souls themselves, a numerous progeny of sons ensuring to the dead sacrifices and worship for many generations to come and, moreover, high rank in the world of spirits, where those surrounded by a large clan will be the bearers of power and influence, just as in this world.

Thus, as Dr. Edkins has judiciously remarked [1], » filial piety which, in obedience to the lessons of ancient and modern mentors of the nation, takes good care of the graves of parents and grand-parents, has a material reward; on the other hand, the want of it invites a retribution involving poverty, sickness, loss of descendants, degradation in the social scale". By Fung-shui the graves are turned into mighty instruments of blessing or punishment, the spirits of the ancestors, dwelling therein, being the divinities of the nation, with whose protection and goodwill all social happiness is intimately bound up. But souls do not dwell in graves only. They also reside in tablets exposed for worship on the domestic altars, and in temples specially erected to shelter them. There, too, precisely for the same reasons, they ought to be made to live under the favourable influences of Nature. Consequently, Fung-shui is firmly entwined with house-building and the construction of ancestral temples. It plays an important part even in the erection of altars and sanctuaries dedicated to gods and saints of whatever kind or description.

Thus being an essential part of the Chinese Religion in its broadest sense, Fung-shui demands a place among the subjects to be treated of in this work. In the present volume we must, however, confine ourselves to noting the part it plays in grave-building, and reserve for an other volume most of what we have to say on its influence in other branches of the Religious System.

Nature having never been studied in China in a scientific manner, Fung-shui is not based on any sound ideas acquired by an experimental and critical survey of the heavens and the earth. Starting with the hazy notion that Nature is a living organism, the breath of which pervades everything and produces the varied conditions of heaven and earth, and with some dogmatic formulae to be found in the ancient works and confided in as verdicts of the most profound human wisdom, Fung-shui is a mere chaos

---

1 The Chinese Recorder and Missionary Journal, vol. IV, p. 275.

of childish absurdities and refined mysticism, cemented together, by sophistic reasonings, into a system, which is in reality a ridiculous caricature of science. But it is highly instructive from an ethnographical point of view. The aberrations into which the human mind may sink when, untutored by practical observation, it gropes after a reasoned knowledge of Nature, are more clearly expounded by it than by any other phenomenon in the life and history of nations. It fully shows the dense cloud of ignorance which hovers over the whole Chinese people; it exhibits in all its nakedness the low condition of their mental culture, the fact that natural philosophy in that part of the globe is a huge mount of learning without a single trace of true knowledge in it.

Embracing, as it does, the whole extent of Chinese natural philosophy, we have not space here to lay the Fung-shui system before our readers in detail. Such a work would require many years of painstaking study, and yet produce but meagre results; in fact, the cobwebs of absurd, puerile speculation, built up by the system, are hardly worthy of serious study. All we can give our readers here is a very brief outline, a rough sketch, chiefly drawn up from information received by us at Amoy from professional experts and supported by evidence gleaned from the native literature.

Besides, to thoroughly understand what Fung-shui is, it is quite unnecessary to scrutinize and unravel the farrago of absurdities which constitute its details. Some knowledge of the main principles upon which it is founded will suffice, if those principles be understood in the sense in which the people and the professors of the art understand and practically apply them. Fung-shui is, in point of fact, a practical art. Its theories, as expounded in the books, are seldom taken notice of, even by the most distinguished professors among the initiated. Being a quasi science, it is practised as a quasi science, that is to say, as charlatanism. Every member of the learned class considers himself an adept in it, on the sole ground of his having made some study of the Classics and of his understanding the leading principles of the national philosophy. The people even consider themselves morally obliged to possess some expertness in Fung-shui matters, and the current adage runs: » No son of man should be ignorant of matters relating to grounds and mountains, nor of medical art" [1]. Indeed, how can a filial son properly observe

---

[1] 爲人子不可不知山、不可不知醫.

the tender care he owes to his parents, unless he be able to control the professors who assign to them their graves, thus holding in their hands the weal and woe of their souls, and the quack physicians, who may harm, nay kill, his parents by administering wrong medicines to them? It is no wonder then that even the least educated among the people show an astounding amount of knowledge of Fung-shui. Women and children may be heard chattering and talking about it with great authority; and when there is an altercation about imaginary injuries done to the Fung-shui of a grave or a house, old matrons are generally loudest in expressing a decided opinion.

Every Chinaman being more or less initiated in the secrets of the system, a practical intercourse with the people is sufficient for a foreigner to gain a tolerably clear idea of what it is and of the part it plays in the several branches of religious life. Our exposition will be found to deviate but little from that which was given, twenty-two years ago, by Dr. Eitel, in a treatise entitled: Feng-shui, or the Rudiments of Natural Science in China. Insignificant differences which our readers may observe between the conclusions of this distinguished Sinologist and our own, are to be ascribed chiefly to the circumstance that his investigations were made in Canton or Hongkong, and ours in the south-eastern part of the province of Fuhkien.

2. Fung-shui as regulated by High Grounds and Watercourses.

In China, the people are not bound, either by law or custom, to bury the dead in grave-yards. Every one has full liberty to inter his dead wherever he chooses, provided he possesses the ground, or holds it by some title acquired from the legal owner. The question whether a spot be suitable for a burial ground is decided by the Fung-shui theories.

Fung-shui, or *Hong-súi* according to the local pronunciation at Amoy and in the surrounding districts, is denoted by some other names. The principal amongst these is Khan-yü [1], pronounced *Kham-ú* in the Amoy language, and specially used in literary style. Khan means the canopy of heaven, and yü a cart or chariot, or, metaphorically, the earth which contains and bears the human

---

[1] 堪輿.

race; the term K h a n - y ü may accordingly be translated by: »the system which occupies itself with heaven and earth". A third name is T i l i (Am. *Tē lí*)[1], »the natural influences that pervade the earth". The experts or professors of the art, who make a livelihood from searching out favourable spots for burying the dead and building houses and temples, are called s i e n s h e n g[2] (Am. *sien sing*) or s h i[3] (Am. *su*), with the prefix F u n g - s h u i, K h a n - y ü or T i l i. S i e n s h e n g signifies »an earlier born man", and may be rendered by »an elder, a master, a professor"; s h i means »a leader, a master"; and both words are terms of respect denoting men of learning, including teachers, soothsayers, quack-doctors, etc. Foreigners are in the habit of calling the Fung-shui experts geomancers, which is correct, provided the earth be also considered as a depository of influences continuously poured down upon it by the celestial sphere. Besides the six terms above, the professors are often styled Y i n Y a n g s i e n s h e n g[4] (Am. *Im Ióng sien sing*) or Y i n Y a n g s h i[5] (Am. *Im Ióng su*), »Masters of the Yin and Yang", which two supreme powers of the Universe are respectively identified with Earth and Heaven, as our readers know.

The word Fung-shui indicates that the first thing to be attended to in selecting a spot for a grave, house, temple, village or town, is wind or air, f u n g. Noxious winds must as far as possible be prevented from striking a tomb or building at the back or flank. Hence, a mountain slope flanked by two ridges forking out from it, and affording a rather wide view in front, is deemed to be good ground for burying and building, especially if those ridges form a double fence, both visible from the grave or building. Their utility is not in the least reduced by distance. Even when so far off that they are hardly discernible, professors take them into account as elements of the highest importance, for theoretically they screen off the winds, and, in Fung-shui matters, theory and speculation are everything.

Pernicious and life-destroying influences of the winds or the air are denoted in the special Fung-shui nomenclature by the term f u n g s h a h[6] (Am. *hong soah*), »noxious effects of the winds". There exist various means to ward them off. Suppose it is feared they will burst forth from some break in the mountains, it is then

___

1 地理.   2 先生.   3 師.
4 陰陽先生.   5 陰陽師.   6 風煞.

deemed necessary to build the grave in such a way that this opening cannot be seen from the spot where the corpse must lie, or so that it is hidden from view by some mountain boulder, house or other object. In many cases, the dangerous gap is artificially rendered invisible by means of stones piled up at a correct distance from the grave, in accordance with the indications given by Fung-shui professors. Such so-called Fung-shui tʻah[1] or »Fung-shui pagodas" are very numerous in the mountainous provinces of the South. As a rule they are so far from the spot they are supposed to protect, that in reality they do not screen it from the wind at all, thus proving the Fung-shui wisdom in evading dangers to be on a level with that of the ostrich.

Gaps or breaks in the mountains being harmless to a grave if they are invisible from the place where the corpse lies, it follows that the danger may be avoided by burying the corpse sufficiently deep. But this expedient is not very often resorted to, as, in most cases, it would cause the dead to lose the protecting ridges and brows of the mountains from view and thus annihilate their useful effects. For, as Fung-shui combines logic with wisdom, it cannot but conclude that, whereas unseen dangers are no dangers, unseen protection is no protection.

As a matter of course, a grave surrounded by mountains without either gaps or deficiencies is hardly obtainable. Nor is it easy to find a spot from which the person, who is buried there, can see a surrounding range of hills. These difficulties are ingeniously overcome by building around the tomb, at the back and the sides, a well finished artificial ridge. This is a low embankment of earth (see Plate 2, p.211) which at the same time serves to prevent the rain water, flowing down from the surrounding high ground, from washing away the tumulus. Our readers know the Chinese coffins are usually high, bulky, and, among the well-to-do, considerably broader at the head than at the foot. When such a coffin is buried in the proper way, viz. with the head up against the slope, and in a shallow pit, lest the dead should lose the brow of the mountains out of sight, the tumulus thrown up over it naturally obtains an ellipsoidal shape, the broad side of which, like that of the coffin, lies highest. This tumulus again in its turn determines the shape of the embankment. The latter embracing the three larger sides, its form becomes necessarily that of a horse-shoe, or, oftener still, of

---

[1] 風水塔.

an Ω, the ends being bent outward, in order that the noxious influences of the winds, on striking against the embankment, may glide
along it and be forced to roll away from the grave to the right and
left. Many of these embankments are built of masonry, or of puddled
clay mixed with lime, and plastered over with white mortar, forming
low walls, one or two feet in height. Some few are of solid granite.
Several graves have a double fence, the one of solid masonry or
granite, and then a much broader one of earth, the latter being
always on the outside of the first. Both are called at Amoy *bōng moa*[1],
which may be rendered: »the piazza or side gallery of the grave", the
term being an allusion to the verandahs on the right and left of mansions
and temples.

A *bōng moa* never extends along the front. For, according to
theory, there is no necessity whatever to ward off any fung shah
from that side, as graves and buildings of every kind, though they
may in fact face any point of the compass, are supposed to be
turned towards the mild and blessed south, the cradle of warmth,
light, life and productive summer rains. There are, furthermore,
stringent reasons forbidding the presence of sight-obstructing objects
in front of graves, which we shall pass in review on pp. 945 *seq*.

No attempt to attract the good influences of the winds unto
graves, houses or temples is, as far as we know, ever made.
Perhaps no expedients to effect this have been invented, as
they are totally superfluous, because of the prevailing notion that
good and beneficial influences naturally obtain their full scope
wherever counteracting or neutralizing evil influences are sufficiently
warded off.

The attempts of the Chinese to control the winds which strike
the graves of the dead, the temples of the gods and the habitations
of living men, are by no means simply intended as a protection
of those beings from the inclemencies of the climate and its immediate consequences, such as sickness and indisposition of all kinds.
The scope of the Fung-shui system extends much farther. The climate being ruled by the winds, the winds become the cause of
all things, good or evil, which Nature showers down upon this
earth. Hence, the grand art of controlling their influences is the
art of regulating the fortunes and happiness of mankind. Winds
blowing from the North and North East, as they generally do in

---

1 墓厝 or 墓廊.

China from October till February or March, freeze up the northern provinces, and in the South scarcely send down a single drop of rain, thus destroying the vegetable kingdom and putting a stop to agricultural pursuits. The southern or south-western winds which prevail during the other half of the year, on the contrary, produce warmth and growth, blessing the Empire with copious rains and abundant crops. But, should these monsoons deviate from their regular course, or become disturbed, calamities are sure to ensue. Dry winds in summer entail poor crops and dearth, dooming the people to starvation. When typhoons rage, whole provinces in the South are deluged by rains, which cause the streams and rivers to overflow and destroy the crops in innumerable fields. No wonder, therefore, that the Chinese people are deeply conscious of their dependence on the winds, and feel the greatest reverence and sympathy for a system which promises everybody protection against their baneful influences, ever holding up before their eyes the irrefutable device: » When the winds (fung) blow harmoniously and the rains (shui) come down regularly, the Realm shall flourish and the people live in peace and comfort" [1]. This tenet occurs in a very old book, viz. the Historical Records, in the following words: » If the course (Tao) of the Universe » be such that cold and heat do not come in due season, diseases » will prevail; and if it be such that winds and rains do not come » at the proper time, there will be famine" [2].

Winds in the very first instance commanding the influences of Nature upon earth, Fung-shui professors are perfectly correct in considering them as the first and principal element of their system. They do not, however, go so far as to attribute constant beneficial influences to certain points of the compass, and pernicious influences to others. Even the cold and rigorous blasts from the North may be salutary, the mildest southern zephyrs extremely dangerous, according as they have been in contact with certain celestial or terrestrial influences. Every geomancer entertains private views on this subject, which it is scarcely possible, and certainly quite useless, to endeavour to unravel.

Water courses

Nor do geomancers devote less of their attention to the chief results of the favourable operation of the winds, viz. to rains and water, indicated by the second syllable of the word Fung-shui. Water

---

[1] 風調雨順國泰民安.

[2] 天地之道寒暑不時則疾、風雨不節則饑. *Shi ki*, ch. 24, l. 17.

oeing an element indispensable to life, and especially necessary for an agricultural people like the Chinese, neither living men in their dwellings, nor disembodied souls in their graves and temples, nor divinities in their sanctuaries, can ever be at ease or enjoy prosperity, unless its blessed influences be concentrated upon those spots. These influences are called s h u i s h e n [1] (Am. *tsúi sín*): »aquatic spiritual agencies".

Rivers and rivulets, brooks and gullets, lakes, tanks, ponds and seas, being the bearers of the waters showered down from the heavens, are all bearers of these s h u i s h e n. Even when. perfectly dry, they are still regarded as such, Fung-shui philosophy contenting itself with theories. The sources of the water-courses which cross inhabited glens and valleys, and the mountains and mountain ranges in which they take their rise, are specially held to control human destiny, because they send down the precious fluid on which agriculture depends. Their position is carefully considered whenever a site for a grave, house or temple has to be selected.

Neither a wet nor a dry watercourse is allowed to run straight onwards to a grave, a human dwelling or a sanctuary. Otherwise, this building would become an obstacle in the way of the descending aquatic influences, nay, a rude declaration on the part of the living that they do not desire to have anything to do with these influences. Without a doubt the insulted element would avenge itself by accumulating evil on the spot, or, in any case, by flowing away to the right and left without benefiting the place in the least. A good Fung-shui may be obtained when the water flows down from the right or left, either in front of the spot in question or at the back of it, and then, passing along the front, finds its outlet in a lateral direction. It is all-important, however, that the water, in flowing away, should be invisible from the place where the corpse lies, or from the tabernacle in which the soul or the god is seated, as, otherwise, the soul or god would be able to see the beneficial aquatic influences flowing away and thus derive no advantage from them.

As no water may flow down straight in front, it follows that it is always dangerous if the prospect in front is screened by a mountain slope which may send down water in that direction. Besides, such a slope may obstruct in their free natural course the aquatic influences coming down from the opposite side and consequently, in the case of a grave, obstruct the free expansion

---

[1] 水神.

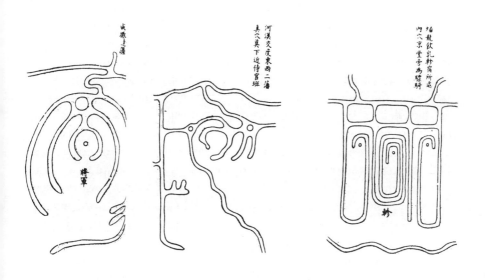

Water Patterns

Illustrations showing the location of the focal points of Dragon's Breath – the ideal site, shown in these diagrams as a small circle – within various confluences.

From *Shui Lung Ching*, The Water Dragon Classic, Book 2. (*Imperial Encyclopaedia*, Section XVII, part 672.)

and development of the prosperity of the family to whom it belongs, not only rendering them poor and miserable, but even causing them to die out. Hence it is an established principle of geomancy that »Fung-shui which is cramped up too much" — *hong-súi khah pik*[1], as the Amoy Chinese say —, is bad Fung-shui. This does not mean that mountains in front are always harmful. They may even exercise a salutary influence, if they are located at a sufficient distance or answer to certain conditions; and it is the professors who decide this by their wise calculations.

Bad effects may likewise be exercised upon a grave by walls, houses or boulders obstructing the prospect in front. For this reason, the walls surrounding the gardens and grounds of European houses in some of the Treaty Ports have not seldom a spot of open-worked masonry, or a few small holes, made therein at the request of the owner of some grave behind, for the purpose of preserving both his prosperity and posterity from destruction. For the same reason, in the province of Fuhkien trees or shrubs are hardly ever allowed to grow in front of a grave. Every thing that happens to strike root there is ruthlessly destroyed, and geomancers, with the remarkable acuteness and wit which distinguish them, are constantly pointing out herbs and shrubs which are injurious. Trees growing at the back or the sides of a grave are, however, generally considered as beneficial, they having the same effect as a *bōng moa*. Yet, as grounds deemed suitable for burying are usually studded with graves, such trees are rare, owing to the fact that they might exert bad influences upon the graves of others. As a consequence, grave grounds in the mountainous South are generally dreary wastes, sparsely covered with grass and weeds and looking but little adapted to serve the dead as an agreeable resting place, especially in summer, when they are burnt and scorched by the tropical heat. But such considerations do not seem to occur to the minds of the Chinese when the question is asked: where shall we bury our dead.

This fact is also to be ascribed to the doctrine that Fung-shui may not be cramped in front of a grave, viz. that stone images of men and animals have seldom, if ever, been erected there in recent times. It proves that objects nowadays considered harmful to a grave, were not so regarded in former times, and it illustrates the powerful hold Fung-shui has upon the nation, since the highest classes have now given up

----

[1] 風水復逼.

in obedience thereto a time-hallowed privilege which, being conferred by the Sons of Heaven, shed the greatest lustre and distinction
on the memory of their dead.

Just as the æolian influences, so those of the watery element can
be artificially controlled. Should no natural water-course run past
a grave, house or temple, this deficiency is often remedied by
constructing a tank in front of it, to receive the water which flows
down from all sides when it rains; this tank becomes a receptacle for
aquatic influences, whence they extend themselves beneficially over the
immediate surroundings. In the case of large mansions, palaces and
temples, the tank is situated in the centre of the court-yard which was
anciently painted partly or entirely red, and hence such tanks are
generally styled t a n c h ʿi [1], »vermilion court-yards". As a rule, they
are curved on one side; the opposite straight side runs parallel with
the front line of the grave or building, and the curved side is turned
away therefrom. Great temples and palaces have the largest and
deepest, which are generally paved at the bottom, and lined on all
sides with square blocks of granite, marble or dolomite. Those in
front of graves are small, hardly ever deeper than one or two feet,
and of plastered masonry, or of earth mixed with lime; in some few cases
they are square, sometimes circular.

The Fung-shui doctrines prescribe that the greatest attention
should be bestowed upon the opening through which the water
leaves such a tank, for, as our readers will easily understand, it
commands entirely the influences of the s h u i s h e n accumulated in
this latter. It may neither be too small, nor too large, or, in other
words, the water must not flow away either too slowly or too
quickly; the situation of the opening is also calculated with the
utmost nicety and must, at all events, be invisible from the site
where the corpse lies or, in the case of a temple, from the tabernacle occupied by the ancestral tablets or the images of the gods. It
makes no difference if such tanks stand dry. They do not lose
their efficacy thereby, any more than the brooks or gullets do.
Those in front of graves are often made without any intention
of their being filled with water, the grave being thereby kept drier
and less exposed to the attacks of termites.

Grave tanks and grave brooks certainly do not date from recent

---

[1] 丹墀.

times. They are mentioned in Chinese literature in connection with the mausolea of Hoh Lü and his daughter, who lived in the fifth century before Christ, and also in certain accounts of the burial of Shi Hwang and the imperial mausolea of the Han dynasty. It may be surmised that the custom of this family to place each of their sepulchres in an excavated plot of ground, is to be ascribed to a desire that water might flow towards it from many sides and be collected in a tank or brook dug near its immediate vicinity. Ponds and moats were also constructed near the grave of the magnate Chang Poh-nga, who lived under the Han dynasty. It is a question whether their origin may not even be traced up to those misty ages when, as a consequence of the custom of burying the head in the houses in which they had dwelled during their lifetime, burial grounds were actual villages occupied by the dead and, in imitation of real villages, were protected by walls and, on the chief or front side, by running water, — uncivilized man generally having chosen the banks of rivers for a dwelling place.

We may note here by the way that the curious custom of coffining the dead at flood tide or while some pails of sea water, taken at high tide, are standing in the same apartment (see note 1, p.147), likewise belongs to those practices which purport the concentrating of aquatic influences in the graves. Nobody doubts but this water, drawn at *high* tide, will *fully* work upon the corpse while it is being encoffined, and its influences are thus, so to say, enclosed in the coffin and afterwards deposited in the tomb.

Doubtlessly it is with the same object of imbuing corpses with aquatic influences, that the Chinese of Amoy place them, while they are being conveyed to their last abode, under a cover embroidered with clouds and dragons, dragons having been in China, since very ancient times, the emblems of fertilizing rains (see note 2, p.147). It is considered a very auspicious omen when rain falls whilst a grave pit is being filled up? indeed, Nature itself then showers down its most beneficial influences, which cannot but yield precious fruits of felicity to the offspring of the deceased man.

The foregoing pages sufficiently prove that mountains and hills, or, more correctly speaking, the configurations of the earth, are an all-important element in the Fung-shui system. Indeed, controlling, as they do, the influences of the winds, they regulate the principal benefits of Nature, especially rain and water; besides it is from the mountains that water-courses take their rise and carry the beneficial influences of the principal element of Nature far away on all sides, through valleys and districts, even through entire provinces, kingdoms and empires.

The configurations of the ground are important also in another respect. They are bearers, depositories of the influences of the heavens, and as such can work most beneficiently upon the fate of man.

Our readers know already what these influences are, viz. the so-called t'ien khi[1] or »Celestial Breath", the energy of the Yang or highest power of the Universe, specially identified (see note 3, p.147) with Heaven, as it embraces Light and Warmth. It shares the supreme sway in Nature with the »Terrestrial Breath" ti khi[2], or the energy of the principle Yin which represents Darkness and Cold and is identified with Earth. By the co-operation of these two principles life is created; in other words Yang and Yin alternately bearing sway in Nature and blending their influences together, are the causes of constant growth and decay, of life and death, of the annual rotation of production and destruction. Indeed, the *Li ki* (ch. 38, l. 11) explicitly states: »Everything which exists is engendered after Heaven and Earth »have joined together"[3], and (ch. 20, l. 37) »when in the first »month of the vernal season the Celestial Breath descends and »the Terrestrial Breath ascends, Heaven and Earth unite har- »moniously and the vegetable kingdom is disclosed and set in »motion"[4]. The *Yih king* also declares that: »When Heaven and »Earth exert their influences, all things are transformed and vivi- »fied"[5]. Lü Puh-wei in the third century before our era pronounced the same opinion: »The first causes of production", he wrote, »are Heaven and Earth"[6]. And Chu Hi, the authoritative philosopher

---

[1] 天氣.

[2] 地氣.

[3] 天地合而後萬物與焉. Sect. 郊特牲, III.

[4] 孟春之月天氣下降、地氣上騰、天地和同、草木萌動. Sect. 月令, I.

[5] 天地感而萬物化生. Ch. 10, or sect. 象下傳.

[6] 始生之者天地. *Lü-shi ch'un ts'iu*, chapter I, § 本生.

who lived in the twelfth century, formally subscribed to these ancient doctrines, declaring that » the Two Breaths by uniting and exciting each other produce and reproduce everything" [1].

As a matter of course, in every part of the ground, in every chain of mountains, in every bluff or rock, Nature has laid down a certain quantity of Yin or Terrestrial Breath. But, according to the above doctrines, it cannot exert any life-producing influences unless it be at the same time imbued with some Yang or Celestial Breath. Geomancers alone are capable of deciding whether this latter be represented in an adequate proportion, and whether the ground has any value for building purposes and grave making. They derive their conclusions from the outlines and forms of the surroundings. Starting from the fact that the celestial sphere has, since ancient times, been divided into four quarters, viz. the Azure Dragon, the Red Bird, the White Tiger and the Black Tortoise, identified respectively with the East, the South, the West and the North, their wise predecessors have taught, during a long series of ages, that no part of the soil can be fully impregnated with the beneficial influences of Heaven unless those four quarters operate upon it conjointly, that is to say, unless it be surrounded by mountains, bluffs, boulders or buildings which can be identified with those symbolic animals. Graves and edifices being, in theory, turned to the South, they must have a Tiger on the right or theoretical western side, a Dragon on the left, a Tortoise at the back, and a Bird in front. All-important is the presence of a Tiger and a Dragon. For, these animals represent all that is expressed by the word Fung-shui, viz. both æolian and aquatic influences, Confucius being reputed to have said that » the winds follow the tiger" [2], and the Dragon having, since times immemorable, in Chinese cosmological mythology played the part of chief spirit of water and rain.

So, for instance, Amoy is unanimously declared by all the wise men of the town to be indebted for its prosperity to two knolls flanking the inner harbour, and vulgarly styled *Hó-t͘aó soan* [3] or » Tiger-head Hill" and *Líng-t͘aó soan* [4] or » Dragon-head Hill".

---

[1] 二氣交感化生萬物. » Illustrated Dissertation on the Great Ultimate Principle" 太極圖說, quoted in the Khanghi Dictionary, *in verbo* 氣.

[2] 風從虎. See the *Yih king*, chapt. 16, or sect. 文言傳.

[3] 虎頭山.   [4] 龍頭山.

This latter, which is situated on the opposite shore, on the islet of Kulangsu, is crowned with huge boulders poised in a fantastic manner, upon which professors have had several blocks of granite arranged for the purpose of helping the imagination to discover the outlines of a dragon on the spot. The costs of these improvements were borne by some well-to-do citizens, anxious to promote their own prosperity and that of their fellow townsmen. Of the city of Canton » the favourable situation lies herein, that it is placed in » the very angle formed by two chains of hills running in gentle » curves towards the Bogue, where they almost meet, forming a » complete horse shoe. The chain of hills known as the White Clouds » represent the Dragon, whilst the undulating ground on the other » side of the river forms the White Tiger. The most favourable sites » in Canton are therefore on the ground near the North gates, » whence the Tiger and the Dragon run off to the right and left" [1].

Similarly, Peking is protected on the North-west by the Kin-shan [2] or Golden Hills, which represent the Tiger and ensure its prosperity, together with that of the whole Empire and the reigning dynasty. These hills contain the sources of a felicitous water-course called Yuh-ho [3] or » Jade river", which enters Peking on the North-west and flows through the grounds at the back of the Imperial Palace, then accumulates its beneficial influences in three large reservoirs or lakes dug on the west side, and finally flows past the entire front of the inner Palace, where it bears the name of The Golden Water. Its course therefore perfectly accords with the principles which are valid for grave brooks and grave tanks (comp. page 944).

In thus making use of the configurations which render the relative position and extent of the influences of the four Celestial Animals favourable or unfavourable, there is room for countless combinations. Every mountain, rock, bluff, house or tower may form a good Animal, and at one spot serve for a Tiger and at the same time as a Dragon, Bird or Tortoise for another spot, the fancy and imaginative ingenuity of geomancers being allowed free scope in all cases. With endless manipulations of their compass, consisting of a small magnetic needle around which all the elements that enter in their calculations are inscribed in concentric circles, these men deliberately point out whether the Tiger

---

1 Eitel, Feng-shui, page 23.

2 金山, more generally called Wan-sheu shan 萬壽山.

3 玉河.

and Dragon unite harmoniously, or, as they call it, »lie in a bow-shaped line in mutual embrace"[1], or whether their forms are spoiled or done away with by other conjunctions, finally deciding with an air of profound wisdom and a flood of technical terms which overawe their clients, whether the site to be fixed upon for burial or building purposes forms »a perfect complex", ch‘ing küh[2]. If so, the Fung-shui is good, provided it answers to certain other requirements which we must still pass in review. Every son of man who buries an ancestor in such a spot, or builds his house there, shall be rich, prosperous and blessed with a numerous offspring that shall not die out unto the last day. They shall rise high in the social scale and gain glorious positions in the civil and military service, for the Dragon symbolizes the Emperor and his beneficial civil government, and the Tiger martial power and intrepidity. Sad to say, however, the value of such predictions is generally somewhat detracted from by the diversity of opinions prevailing among geomancers, each of whom is imbued with professional jealousy and cherishes the rather arrogant conviction that his own wisdom is always necessary for the correction of the opinions pronounced by his colleagues.

Dragons and Tigers are by no means equally important in the Fung-shui system. Professors are wont to say: »Any spot is felicitous that has a Dragon and no Tiger; but a spot is not of a certainty unfelicitous if it has only a Tiger and no Dragon"[3]. This pre-eminence of the Dragon is due in the first place to its heading the list of the four Celestial Animals and to its being the emblem of spring, which is the first of the seasons, and further, to its identification with Water, the all-important element without which all Fung-shui is null and void. Practically, Fung-shui professors are accustomed to speak of a Dragon when referring in reality to a Dragon and Tiger; in short, the word Dragon comprised the high grounds in general, and the water-streams which have their sources therein or wind their way through them. Hence it is that books on Fung-shui commonly commence with a bulky set of dissertations, comprised under the heading: »Rules concerning the Dragon"[4], in reality dealing with the doctrines about the

---

1 龍虎二山弓抱.
2 成局.
3 有龍無虎亦爲吉、有虎無龍未是凶.
4 龍法.

situation and contours of mountains and hills and the direction of
water-courses. In these dissertations every imaginable combination
of hills and peaks is amply discussed and illustrated by coarse woodcuts. Such combinations generally are indicated by special fancy
names, mostly derived from objects they bear a likeness to. These
names too are believed to exercise a mighty influence upon the
destiny of those who live under the Fung-shui of such configurations,
all of them being calculated to call up before the mind ideas
associated with either felicity or mishap.

The doctrine that the configuration of the ground is a sure index
to the presence of celestial influence, is better understood when
we bear in mind that objects, such as soul tablets and images,
which call up before the mind spirits or so-called s h e n, are generally believed by the Chinese to be inhabited by such spirits, and
are consequently made for the dead and the gods in order that the
latter may radiate their beneficial influences therefrom over mankind.
Such s h e n being composed of Y a n g or Celestial Breath, the Chinese
have every reason to believe that the s h e n of the four Animals or
quarters of the sphere will settle in objects such as hills, mountains or
other configurations, which by their shape and situation call them up
before the mind.

The active operation produced in the earth by the Celestial and
Terrestrial Breath properly intermixing, is denoted by the term
s h a n l i n g [1], »effective operation of high grounds"; we might call
it the living and active animus of a configuration. Each configuration
is a complex of mere lifeless forms when the two Breaths, confined
in it, are latent and inactive. Its Fung-shui in such cases is, as
geomancers express it, dead.

Like a current of vital power, the s h a n l i n g flows in every
direction through favourable sites, especially through ledges and
edges of hills which geomancers cleverly identify with the limbs of
Dragons, Tigers, Tortoises and Birds. Thanks to the wisdom and
experience of these men, it is possible to learn which limbs are
thoroughly imbued with s h a n l i n g and accordingly the most pre-
ferable for making graves or building houses on. Sloping ledges
are generally considered to be favourable spots in this respect:
indeed, even a child can understand that s h a n l i n g with a descending motion must develop great vigour and energy, particularly
at the end of its downward course. Moreover, it accumulates wher-

---

[1] 山靈.

ever in its downward course it meets with some eminence sufficient to absorb and collect it, or to impede its course and prevent
its flowing away. Such sites are called l i n g m e h [1] or »(s h a n-) l i n g
pulses", where the animus lives and throbs as does the vital power
in the pulses of man. The ledges in question geomancers denote
by the term l i n g t s i h [2]: »back-bones of the (s h a n-) l i n g".

A body imbued with vitality is generally a breathing body. Geomancers, inverting this theorem, teach that formations of the ground
possess no s h a n l i n g unless they contain what is styled l i n g
k h i [3], »(s h a n-) l i n g breath". Again it is the configuration which
indicates the presence of the latter. It is found exclusively in undulating grounds; hollow, flat or straight-lined formations do not respire,
and are therefore of little or no use for burying or building purposes. In making graves, attention should also be paid to the fact
that hard, rocky soil is breathless; compact, reddish loam on the
contrary is full of breath and life and consequently prevents a quick
decay of the coffin and the corpse, rendering the bones hard,
white, and suitable for binding the soul for a long time to the
grave. Besides, white ants and other voracious insects do not harbour
in such loamy soil, which fact geomancers ascribe to the influence
of the breath. The breath can be active or latent, accumulated
or expanded, powerful or weak, floating on the surface or hidden
underneath, unalloyed or mixed with other substances, and the
astuteness of the professors must detect all these qualities. By various circumstances, which they alone know how to trace, the breath
may also partly or entirely vanish, which is a proof that the operation of the s h a n l i n g has been put a stop to and the Fung-shui
of the spot is dying, or dead.

Even though a configuration be such as to leave no doubt as
to the presence of an abundant quantity of Y a n g and Y i n, it is
not yet certain that these two Breaths produce s h a n l i n g and
would thus co-operate beneficially on the grave. They may be inert
and exercise no influence upon each other; however, this state
of latency cannot last long. In the end they must awake from their
torpor, as is the case in spring, when they fill the Universe with
vital energy and re-vivify the vegetable kingdom. Not seldom, at
burials, geomancers deem it necessary to arouse the two Breaths
from their lethargy, in order that the family may forthwith begin
to reap profit from the grave. It is plain enough to our readers that the

[1] 靈脉.   [2] 靈脊.   [3] 靈氣.

object of the strange demeanour of the professor while standing on the *t'ien-tik hng* or »the spot in which the beneficial celestial influence or breath is concentrated", is to actuate it there; subsequently, when he rushes down in the direction of the grave, he rouses it also in the »pulse" which connects the *t'ien-tik hng* with the latter, thus bringing forth an energetic downward current and accumulating a large store of s h a n l i n g over and around the corpse.

Since time immemorial, the four heavenly quadrants or Animals have each been subdivided into seven constellations, called s i u [1]. These twenty-eight groups, about which we shall have more to say on pp. 971 *sqq.*, are irregularly distributed over the sphere as it is visible in China. Hills and mountain-ranges being the embodiment of the influences of the Four Animals, their several parts are deemed to stand each under the influence of a s i u. In this manner, geomancy is ingeniously combined with astrology and the field of speculation greatly widened. The s i u being important elements in astrological science, they contribute much to rendering Fung-shui a black art so mysterious that it can only be practised with success by the proficients who derive a livelihood from it.

Geomancers in their theories also give a place to other groups of stars which they believe to correspond with certain parts of the Earth and to determine the fate thereof. It is, in fact, constantly on their lips as an axiom of their system, that » the stars of the Heavens above, and the configurations of this Earth beneath correspond with each other" [2]. This dogma directly arises from the great fundamental principle of both ancient and modern astrology, viz. that every human affair has a star or asterism controlling it. Practically, however, the combination of astrology with geomancy plays a very inferior part; so we need not dive into its vagaries.

Hills and mountains are also very powerful in their influence upon the destiny of man if their outlines are such as to allow the imagination to see in them felicitous or infelicitous omens. For instance, if a hill bears on its top a boulder of large dimensions, weighing heavily upon it, the fortunes of the people around may be crushed down and poverty and misfortune for ever prevail among them. If people, however, consider they recognize in its outlines some animal portending good luck or misfortune, those who dwell under the shade of its Fung-shui will enjoy that luck or suffer

---

[1] 宿.　　　　　[2] 天星地形上下相應.

from the misfortune. Thus the shape of a snake is calculated to make them rich, provided there be near its head a rock or stone which calls up before their minds the idea of its vomiting forth a pearl. If one dwells on a mountain on the top of which there are three small peaks side by side in a row, his sons and grandsons will gain literary laurels by study and scholarship and be promoted to high offices; indeed, students are accustomed to have upon their writing table an instrument of stone or wood, cut in the shape of such peaks, on which they rest the point of their writing brush to prevent the ink from blotting the table. As such association of ideas with the contours of mountains may be spun out endlessly, the field for imaginative ingenuity is again widened, and both experts and adepts of the geomantic art take good care to explore that field in every sense and direction. Some books of geomancy give long lists of objects which have disastrous or beneficial effects when detected in the outlines of hills and mountains.

The Five Elements

It may be supposed that in a system which purports to command the influences of Nature, a place of importance is also allotted to the elements out of which Nature is built up and which play a chief part in its organisation, viz. water, fire, wood, metal, and earth. No configuration is perfect unless these five elements work in it harmoniously.

In the *Shu king* the five elements form the first topic in a treatise entitled: »The Great Plan" [1], a curious scheme of government, intended as a guide to sovereigns in the discharge of their duties towards themselves and their subjects. This fact proves that already at the dawn of history the conviction prevailed that the happiness of the nation, and even the life of the people, entirely depend upon those elements and that mankind cannot exist without their beneficial influence. Being produced, like everything else in the Universe, by the Yang and Yin, they are the natural agents of this dual Breath, operating favourably or unfavourably upon the living and the dead. Is it not evident, for instance, that wherever fire or heat, which is an emanation from the Yang, predominates, disaster will ensue, unless it be properly counter-balanced by another element, such as water, which is produced by Yin, the opposite breath? Is it not evident also that, if the element earth is overruled

---

[1] 洪範.

by water, or suffers from want of water, there is no fecundation, no production of food and raiment? Crops are devastated in this case, nay, the entire element wood may be destroyed and mankind thus be decimated by famine. Woe therefore to those who disturb the harmony of the elements! It shall fare with him as with the father of the illustrious founder of the Hia dynasty, of whom the Great Plan states: »Formerly, Kwan, in damming up » the inundating waters, disarranged the five elements. The Em-» peror (of Heaven), aroused to anger, did not give him the nine » divisions of the Great Plan, in consequence of which the sundry » relations of society were disturbed and he himself was kept im-» prisoned till his death" [1].

No wonder then that the Chinese pay great attention to their geomancers who, selecting sites for every house and grave, restrain them from stupid acts à la Kwan, thus preserving them from the wrath of Heaven both in life and death. How carefully do these men inspect every rock and every stone, every inch of the surface of the ground, to detect the element which predominates in it! A stony ground, barren rocks, and boulders not cemented together by loam or clay in considerable quantities, embody the element fire, as the capricious outlines remind us of notched flames, and the dryness of the stones and rocks is a proof of plutonic propensities. A coffin, imbedded in such ground, would quickly moulder and not long afford a shelter to the corpse and the manes. Likewise, any mountain, bluff or knoll rising up like a peak or rather sharp pointed ∧ ∧ ∧, represents the element fire. If the top be gently rounded ⌒, metal predominates in it. If it rises up steep, bold and straight, running out into a rounded or flat point ⋂, it is declared to represent the element wood, probably because its shape calls to mind the trunk of a tree. Should the top form a plateau composed of soft clay or earth ⌐⌐\, the element earth predominates in that mount; but if the plateau has an irregular surface, its contours reminding us of a lake or river ⌒ ⌒, it passes for an embodiment of the watery element. Of course, any eminence may combine in itself two or more of these fundamental forms, and thus represent just

---

[1] 在昔鯀陻洪水、汨陳其五行。帝乃震怒、不
畀洪範九疇、彝倫攸斁、鯀則殛死.

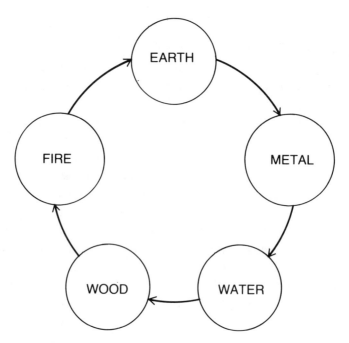

The 'productive' order of the Five Elements (see pages 35 and 37)

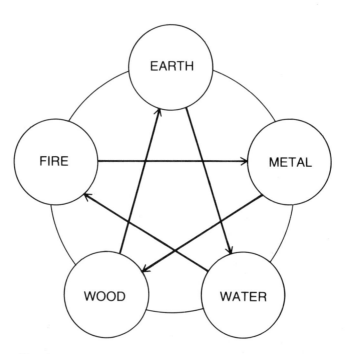

The 'destructive' order of the Five Elements (see pages 35 and 37)

so many elements. In truth, one professor as a rule sees fire where another detects water or metal; but this is no drawback at all, as they can thus perpetually confute each other's statements in the interest of the public and of their own purse.

Now, with reference to any given locality it is all-important to determine whether the elements represented by the configurations of the ground form a harmonious conjunction. It would, for instance, be highly detrimental if hills or boulders representing both fire and wood were in close proximity to graves or houses, as this would certainly render those houses liable to frequent conflagration. Human settlements often suffer from murderous raids of robbers and rebels if they are situated at the foot of a big hill representing metal, or if the graves of the dead are laid out near such a spot. And so forth. On the other hand, there are numerous beneficial combinations of elements. Fire and water, for instance, when united in harmony and in adequate proportions, further fecundation, and may therefore render the fields productive and cause the inmates of a house, or the offspring of a buried corpse, to give birth to a numerous progeny.

Bad elements also may produce good ones and neutralize nefarious elements. This doctrine, which allows fancy and speculation even a wider play, is based upon the wisdom of antiquity. In the writings of Liu Ngan, who lived in the second century before our era, it is stated that » wood overpowers earth, earth » conquers water, water vanquishes fire, fire conquers metal, and » metal overpowers wood" [1]. Pan Ku, a celebrated scholar and historian of the second century, known especially as the compiler of the Books of the Early Han Dynasty, wrote: » Wood (produces » fire, fire produces earth (*i. e.* ashes), earth produces metals, metals » produce water, and water produces wood (viz. vegetation). If » fire heats metal, the latter produces water (that is to say, it » liquifies); hence water, destroying fire, operates inimically » upon the very element which engenders it. Fire produces earth, » and earth impairs water; nobody can frustrate such phenomena, » for, the power which causes the five elements to impair each » other is the natural propensities of Heaven and Earth. A large » quantity prevails over a small quantity; hence water vanquishes » fire. Unsubstantiality prevails over substantiality; so fire con- » quers metal. Hardness prevails over softness; hence metal con-

---

[1] 木 勝 土、土 勝 水、水 勝 火、火 勝 金、金 勝 木·
Hung lieh kiai, ch. IV, l. 8.

» quers wood. Density has the upper hand over incoherence; there-
» fore wood overpowers earth. And solidity overrules insolidity; *ergo*
» earth vanquishes water" [1].

That such vagaries are much older than the age in which Liu
Ngan lived, is proved by the *Tso ch'wen*, in which we read that
a certain oneiromancer, in explaining a dream, declared that » fire
vanquishes metal" [2]. They have stood their ground as wisdom of
the highest order down to the present day, and helped to swell
numerous philosophical works — sources from which the Fung-shui
professors of all ages have drawn at discretion. These men have also
invented the art of regulating the operation of the elements by improving the natural configurations of the ground, and even carried
this art to a high stage of perfection. Hence it is that clever geomancers at present find no difficulty in quenching, for instance,
the evils emanating from a rock which represents fire, by having
a grave tank made of proper dimensions and calculated to an inch.
They can also cut off the point of a dangerous rock, and thus
convert fire into wood, metal, or any element they please, or turn
a brook in a favourable direction, in order to quench the fire of
such a rock. Or, if a flat elevation disturbs the harmony of the
configuration, they merely have to place a convex or pointed pile
of stones on the top, as high and broad as they deem fit. With
the object of thus correcting the Fung-shui of cities, towns and
valleys, there have been erected towers or pagodas in large numbers
throughout the Empire, at the cost of much money and labour.
Thus may man's foresight and energy rule the influences of the
Universe; and so he can turn his own destiny and fortunes, and
those of his offspring, into any channel he pleases.

The above philosophical nonsense about the elements and their
influences intimately connects the geomantic art with the celestial
sphere. For a long series of centuries it has, for occult reasons,

---

[1] 木生火、火生土、土生金、金生水、水生木。
其火爍金、金生水、水滅火報其理。火生土、土
則害水、莫能而禦、五行所以相害者天地之性。
衆勝寡、故水勝火也。精勝堅、故火勝金。剛勝
柔、故金勝木。專勝散、故木勝土。實勝虛、故土
勝水也. *Poh hu t'ung i*, chapt. II, § 五行.

2 火勝金. Thirty-first Year of the Ruler Chao's Reign.

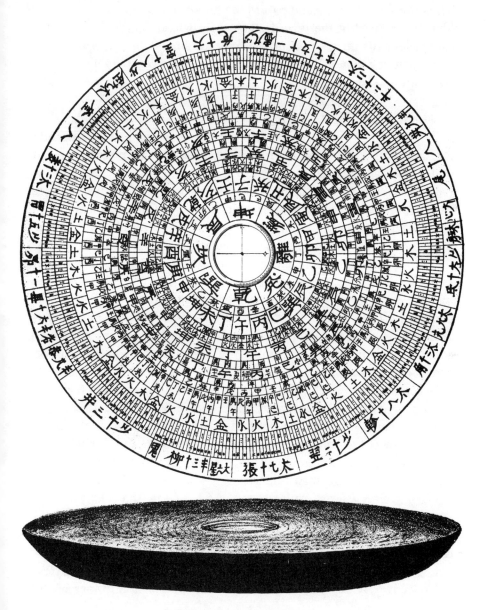

A Geomancer's Compass.

been customary among the Chinese to consider the five planets as embodiments of the influences of the five elements and to denote them by the names of these latter: Venus they call the Star of Metal [1], Jupiter that of Wood [2], Mercury that of Water [3], Mars the Star of Fire [4], and Saturn the Star of Earth [5]. (See Appendix 2) Thus every part of the terrestrial surface, when identified with one or more elements on account of its shape, is under the influence of the corresponding planets, and also under that of the constellations through which those planets move.

The Geomancer's Compass

To solve the problems relating to the construction of dwellings for the living, graves for the dead, temples for the ancestors and the gods, geomancers have invented a curious instrument, in which the principal matters and factors that play a part in their art are combined for handy use. It is a circular piece of wood, rounded down at the bottom like a tea-saucer; the upper surface has, in the centre, a round excavation containing a small magnetic needle, seldom longer than one inch, which moves freely upon a pivot and is kept in its place by a glass cover fixed in the rim of the excavation. A straight line at the bottom of this needle-house gives the direction from North to South. The surface of the instrument, which is generally painted yellow and varnished, is inscribed with several concentric circles, containing the sundry geomantic factors. Small compasses have a smaller number of circles, larger ones have a larger number, and these latter enable the geomancers to take more precise bearings. The average diameter is about two decimetres, but we have seen several both of a larger and a smaller size. In many cases, the reverse side is lackered black and bears a short table giving the contents of the circles, as also the name of the manufacturer of the instrument.

Such compasses are called lo king [6], or, in the Amoy dialect, *ló king*. This term, which signifies »reticular tissue", is probably an allusion to the circular lines on the surface, which, being intersected by other lines radiating from the centre, remind one of a net. The concentric circles are called ts'eng [7], »stories, or layers".

To convey a clear idea to our readers of the inscriptions of geo-

---

[1] 金星.   [2] 木星.   [3] 水星.   [4] 火星.
[5] 土星.   [6] 羅經.   [7] 層.

mantic compasses and the relative position of the circles, we show
opposite page 958 a reduced picture of one of average size. The
centre in which the needle revolves is understood to represent the
Tᶜai Kih[1] or »Great Ultimate Principle" which, according to ancient philosophy, is the genitor of the so-called Liang I[2] or »Two
Regulating Powers", viz. the superior Breaths Yang and Yin
which, as our readers know, create the phenomena of Nature by
their co-operation. The first or inmost circle contains eight characters, which indicate Heaven and Earth or the two principal agents
of the Universe, and six chief powers and elements which work in
this latter; all these powers are produced by the Two Regulators,
who, mutually extinguishing and giving way to each other, keep
at work a ceaseless process of revolution which produces the phenomena of existence. They are:

Khien 乾, Heaven, the sky, the celestial sphere.

Tui   兌, watery exhalations, vapours, clouds, etc.

Li   離, fire, heat, the sun, light, lightning.

Chen 震, thunder.

Sun   巽, wind, and wood.

Khan 坎, water, rivers, lakes, seas, etc.

Ken   艮, mountains.

Khwun 坤, Earth, terrestrial matter.

This system of cosmogony and natural philosophy, represented
by the compass, has been handed down from time immemorial.
It is the basis of a system of divination laid down in the *Yih
king* or Canon of Metamorphoses, and invented and expanded,
according to tradition, by the royal founders of the Cheu dynasty.
We read in the said Classic (chapter 14, ll. 16 and 17): »Hence
» there is in the system of the metamorphoses of Nature the Great
» Ultimate Principle, and this produces the two Regulating Powers.
» These Powers produce the four Forms, which again produce the
» eight Trigrams. These Trigrams determine good and evil, and
» good and evil cause the great business of human life"[3].

---

[1] 大極.   [2] 兩儀.

[3] 是故易有大極、是生兩儀。兩儀生四象、四象
生八卦。八卦定吉凶、吉凶生大業. Sect. 繫辭傳, I.

To entirely understand this passage, it is necessary to know that, in the *Yih king*, the principle Y a n g is represented by an un-broken line ━━━, and Y i n by a line broken in two ━ ━, and that from these lines are deduced four diagrams representing the four Forms, viz.

≡ called the Major Y a n g 太陽, representing the sun, heat.

≡ ≡ called the Major Y i n 太陰, representing the moon, cold.

≡.≡ the Minor Y a n g 少陽, or Y a n g *under* the Y i n, corres-ponding to the stars, daylight, etc.

≡ ≡ the Minor Y i n 少陰, or Y i n kept under by the Y a n g, corresponding to the planets, night, etc.

Placing each of these lineal figures under an unbroken and a broken line, the eight trigrams are obtained, of which the above extract speaks. They are called k w a [1] by the *Yih king* and repre-sent the eight aforesaid powers and elements, showing the relative quantities of Y a n g and Y i n breath present in each of these:

Khien	Tui	Li	Chen	Sun	Khan	Ken	Khwun

The principal k w a are K h i e n and K h w u n, or Heaven and Earth, entirely composed of Y a n g lines and Y i n lines, and therefore styled »unalloyed Y a n g"[2] and »unalloyed Y i n"[3].

Thus the geomantic compasses teach us that a prominent place is given in the Fung-shui doctrines to the *Yih king*, the same ancient book which the sages and learned men of all ages have held in high veneration as a clue to the mysteries of Nature and as an unfathomable lake of metaphysical wisdom explaining all the phe-nomena of the Universe. On many compasses, the lineal figures representing the k w a are inscribed around the needle, instead of the characters that denote them. Being combined by the *Yih king* with the seasons and the eight cardinal points, the k w a allow a wide play to the imaginative ingenuity of geomancers. » All things » endowed with life", that Classic says (chapter 17, l. 7), »have their » origin in C h e n, as C h e n corresponds to the East. They are » in harmonious existence in S u n, because S u n corresponds with » the East and the South. L i is brightness and renders all things

---

[1] 卦. [2] 純陽. [3] 純陰.

» visible to one another, and it is its kwa which represents
» the South. Khwun is the Earth, from which all things en-
» dowed with life receive food. Tui corresponds to the middle of
» autumn. Khien is the kwa of the North-west. Khan is
» water and the kwa of the exact North and distress, unto
» which everything endowed with life reverts. Ken is the kwa
» of the North-east, in which living things terminate and also
» originate" [1].

Little shrewdness is required to understand this extract in
detail. The East is reasonably represented as the quarter in which
is rooted the life of everything, the great genitor of life being
born there every day. It is identified also quite correctly with the
kwa Chen, which represents thunder (see page 960); indeed, the
vernal season, identified with the East because it is, so to say,
the morning of the year, is particularly characterized in China by
heavy thunderstorms caused by the return of the southern monsoon.
The *Li ki* (chapter 21, l. 11) says: »In the month of mid-spring,
» when day and night are of equal length, thunder utters its voice
» and it begins to lighten" [2]. For just as plausible reasons, the
South, where the God of Light daily reaches the zenith of his
glorious course, is identified with brightness; the North, which he
never frequents, with death. Tui, declared to correspond to the
middle of autumn or the evening of the year, naturally belongs
to the West or the evening of the day, this corroborating the identification of the East with the middle of the spring and naturally
implying an identification of the South with midsummer, of due
North with mid-winter. Finally, in Ken, the kwa of the North-
east, everything which has life is stated to terminate and to
originate, the North being identified with death, and the East
with life.

---

[1] 萬物出乎震、震東方也。齊乎巽、巽東南也。
離也者明也、萬物皆相見、南方之卦也。坤也者
地也、萬物皆致養焉。兌正秋也。乾西北之卦也。
坎者水也、正北方之卦也、勞卦也、萬物之所歸
也。艮東北之卦也、萬物之所成終而所成始也.
Sect. 說卦傳.

[2] 仲春之月、日夜分、雷乃發聲、始電 Sect. 月
令, II.

All these data may be placed, in imitation of the Chinese, in the following order:

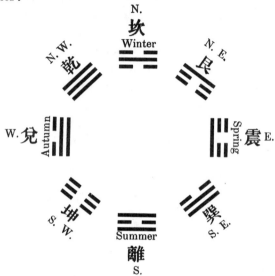

This arrangement however is not used for Fung-shui purposes. All the geomantic compasses we have seen bore the following arrangement, said to be much older, having been devised by Fuh Hi[1], a fabulous sovereign from whose reign the Chinese commence their chronology. It is likewise based upon certain sayings of the *Yih king*:

In this plan, **Khien**, which represents Heaven or the unalloyed **Yang**, is logically placed at the South, this being the chief seat

---

[1] 伏羲.

of warmth and light and, therefore, the region in which Yang
is in the zenith of its power and influence. So, also, Khwun,
the unalloyed Yin, is placed at the North, where Yin reigns
supreme. Li, or fire and heat, is identified with the East, the region
where the sun rises; Khan with the West, because it represents
water and is thus the opposite of fire; and so forth.

Not only do the eight kwa answer to the eight points of the
compass and the seasons of the year, but they symbolize also the
virtues and properties attributed to those points and the seasons.
Moreover, to each of them the *Yih king* [1] ascribes a series of
qualities, such as the following:

Khien 乾 corresponds to immobility and strength. It represents a
horse, the head, the heavenly sphere, a father, a prince, roundness,
jade, metal, cold, ice, red colours, a good horse, an old horse, a
thin horse, a piebald horse, fruit of trees, etc.

Khwun 坤 represents docility and, consequently, bovine cattle;
further, the belly, Mother-Earth, cloth, caldrons, parsimony, a heifer,
large carts, figures, a multitude, a handle, black colours, etc.

Chen 震 indicates motion. It represents a dragon, *i. e.* the animal
identified with the spring of the East of which, according to the posterior
arrangement, C h e n is the k w a. It also indicates the feet, an eldest
son, thunder, dark-yellow colours, development, high roads, decision
and vehemence, bamboo, rushes, the best neighers among horses,
etc.

Sun 巽 means penetration and indicates a fowl, the thighs, an eldest
daughter, wood, wind, whiteness, length, height, a forward motion,
a backward motion, baldheadedness, a broad forehead, three hundred
per cent. gain in the market; and so forth.

Khan 坎 signifies peril, a pig, the ears, a son who is neither the
eldest, nor the youngest, water, channels and streams, hidden things,
alternate straightness and crookedness, a bow, a wheel, anxiety,
distress of mind, pain in the ears, a blood-red colour; a horse with
an elegant spine, high spirits, drooping head, thin hoofs or a shamb-
ling step; finally it means the moon, this planet being identified
with the West, as the sun is with the East (comp. the next kwa);
thieves, strong trees, etc.

Li 離 means beauty and brightness. It represents a pheasant, *i. e.*
the bird identified with the South (see p. 949), of which region Li is

---

1 In ch. 17, ll. 11 *sqq.*, being the section 說 卦 傳.

the k w a according to the posterior arrangement. Further it means the eyes, a daughter who is neither the eldest nor the youngest, the sun, lightning, cuirasses and helmets, spears and swords, a large-bellied man, dryness, turtles, crabs, spiral univalves, mussels, tortoises, etc.

Ken 艮 indicates stoppage, a dog, the hands, a youngest son, paths and roads, small rocks, gates, fruits and cucumbers, porters or eunuchs, finger rings, rats, birds with large bills, etc.

Tui 兌 means pleasure, a sheep, the mouth, a youngest daughter, spiritual mediums between men and the gods, the tongue, a concubine, and so forth.

Like the whole contents of the *Yih king*, the above speculations about the k w a and their attributes have, throughout all ages, been looked upon by the wise men of the nation as the outcome of the profoundest classical wisdom, and as such have been greatly enlarged and dilated upon by [authors of renown. They consequently afford ample means to the Fung-shui professors to define minutely the proprieties of all the spots situated near any given place, and to derive therefrom sage conclusions as to the desirability of constructing dwellings, temples or graves there. We must now have recourse to the other circles of the compass, to penetrate somewhat deeper into the computations of those men.

The third circle divides the compass in twenty-four points. S. E., S. W., N. W. and N. E. are designated respectively by the k w a Sun 巽, Khwun 坤, Khien 乾 and Ken 艮, which correspond to these cardinal points according to the posterior plan of arrangement; the twenty remaining points are indicated by the characters of the two cycles known as the Ten k a n [1] and the Twelve Branches. (See Commentary 5, p.157).

Kiah 甲 .... is E. N. E. by E.

Mao 卯 is East.

Yih 乙 .... is E. S. E. by E.

Ch'en 辰 is E. S. E. by S.

Sun 巽 .... is S. E.

Szě 巳 is S. S. E. by E.

Ping 丙 .... is S. S. E. by S.

Wu 午 is South.

---

[1] 十干.

Ting 丁 .... is S. S. W. by S.

Wei 未 is S. S. W. by W.

Khwun 坤 .... is S. W.

Shen 申 is W. S. W. by S.

Wu 戊 .... }
Ki 已 .... } are the Centre.

Keng 庚 .... is W. S. W. by W.

Yiu 酉 is West.

Sin 辛 .... is W. N. W. by W.

Suh 戌 is W. N. W. by N.

Khien 乾 .... is N. W.

Hai 亥 is N. N. W. by W.

Jen 壬 .... is N. N. W. by N.

Tszĕ 子 is North.

Kwei 癸 .... is N. N. E. by N.

Chʻeu 丑 is N. N. E. by E.

Ken 艮 .... is N. E.

Yin 寅 is E. N. E. by N.

Wu 戊 and Ki 已 do not designate points proper of the compass, but the centre, which corresponds to the element earth. The *Li ki* says (ch. 23, ll. 14 and 15): » The centre is earth, and its days are Wu and Ki" [1].

The above method of representing twenty points of the compass by characters derived from the denary and the duodenary cycles, is very old, as Liu Ngan uses it in enumerating the twenty directions in which the tail of the Great Bear points during its apparent yearly revolution round the pole [2]. It is used also in the Historical Records, in the twenty-fifth chapter, which is devoted to natural science for divining purposes, and which denotes the cycles as » the Ten Mothers" [3] and » the Twelve Children" [4].

The second circle of the compass likewise contains characters

---

[1] 中央土、其日戊已. Sect. 月令, IV.

[2] *Hung lieh kiai*, ch. III, ll. 7 *seq*.

[3] 十母.　　　　　　　[4] 十二子.

drawn from those cycles, arranged in an order the leading idea of which we cannot grasp. Some characters appear in it two or three times. The fourth circle gives the characters of the denary cycle in alternate succession, in twelve combinations of five; between every two combinations a blank is left, two characters being skipped over. With this circle the tenth corresponds, but the inscriptions on it are shifted slightly to the right.

The fifth circle gives the five elements twelve times, in varied permutations. It combines the influences of the elements or planets with the points of the compass inscribed on the third and fourth circles.

The sixth and the eighth circles are identical with the third. They do not, however, like this latter, indicate the centre of each of the twenty-four points of the compass, but their extreme limits, thus insuring accuracy in taking bearings. For some occult reason, each character in these circles is combined, through the next cycle, with the characters 丁辛 or 丙庚, borrowed from the denary cycle.

The eighth circle contains, moreover, the twenty-four subdivisions of the year, and is therefore a calendar indicating the season during which a house, temple or tomb, for which a favourable locality is assigned by the compass, ought to be built. According to the national philosophy, these seasons are wrought by Yang and Yin, the two »breaths" which through the course of every year blend together in constantly varying proportions, Yang having the upper hand in the hottest weather, and Yin in the coldest. Hence they are logically called tsieh khi[1], »breaths of the divisions (of the year)", or simply khi[2], »breaths".

They are arranged on the circle in such a way that mid-spring corresponds to due East, midsummer to due South, mid-autumn to due West, and mid-winter to due North, this being, as stated on page 962, in perfect accordance with the speculative philosophy of the ancients. Also in the writings of the philosopher Kwan I-wu (see note 4, p.147), who lived in the seventh century before our era, it is stated that »the seasons appertaining respectively to the East, »South, West and North are the spring, the summer, the autumn »and the winter"[3].

---

[1] 節氣.   [2] 氣.

[3] 東方…其時日春、南方…其時日夏、西方… 其時日秋、北方…其時日冬. *Kwan-tsző* 管子, ch. 14, § 40, 四時.

On a great many compasses the twenty-four seasons occupy a separate circle. They bear the following names:

Spring.		Autumn.	
立春	Beginning of Spring.	立秋	Beginning of Autumn.
雨水	Rain Water.	處暑	Limit of Heat.
驚蟄	Resurrection of hibernating Insects.	白露	White Dew.
春分	Vernal Equinox.	秋分	Autumnal Equinox.
清明	Pure Brightness.	寒露	Cold Dew.
穀雨	Rains over the Grain.	霜降	Descent of Hoar Frost.

Summer.		Winter.	
立夏	Beginning of Summer.	立冬	Beginning of Winter.
小滿	Grain filling a little.	小雪	Little Snow.
芒種	Grain in Ear.	大雪	Heavy Snow.
夏至	Summer Solstice.	冬至	Winter Solstice.
小暑	Slight Heat.	小寒	Little Cold.
大暑	Great Heat.	大寒	Severe Cold.

The division of the year into the above seasons dates from early times. A calendar of the Hia dynasty, still extant under the title of *Hia siao ching* [1], mentions the Resurrection of hibernating Insects under the name Emergence of hibernating Insects [2], and also the Winter solstice. In the writings of Kwan I-wu [3] the appellations Pure Brightness, Great Heat and Slight Heat are employed to denote certain periods of the year; and the *Kwoh yü* [4] or »Discussions about the States", a narrative of events in several feudal kingdoms during the Cheu dynasty, said to have been composed by the author of the *Tso ch'wen*, mentions the appellation Limit of Heat as having been used by one Fan Wu-yü [5], who lived in the sixth century before our era [6]. The section of the *Li ki* known as the Monthly Precepts

---

[1] 夏小正.

[2] 啟蟄.

[3] *Kwan-tszě*, ch. III, § 8.

[4] 國語.

[5] 范無宇.

[6] Chapter 17, being the first part of the »Narratives of Ch'u" 楚語.

contains the expressions Beginning of Spring, of Summer, Autumn, and Winter; it also speaks of »Rain Water beginning to fall in » the month of mid-spring, and of the insects in their burrows » then all coming into motion" [1], and further says: »Slight Heat » comes in the month of midsummer [2], White Dew descends in » the first month of autumn [3], and Hoar Frost begins to fall in » the last month of this season" [4]. All the above facts merely serve to prove that many of the twenty-four appellations of the seasons were in vogue before the Han dynasty, but they do not give us any certainty that they formed in those times a series like the one in present use. Slight evidence that this series really was used during the reign of the House of Cheu, we have in the fact that it is given entire by the »Books of the Cheu dynasty obtained from the tomb in Kih", in the section entitled: »Explanation of the Doctrines about the Seasons"[5]. But it is far from certain whether this work is the product of the time expressed in the title, and it may probably contain spurious references to matters of posterior date. It indicates the seasons by the same word k h i by which they are at present known. Liu Ngan, summing up the principal phenomena proper to the successive periods of fifteen days, which he calls t s i e h, gives these twenty-four seasons in nearly the same sequence in which they are placed nowadays[6]. They are enumerated also in the section on chronology contained in the Books of the Early Han Dynasty[7], and have probably had an official status in China ever since, down to this day.

Returning to the geomantic compass after this historical digression, we see that the eleventh circle is divided into one hundred and twenty compartments and consists of two lines of characters of little interest. The inner line contains the same characters as the seventh and the ninth circles, but they are shifted a little into a different position, and the open spaces between them are filled up with other characters of the denary cycle ; — the outer

---

1 仲春之月始雨水、蟄蟲咸動. Ch. 21, ll. 3 and 11.
2 仲夏之月小暑至. Ch. 22, l. 23.
3 孟秋之月白露降. Ch. 23, l. 30.
4 季秋之月霜始降. Ch. 24, l. 30.
5 時訓解. Chapter 6, § 52.
6 *Hung lieh kiai*, ch. III, ll. 7 *seq.*
7 Chapter 21, II, ll. 14 and 15.

line divides the compass into twelve points, indicating these by
the characters of the duodenary cycle, each repeated four times
(compare this with the third circle). The next circle, the twelfth,
is more important. It is divided into sixty portions of unequal
sizes, inscribed with the names of the five elements in varied
sequence, so that each element recurs twelve times. This useful circle
enables the geomancer to judge by which element or planet any
spot whatsoever is influenced, and whether the adjoining places be
dominated by elements which might work either productively or
destructively upon it. Suppose, for instance, a certain spot indicated by the compass as representing water, is shown by this
instrument to have the element earth at its side, its useful effects
may be greatly reduced, nay, rendered null and void, because earth
neutralizes water (see page 957). Should, however, metal lie close
by, the aquatic effects will be greatly invigorated, since metal
produces water. Thus clever geomancers are competent continually
to discover favourable and unfavourable conjunctions of all kinds
and descriptions, without torturing their brains about the question
as to whether a leading idea underlies the arrangement of the elements on this circle, or whether these latter are merely distributed
arbitrarily upon it.

The same circle is also very useful in another respect. Enabling,
as it does, geomancers to discover in the surroundings of a place
the elements by which they are influenced, it reveals to them
at the same time certain of the idiosyncrasies of those surroundings, viz. those which the books on philosophy, and the venerable
Shu king in particular, attribute to the elements themselves. This
Classic contains the following profoundly wise remarks: » Water
» may be described as moistening and descending, fire as blazing
» and ascending, wood as being crooked or straight, metal as flexible
» and changeable, while the virtue of earth is seen in sowing and
» reaping. That which moistens and descends produces a salt taste,
» that which is crooked or straight produces sourness, that which
» is flexible and changeable an acrid taste, and sowing and reaping
» produces sweetness" [1].

The next two circles represent the division of the globe into 360

---

[1] 水曰潤下、火曰炎上、木曰曲直、金曰從革、
土爰稼穡。潤下作鹹、炎上作苦、曲直作酸、從
革作辛、稼穡作甘. The Great Plan, 洪範.

(De Groot omits 'that which is blazing and ascending produces a spicy taste'.)

degrees. Some of these, indicated by a red spot, are lucky; others, indicated by a black cross, are unlucky; the rest, which are either marked black or not marked at all, may be both, or neutral. Odd numbers mark the degrees of each of the twenty-eight siu mentioned on page 954, of which the names are inscribed on the last or outermost circle of the compass. This circle thus serves to determine under the influence of which of these constellations any spot pointed out by the compass is placed. To the right of the name of each siu there is a cipher, indicating how many degrees it embraces.

The part the twenty-eight constellations play in geomancy has been already touched upon at page 954. The following is a list of their names, indicating the season and the celestial quadrant or Animal, to which each group of seven corresponds.

The Blue Dragon or Eastern Quadrant, corresponding to the Spring

1 Kioh　　角, consisting of Spica and some other stars of Virgo.

2 Khang 亢, certain stars of Virgo.

3 Ti　　　氐, α, β, γ and ι Libræ.

4 Fang　　房, some stars of Scorpio.

5 Sin　　　心, Antares, and a couple of stars of Scorpio.

6 Wei　　尾, some stars of Scorpio.

7 Ki　　　箕, four stars in the hand of Sagittarius.

The Red Bird or Southern Quadrant, corresponding to the Summer

8 Teu　　斗, the principal stars of Ursa Major, and some of Sagittarius.

9 Niu　　牛, stars of Capricorn and Sagittarius.

10 Nü　　女, part of the sign Aquarius.

11 Hü　　虛, β Aquarii and α of Equleus.

12 Wei　　危, α Aquarii, and some stars of Pegasus.

13 Shih　室, α and β Pegasi.

14 Pih　　壁, γ Pegasi and α Andromedæ.

The White Tiger or Western Quadrant, corresponding to the Autumn

15 Khwei 奎, stars of Andromeda and Pisces.

16 Leu　　婁, the stars of the head of Aries.

17 W e i　胃, part of Musca Borealis.

18 M a o　昴, the Pleiades.

19 P i h　畢, the Hyades, and some stars of Taurus.

20 T s z ě　觜, stars of the head of Orion.

21 Tsʻan　參, Betelgeux, Rigel, and the other principal stars of
　　　　Orion.

The Black Tortoise, or the Northern Quadrant, corresponding to the Winter

22 T s i n g　井, stars in the knees and feet of Gemini.

23 K w e i　鬼, some stars in Cancer.

24 L i u　柳, certain stars in Hydra.

25 S i n g　星, stars in the heart of Hydra.

26 C h a n g　張, the stars of the second coil of Hydra.

27 Y i h　翼, a couple of dozen stars in Crater and the third
　　　　coil of Hydra.

28 C h e n　軫, certain stars in Corvus [1].

These constellations very likely represent the most ancient division of the Chinese sphere. Their origin lies hidden in the mist of ages. H ü (11) and M a o (18) are named already in the very first section of the *Shu king*, the so-called Canon of Yao, in connection with some orders given by Yao, whose reign chronologists place in the 24th. century before our era, to his officers with regard to certain astronomical observations to be made. F a n g (4) is mentioned in the same Classic [2] as the place in which an eclipse of the sun took place in the 22nd. century B. C. The *Hia siao ching* mentions T e u (8) and Tsʻan (21), the latter also in its remarks about the third and fifth months of the year, and M a o (18) in speaking of the fourth month. In the *Shi king* the appellations of

---

1 The stars corresponding to the above s i u are only given approximately. It would be idle to try to identify the latter precisely, for Chinese authors draw them in a very slipshod way and, moreover, differently. This explains why the identifications given by some authors, such as Mr. Reeves, for instance, in Morrison's Dictionary of the Chinese Language (part. II, vol. I, pp. 1065 *sqq.*), Schlegel in his »Uranographie Chinoise" and Mayers in his Chinese Reader's Manual (page 356), differ on many points.

2 In the section 肩征.

nearly one fourth of the whole series occur, viz. Ki (7), Teu (8), Niu (9), Mao (18), Pih (19) and Tsʻan (21) [1]. The *Cheu li* refers to the series a couple of times, stating that » the Observers have to » attend to the duodenary cycle of years, months and hours, the » denary cycle of days and the position of the twenty-eight aster- » isms" [2], and that » the Destroyer of the Nests, who is charged to » upset the nests of birds of bad omen, must write upon a board the » ten appellations of the days, the twelve appellations of the hours, » months and years [3], and the twenty-eight names of the constel- » lations; then he must suspend this board over the nests and remove » the latter" [4]. In the section of the *Li ki* entitled the Monthly Precepts [5], which is a record of the proceedings of the government in every month of the year, nearly all the constellations are men- tioned, it being there stated for each month in which of them the sun is, and which of them then culminates at dusk and at dawn; two of them, however, are passed over in silence and two others are denoted by other names. In quite the same way they are enumerated in the *Lü-shi chʻun-tsʻiu*, in twelve paragraphs which respectively open the first twelve chapters and bear a striking resemblance to the aforesaid Monthly Precepts; they are mentioned again in the thirteenth chapter of that work. The Historical Records call them by the name of shé, which term Szĕ-ma Kwang explains as follows: »Shé has the meaning of 'to reside or stop some- » where' and siu means an abode; and both words express the » idea of the sun, the moon and the five planets in their revolutions

---

1 Ki, Teu, Niu and Pih are mentioned in the section 小旻, ode IX, and Ki, moreover, in ode VI. Pih also occurs a second time, viz. in the section 都 人士, ode VIII. Tsʻan and Mao are spoken of in the sect. 召南, ode X.

2 馮相氏掌十有二歲、十有二月、十有二辰、 十日、二十有八星之位. Chapter 26, l. 13.

3 These two extracts show that, during the Cheu dynasty, the years, months and hours were counted with the aid of the Branches, and the days with that of the kan.

4 硩蔟氏掌覆夭鳥之巢、以方書十日之號、十 有二辰之號、十有二月之號、十有二歲之號、二 十有八星之號、縣其巢上、則去之. Chapt. 37, ll. 39 *seq.*

5 月令.

» residing alternately in the divisions of the sphere indicated as » twenty-eight abodes" [1].

The use of the magnetic needle for geomantic observations suggests that the Chinese are perfectly aware that an oblong piece of iron, freely suspended, naturally points north and south. There is, however, not the slightest indication that they possess any knowledge of the variation of the compass, or that they are able to make a distinction between the magnetic North and the exact North.

The chief use of the geomantic compass is to find the line in which, according to the almanac, a grave ought to be made, or a house or temple built. Indeed, in this most useful of all books it is every year decided between which two points of the compass the lucky line for that year lies, and which point is absolutely inauspicious. (See note 5, p.148) This circumstance not only entails a postponement of many burials, seeing it is not always possible to find a grave, answering to all the geomantic requirements, in the lucky line of the year; but it regularly compels the owners of houses and temples to postpone repairs or the rebuilding of the same until a year in which the line wherein their properties are situate is declared to be lucky. Many buildings for this reason alone are allowed to fall to ruin for years, and it is no rare thing to see whole streets simultaneously demolished and

---

[1] 舍止也、宿次也、言日月五星運行或舍於二十八次之分也. See chapter 25, l. 4.

It is a well known fact that the Hindus, Parsis and Arabs also are in possession of a similar system of division of the heavens into twenty-eight parts. The Hindu divisions are styled *nakshâtra*, » stars or asterisms", the Arab divisions *manâzil al-kamar*, » lunar mansions, stations of the moon", which term bears a marked resemblance to the Chinese appellations s i u and s h é according to the above explanation of Szĕ-ma Kwang. Elaborate dissertations on the coincidence between the Hindu and Arab systems have been written by Sir William Jones in the Asiatic Researches for 1790, and by Colebrooke in the Asiatic Researches for 1807, vol. IX (see also his Essays, vol. II, page 321); but the identity of the Chinese system with the Hindu and the Arab was first demonstrated and established by M. J. B. Biot, assisted by his son, the translator of the *Cheu li* (see p. 19), in a series of articles published in the Journal des Savants for 1840. The conclusions arrived at by this eminent scholar were, that this system of celestial division was invented by the Chinese and borrowed from them by the Hindus and Arabs for purely astrological purposes. To this day no considerations of importance have cancelled these views, and though they have been vigorously combated by Weber, Max Müller and other authorities of renown, yet it seems that most investigators of oriental astronomy silently subscribe to them.

rebuilt in years auspicious to the direction in which they are placed.

Chinese books make no mention of the inventor of the compass. Without doubt, such combinations as we find on the compasses at present, were used for geomantic purposes at an early date, the chief of them being, indeed, simple representations of the pre-Christian doctrines respecting the eight k w a and their relation to the seasons and the points of the compass. It is very probable that, prior to the invention of better writing material, those combinations were written upon small boards, which, being improved, in course of time have become the well-finished compasses of the present day.

Taking into consideration that the geomancer's compass comprises all the principles of Chinese physical science, and that the characters and cycles inscribed on it are supposed to exercise to a great extent the same influences as do the powers they represent, we cannot wonder at its being regarded by the people with reverential awe. Geomantic professors themselves are fully conscious that, in manipulating it, they concentrate the benefits of those powers upon any spot which they select for a grave or building, viz., to recapitulate, those of the two great Breaths of the Universe and the elements and agencies represented by the k w a, those of the four, eight, twelve and twenty-four points of the compass, the elements or planets, the seasons and days of the year, the 360 degrees of the globe, the twenty-eight stellar-divisions, etc.; all which renders the compass to every Chinaman an invaluable compound of supernatural wisdom and one of the most useful instruments ever contrived by the human brain. It borrows an odour of sanctity from antiquity, the characters inscribed on it, their arrangement in cycles and the peculiar position of the circles with regard to each another dating, as we have shown, according to tradition, from the holy founders of the Cheu dynasty, nay, even from the age of the mythic Fuh Hi. To the uninitiated, who know all the terms and cycles by name, but comprehend next to nothing of the numerous bewildering conjunctions that can be computed therefrom for any spot in particular, the compass becomes, in the hands of the professors, a powerful magic box containing an inexhaustible source of predictions which, promising money and bliss to every one, are sold at high price, forming thus a steady source of revenue to the professors. Even the most learned among the people, nay, the sceptics who have not much faith in the system, generally receive the prophecies of those experts with the same superstitious dread with which they

regard Nature herself, notwithstanding the fact that those prophecies are much more often disproved than realized by actual events.

Thus far the chief principles of the Fung-shui system only have
been passed in review. No useful purpose can be served by trying
to penetrate farther into its vagaries and the mechanical play of
idle abstractions; but of numerous other matters which play a
part of more or less importance in the practical application of its
doctrines and theories we must still mention a few. In making a
grave, much importance is attached by the professors to the characters forming the horoscope of the person who is to be buried
therein. It has been stated already how the twelve Branches are
combined with the denary cycle of k a n into a cycle of sixty binominal
terms, which are used for counting, in a perpetual rotation, the
years, months, days and hours, thus furnishing for every individual
a horoscope of seven or eight characters which indicate the year,
month, day and hour of his birth. These characters being firmly
believed to determine his fate for ever, no burial place can answer
to the geomantic requirements if the cyclical characters expressing
the year of the birth of the occupant stand in the compass on the
lower end of the line which the almanac has decreed as auspicious
for the current year and in which, of course, the coffin is to be placed.
Suppose, for instance, this line runs from south to north, so that the
longitudinal axis of the grave should fall within the segment defined on
the compass by the limits of the point 子 or the North, as indicated on
the circles VI and VIII. If then the dead man has been born in a year
denoted by a binomium in which the character 子 occurs, his
horoscope is deemed to collide with the good influences that flow
from south to north and to neutralize their benefits, and no blessings can ever be expected from his grave if it is placed in this
direction. Hence its axis must be shifted a little to the right or
left, without, however, going beyond the northern quadrant; and
if it is feared that the beneficial influences of the auspicious line
will in this way be lost, the burial must be postponed. The month,
day and hour of the birth of the deceased may cause similar col-
lisions, though they are of a less dangerous nature, such dates
forming the less important parts of his horoscope. Conjunctions may
be found, in fact, which neutralize such dangers. But if it is not
possible to discover them, the family is constrained to adjourn the
burial until the almanac assigns another direction as peculiarly
auspicious.

Dangerous Shapes of Towns and Villages

Another geomantic law of importance is, that no road, no row of trees, nor any water-course may run in a straight line towards a tomb. Straight lines, geomancers say, are like dangerous darts which, striking a grave in its core, may inflict a deadly wound. They also show the way to the noxious influences which the peculiar Fung-shui nomenclature denotes by the word s h a h (comp. page 940), and besides, as has been stated on page 953, they indicate that the surrounding configurations are devoid of breath and vitality. It is, indeed, not uncommon to hear people who make a pretence to some knowledge of Fung-shui matters, declare a grave to be of no benefit to the descendants of the man or woman buried therein, because it is, as they express it, »violated by the s h a h of a path or a road"[1], in other words, because a path has been accidentally formed in the front or at the side by the feet of passers-by. It is to be ascribed to this superstition, that the avenue to the mausoleum of the founder of the Ming dynasty near Nanking, and that which leads to the sepulchres north from Peking in which his successors are buried, describe a curve in the part which is lined by stone images of men and animals.

In respect of towns, cities and villages, their own shape is deemed a factor of great significance, a factor indeed which has as much to do with their destiny as the contours and configurations of the environs. Professors of geomancy in Ts'üen-cheu-fu are quite in earnest when they relate that, in times of yore, this city, the contours of which strongly remind one of a carp, frequently fell a prey to the depredations of the people of the neighbouring town of Yung-ch'un[2], because this is shaped like a fishing-net. Fortunately, the ancestors of the present population about a thousand years ago neutralized the evil by erecting in the centre of the town two pagodas, which tower above it to the present day, thus preventing the imaginary fishing apparatus of their unfriendly neighbours from being hauled over their heads. There are many towns in China which have come to grief because of their ominous shape. It is related, for instance, in the *Khi leh p'ien*[3], a small work written in the twelfth century by Chwang Ki-yü[4], that »the people of Ch'u abstain from speaking of the head of » a black tortoise, pretending that, when the capital of that depart-

---

[1] 犯路煞.   [2] 永春州.
[3] 雞肋編.   [4] 莊季裕.

» ment, which was built in the shape of a tortoise, was once
» upon a time attacked, some expert of the occult arts taught the
» assailers to bind the head of the animal, in consequence of which
» the town was taken. Hence its people avoid that expression" [1].

A natural outgrowth of the chief geomantic axiom that auspicious influences concentrated upon a grave produce blessings which
the offspring reap, is the dogma that things of good omen, when placed in
a tomb, will cause the blessings they express or symbolize, to fall to the
share of the descendants of the deceased. It is therefore a settled funeral
custom to place at the bottom of coffins and graves sundry things which
express a numerous progeny and abundance of food and wealth,
such as iron nails, hemp, peas, wheat, millet, paddy and coins
nay, even good wishes are sown therein with the same object. So, also, the
clothes and body ornaments of the dead are deemed to work auspiciously
on the fate of their offspring if they symbolize blessings, and for this
reason they generally do so, as shown in our chapter on Grave Clothes.
This same dogma explains why the people are so partial to dressing their
dead in »longevity garments" and the robes of a mandarin, a long life and
official dignities being the things most coveted by the Chinese. Again, this
dogma accounts for the belief that five suits of grave clothes, or any odd
number thereof, may work disastrously upon the principal family
members of the dead man who is sent to his last resting place so oddly
embaled.

On the same line with these curious outgrowths of geomantic
illusion may be placed the ancient custom of adorning the graves of
emperors with stone images of unicorns (see page 947). As these animals
portend the birth of excellent sovereigns, their images may, through the
graves upon which they stand, work beneficiently upon the fortunes of
the nation, and moreover, preserve the imperial line from dying out, thus
securing to the dynasty an everlasting possession of the Throne.

Symbols being placed in and upon tombs in order to create the
realities which they call up before the mind, it is very natural

---

[1] 楚人諱烏龜頭、云郡城象龜形、嘗被攻、有
術者教以繫其首、而破。故諱之. See the *Kai yü ts'ung khao*,
ch. 38, l. 23.

that many tombs bear inscriptions expressing felicity, such as the characters 福 » happiness and prosperity", 祿 » an official position with a large income", and 壽 » a long life" that is to say the same blessings which, as our readers know, are sown inside the graves by means of the clothes in which the deceased are dressed. Often also, animals symbolizing the same good things, such as bats, stags and cranes, and even unicorns, are carved on slabs of granite forming part of the tomb. Many graves bear also the eight kwa, evidently in order that the influences of Nature, which they represent, may be concentrated upon the tombstone. Probably for a similar reason, over two thousand yeas ago, the sepulchre of the mighty potentate of Ts'in was, as Szĕ-ma Ts'ien tells us, adorned with stars and constellations and with the configurations of the earth. We read also that the grave of Li Szĕ-chao [1], a certain prince of imperial blood, » when » broken open by robbers in the year ki-szĕ of the Ching t'ung » period (A. D. 1449), was found to contain a sepulchral chamber » of chiseled stone and, moreover, representations of the sun, the » moon, the stars and the Great Bear" [2]. For the same purpose of attracting the beneficial influence of the Universe unto the grave, coffins were, during the Han dynasty and in subsequent ages, painted with a sun, a moon, constellations, and with the four Celestial Animals; and the board representing the seven stars of the Great Bear, with which coffins have been furnished since many centuries, is probably used for the same reason.

The Fung-shui doctrines being a mere web of speculative dreams and idle abstractions, the product of a credulous faith in absurd vagaries, we are not surprized to find that, in deciding whether a spot will be a lucky burial place, much value is set on prognostics of all kind. So, for instance, if rain happens to fall while a coffin is being placed in the grave, this is deemed a proof that the Fung-shui of that grave will work beneficiently, Nature herself showing in this way that the influences of an element which holds a place of the highest significance in

---

[1] 李嗣昭.

[2] 正統巳巳盜發嗣昭墓、內鑿石爲壙、有日月 星斗象. *Ku kin t'u shu tsih ch'ing*, sect. 坤輿, ch. 134.

the system, operate upon the spot with vigor. The books contain many
legends illustrating this curious feature of the system. Some of these are of
rather ancient date. The Official Histories of the sixth century, for
instance, relate:

» Wu Ming-ch͏eh was a native of the district of Ts͏in. His
» father, who bore the name of Shu, was a general in the right
» division of the armies of the Liang dynasty. Ming-ch͏eh was still
» a lad when he lost him, and yet he proved himself possessed
» of filial devotion of the highest order. When an auspicious hour
» had been fixed for the burial, a person of the surname I, who
» was a proficient in the art of discovering good burial sites by
» means of divination, said to Ming-ch͏eh's elder brother: ‘On the
» day on which you commit the corpse to the earth a man will
» pass by the burial place, riding a white steed and hunting a
» stag; this portends a high and influential position for a filial
» youngest son’. There was indeed such a prognostic when the
» hour of burial arrived; and Ming-ch͏eh was Shu's youngest son” [1].
It is unnecessary to say he attained to the highest dignities of
the State.

» In the period Siang fu (A. D. 1008—1017), a native of Lien-
» cheu (province of Kwangtung), called Liang Shi, while divining
» about a plot of ground in which to bury one of his parents,
» beheld on a certain mountain a man who was settled there, and
» who told him that, ten days before, several tens of tortoises
» had carried thither a big tortoise on their backs and buried it
» in the mountain. Being of opinion that tortoises are animals of
» a spiritual nature, Liang surmised that the place where they
» had buried that beast might be a felicitous place, and therefore
» he climbed that mount with some of his people, in order to
» look for it. Perceiving something resembling a tumulus, they dug
» it up, and discovered a dead tortoise. After having taken it to
» another spot and buried it there, Liang interred his parent in

_____

1 吳明徹秦郡人也。父樹梁右軍將軍。明徹幼
孤、性至孝。塟用時、有伊氏者善占墓、謂其兄
曰、君葬之日必有乘白馬逐鹿者來經墳所、此
是最小孝子大貴之徵。至時果有此應、明徹卽
樹之最小子也. Books of the Ch͏en Dynasty, ch. 9, l. 8; also the History
of the Southern Part of the Realm, ch. 66, l. 22.

» the pit dug by the tortoises, and afterwards three sons were born
» unto him, named Lih-i, Lih-tseh, and Lih-hien. The two last-
» named took the degree of tsin-shi"[1].... and the three brothers
were all promoted to high official dignities.

According to various legends, lucky grave grounds have, moreover, often been pointed out by unknown or mysterious individuals
to persons destined to become men of wealth and rank. We quote
a couple of instances thereof from the Standard Histories:

» When T°ao Khan (a grandee of the highest ranks who lived A. D.
» 259—334) was still an obscure individual, he had to mourn for
» one of his parents. The time for burying the corpse drew near, when
» some member of his family suddenly missed a cow; and ere they
» had discovered its whereabouts, T°ao Khan met with an old
» man, who said to him: 'Near the knoll there, in front of you,
» I have seen a cow couched down in the mire; if that spot be
» used for a sepulchre, it will produce a man invested with the
» highest official dignities'. And then pointing to another mountain,
» the old man said: 'This is one degree inferior in quality; it
» will produce for some generations a dignity to which an official
» income of two thousand stones of rice appertains'. Having
» spoken thus, he vanished out of sight. Khan now went in
» search of the cow, and having discovered it, he buried his
» parent on the spot. The other mountain pointed out to him he
» ceded to (Cheu) Fang, who, when his father died, buried him
» there and actually became governor of a province. After him,

---

[1] 祥符中廉州人梁士卜地葬其親、至一山中
見居人、說旬日前有數十龜貟一大龜、葬於此
山中。梁以爲龜神物、其葬處或是福地、與其人
登山觀之。乃見有丘墓之象、試發之、果得一死
龜。梁乃遷葬他所、以龜之所穴葬其親、其後梁
生三子、立儀、立則、立賢。立則立賢皆以進士
登科. *Pu pih t'an* 補筆談, »Additions to the Pencil Gossip", being a
supplement to a collection of miscellanies in 26 chapters, written by Ch'en Kwah
沈括 in the eleventh century and entitled *Mung khi pih t'an* 夢溪筆
談, »Pencil Gossip of the Brook of my Dreams". This was a rivulet somewhere
in the south of the province of Kiangsu, on the borders of which the author spent
the latter period of his life.

» three generations of his descendants ruled over Yih-cheu for more
» than forty-one years, as had been prophesied by that man" [1].

— » In the first year of the period Ying lih (A. D. 951),
» Nü Li, finding himself in the environs of the Ya-poh mountains
» on the day after his mother's decease, beheld a giant. Frightened
» to death, he took to his heels, but the giant stopped him, saying:
» 'Do not be afraid, for I am the spirit of the ground. Bury your
» mother here in this spot, and you will soon appear at Court
» and become a man of high position'. Nü Li followed this advice,
» and was many times invested with the dignity of Chamberlain
» of the Stud" [2].

3. The History of Fung-shui

Our exposition of the Fung-shui system has shown that its
leading principles have their origin in remote antiquity. Its first
embryo, indeed, grew out of the worship of the dead, which
already in the mist of ages was the religion proper of the Chinese.
The deceased ancestors were then their principal patron divinities,
who influenced the fate and fortunes of their descendants in every
way. Every one propitiated them systematically, and from this
worship a tendency gradually arose of placing the dead in such
subterranean abodes as would afford rest, comfort and felicity to
their manes. And the answer to the question: which grounds are
best suited for burial places? was naturally sought in the forms
and characteristics of the surroundings.

---

[1] 初陶侃微時、丁艱。將葬家中忽失牛、而不
知所在、遇一老父、謂曰、前崗見一牛眠山汙
中、其地若葬位極人臣矣。又指一山云、此亦其
次、當世出二千石。言訖不見。侃尋牛、得之、因
葬其處。以所指別山與（周）訪、訪父死葬焉、果
爲刺史。自訪以下三世爲益州四十一年如其
所言云. Books of the Tsin Dynasty, ch. 58, l. 18.

[2] 女里應歷初以母憂去一日至雅伯山、見一
巨人。惶懼走、巨人止之曰、勿懼、我地祇也、葬
爾母於斯、當速詣關必貴。女里從之、累遷馬羣
侍中. History of the Liao Dynasty, ch. 79, l. 3.

That the elementary principles of the Fung-shui system were practically applied already under the dynasty of Cheu, cannot reasonably be doubted, since we find that already in the fifth century before our era grave-sites were improved by the hand of man by means of artificial brooks and tanks.

Another great step which the ancients took in the direction of Fung-shui, was to connect the qualities of a grave with the influences supposed to be exerted upon it by the celestial canopy and the cardinal points thereof. This custom, too, can be traced back to the time of Hoh Lü. The sepulchre of this potentate was called the Tiger's Hill, a white tiger having settled on the summit on the third day after it was finished. Doubtless this statement is an allusion to the White Tiger of the sphere, the western quadrant, the influences cf which were supposed to have commenced operating upon the royal remains soon after their entombment.

This view is supported by the author of the Records of the country of Wu, who says that, »according to the Annals of Wu and »Yueh[1], three days after the burial of the king the essence of the »element metal assumed the shape of a white tiger and crouched »down on the top of the grave"[2]. Now, in the pre-Christian era. metal was identified by Chinese philosophers with the West. Kwan-tszĕ wrote: »The breath of the East wind, and wind creates wood. The breath »of the South is Yang, which creates fire. The Centre is earth. The »breath of the West is Yin, which gives birth to metal; and that of the »North is »cold, by which water is produced"[3]. Liu Ngam also stated that »the East appertains to wood, the South to fire, the West to metal, and »the North to water"[4]. These theories are easily explained. The

---

[1] We have not, however, been able to discover this statement in any of the copies we possess of this work.

[2] 吳越春秋云、葬經三日金精化為白虎、蹲其上. *Ku kin t'u shu tsih ch'ing*, sect. 坤輿, ch. 140.

[3] 東方其氣曰風、風生木。南方其氣曰陽、陽生火。中央曰土。西方其氣曰陰、陰生金。北方其氣曰寒、寒生水. *Kwan-tszĕ*, chapt. 14, § 40.

[4] 東方木也、南方火也、西方金也、北方水也. *Hung lieh kiai*, ch. 3, l. 3.

vegetable kingdom, *i. e.* wood, revives in spring, the season identified with the East; fire naturally appertains to the South or the region of heat, and water, its opposite element, to the opposite cardinal point; metal had thus to be assigned to the West, no other place being left for it.

Distinct traces of attempts to place the dead in their graves under proper influences of Nature, are also to be found in the *Li ki*. This Classic states (ch. 12, l. 34): »To bury the dead on the »north and with their heads turned to the north was a custom »generally observed during the three first dynasties" [1]. In another section it says (chapter 30, l. 20): »Thus the dead are placed with »their heads to the north, but the living turn their faces to the »south; all this is done in imitation of primeval usage" [2]. According to the Historical Records, the last sovereign of the Yin dynasty was buried in the north of his capital; and the *Tso ch' wen* likewise proves that we are not here dealing with a mere theoretical practice: it mentions, for instance, that the ruler Chwang was buried twice in the northern suburbs.

From these and other passages the Chinese generally draw the conclusion that the houses of the living, as well as the graves of the dead, in those ancient times used to face the south. As stated on page 942, it is still maintained at the present day, though, in by far the most cases, only theoretically. Of course it is not probable that this rule anciently extended to buildings of minor importance and to the dwellings of the common people. Perhaps it was then chiefly in force for palaces of rulers, and mansions of grandees who assisted them in the administration of the realm, it being noted in one of the appendices of the *Yih king* (ch. 17, l. 7): »The trigram Li represents light and renders »all things visible to each other; it is also the trigram of the »South. Sage rulers face the south when they give audience »to all under the sky, and they turn themselves to that region »of light in administering government" [3]. This rescript has always been observed to the letter by the emperors of succeeding dynasties,

---

[1] 葬於北方北首三代之達禮也. Sect. 檀弓, II, 1.

[2] 故死者北首、生者南鄉、皆從其初. Sect. 禮運, I.

[3] 離也者明也、萬物皆相見、南方之卦也。聖人南面而聽天下、嚮明而治. Sect. 說卦傳.

including the now reigning House. Hence the Imperial Palace, and all the principal buildings within its walls which serve for audiences or other government business, face due south; and this is also the case with the Metropolis, in the centre of which the Palace stands, its walls and gates exactly facing the four cardinal points.

From the fact that the ancient Chinese considered the South to be the principal seat of the blessings of the Universe, their country being regularly visited every year by the deadening influences of the rigorous North, and that they made the influences of the South to bear upon the position and construction of princely residences with the object of accumulating blessings upon the rulers and their subjects, we must conclude that they had made considerable advance in the direction of Fung-shui. We shall find this inference confirmed, if we may place any trust in the Annals of the States of Wu and Yueh; but this work is interspersed with too many anecdotes and romantic tales to be worthy of unreserved credit, and, moreover, it was not composed before the first century of the Christian era. We read therein that »Hoh Lü said to his minister »Wu Tszĕ-sü, (see note 6, p.148): 'In what does the art of ensuring »peace to princes and good rule to their people consist?' The an- »swer was: 'He who wishes to ensure peace to the prince, to have »the people ruled in a proper way, to make strong government »prevail, and to cause perfect rulers to bear sway from close by »over those who live far off, he certainly ought to start by erecting »city walls and moats, by appointing military chiefs, by filling »the granaries and stores, and by properly attending to the arsen- »als: in this the art in question consists'. 'This is all very well »and good', retorted Hoh Lü; 'but, though in building fortifi- »cations, store-houses and arsenals we really take notice of what »ought to be taken notice of with regard to the terrestrial influ- »ences, still there must exist in the domain of the Celestial Breath »some factors of which we may avail ourselves to keep neigh- »bouring kingdoms in fear and awe; is it not so?' — 'Yes', was »the reply. '1 charge you to put those factors into practice', said »Hoh Lü.

»Tszĕ-sü now gave orders for the investigation of the ground and »the examination of the water-courses, and, imitating the confi- »gurations of Heaven and Earth, he built a large city, forty-seven »miles in circumference. It had eight land-gates in imitation of »the eight winds of Heaven, and just as many water-gates corres-

» ponding to the eight good qualities of the Earth. He also built
» a smaller city (inside the other), ten miles in circumference. It
» had three land-gates; but that on the east (where light is born)
» was not opened, in order that the lustre and glory of the (ini-
» mical) realm of Yueh might be exterminated. The Gate of Efful-
» gent Sunlight was built as a representator of the gate of the heavens,
» and to admit the winds of the Gates that are shut upon the
» Effulgent Sunlight; and they made also a Serpent Gate in imita-
» tion of the door of Earth. Desiring westward to defeat the king-
» dom of Ch'u, which was situate north-west from his, Hoh Lü
» had the Gate of Effulgent Sunlight built, to admit the Breath
» of the heavens; therefore they called it also the Gate to defeat Ch'u.
» And as he desired to pacify eastward the kingdom of Yueh,
» which was situated to the south-east, he erected the Serpent
» Gate, in order to subdue this hostile country.

» Wu (Hoh Lü's realm) being situate in Ch'en, which point of
» the compass corresponds to the Dragon, a pair of i-yao fishes with
» reversed fins were placed over the southern gate of the small city,
» to represent the horns of the Dragon. And Yueh being situate in
» Szě, a point of the compass corresponding to the Serpent, there
» was over the great south gate a wooden snake, stretched towards
» the north and pushing its head into the gate, thus indicating
» that Yueh belonged to Wu" [1].

----

[1] 闔閭曰、安君治民其術奈何。子胥曰、凡欲
安君、治民、興霸、成王從近制遠者、必先立城
郭、設守備、實倉廩、治兵庫、斯則其術也。闔閭
曰、善、夫築城郭立倉庫因地制宜、豈有天氣之
數以威隣國者乎。子胥曰、有。闔閭曰、寡人委
討於子。

子胥乃使相土嘗水、象天法地造築大城、周
廻四十七里。陸門八以象天八風、水門八以法
地八聰。築小城、周十里。陸門三、不開東面者、
欲以絕越明也。立閶門者以象天門、通閶闔風
也、立蛇門者以象地戶也。闔閭欲西破楚、楚在
西北、故立閶門以通天氣、因復名之破楚門。欲
東并大越、越在東南、故立蛇門以制敵國。

吳在辰、其位龍也、故小城南門上反羽爲兩

This long extract requires explanation. The duodenary cycle of Branches, indicating the twelve points of the compass and used to denote the years, months, days and hours, is combined for divining purposes with the Twelve Animals in the following way:

Tszĕ	子	appertains to	鼠 the Rat.
Chᶜeu	丑	»	» 牛 the Cow.
Yin	寅	»	» 虎 the Tiger.
Mao	卯	»	» 兎 the Hare.
Chᶜen	辰	»	» 龍 the Dragon.
Szĕ	巳	»	» 蛇 the Serpent.
Wu	午	»	» 馬 the Horse.
Wei	未	»	» 羊 the Goat.
Shen	申	»	» 猴 the Monkey.
Yiu	酉	»	» 雞 the Fowl.
Suh	戌	»	» 犬 the Dog.
Hai	亥	»	» 猪 the Pig.

Accordingly, the Annals of Wu and Yueh lead us to believe that this combination of the Branches and Animals was in vogue in the sixth century before Christ, the book mentioning the Dragon in connection with Chᶜen, and the Serpent in connection with the branch Szĕ *i. e.* the South-east (see page 965). But, as stated above, the work was written in the first century of our era, and the whole episode may owe its existence to the imagination of the author. Yet, at any rate, the conclusion is allowable that the Branches and Animals used to be combined for geomantic and necromantic purposes when its author lived. This is confirmed by the fact that in a contemporaneous work, entitled *Lun heng* [1] or » Discussions and Criticisms", the following odd passage occurs: » The

---

鯢鰌以象龍角。越在巳地、其位蛇也、故南大門上有木蛇、北向、首內、示越屬於吳也. Chapter II, ll. 1 and 2.

1 論衡. This work doubtless is one of the most interesting products of the Han dynasty. Its author, Wang Tᶜung 王統, with great boldness criticises the superstitions of his time and even attacks Confucius and Mencius; the work thus forms a valuable source of knowledge of the ideas and customs prevalent at the beginning of our era.

» influences of the Five Elements attack and impair each other,
» and sanguiferous animals conquer and overpower each other; how
» is this phenomenon to be explained? The answer is: The branch
» Y i n corresponds to the element wood, and its animal is the tiger;
» S u h appertains to earth, and its animal is the dog; C h ʿe u and
» W e i likewise appertain to earth, and their animals are the cow and
» the goat. Now, as wood overpowers earth, it follows that dogs, cows
» and sheep are subdued by the tiger. H a i appertains to water, and its
» animal is the pig, S z ĕ corresponds to fire, and its animal is the
» serpent; T s z ĕ is identical with water, and its animal is the rat;
» and W u appertains to fire, and its animal is the horse. Hence,
» whereas water conquers fire, pigs devour snakes; and because fire is
» impaired by water, horses that devour a rat get a swelled belly on
» voiding excrements" [1]. This idle play with the Cycles and Elements
will be partly explained when we notice what has been brought forward on page 957 concerning the influences exerted by the Elements
upon each other, and when we take into account that the Branches,
denoting the cardinal points (see pp. 965 *seq.*), appertain to the
Elements because these are likewise identified with the cardinal
points (see p. 983). Thus the following combinations are obtained:

Yin	寅	
Mao	卯	appertain to the East and Wood.
Chʿen	辰	

Szĕ	巳	
Wu	午	appertain to the South and Fire.
Wei	未	

Shen	申	
Yiu	酉	appertain to the West and Metal.
Suh	戌	

---

[1] 五行之氣相賊害、含血之蟲相勝服、其驗何
在。曰、寅木也、其禽虎也、戌土也、其禽犬也、丑
未亦土也、丑禽牛、未禽羊也。木勝土、故犬與
牛羊爲虎所服也。亥水也、其禽豕也、巳火也、
其禽蛇也、子亦水也、其禽鼠也、午亦火也、其
禽馬也。水勝火、故豕食蛇、火爲水所害、故馬
食鼠屎而腹脹. Chapter III, § 物勢.

Hai 亥 ⎫
Tsze 子 ⎬ appertain to the North and Water.
Ch°eu 丑 ⎭

That the combination of the Branches with the Animals was in vogue in the beginning of the Christian era, is also proved by the *Shwoh wen*, the famous dictionary which dates from the first century, for it says that » the character Sze represents the shape of a serpent" [1]. The native books show that the Twelve Animals have, since the Han dynasty, played an important part in Chinese life as factors in soothsaying and divination, as they were believed to exercise an influence, according to the attributes ascribed to each, over the years, days and hours denoted by the Branches to which they respectively appertain.

The cycle of Animals is generally styled » the Twelve Animals" [2] and the combination of the two cycles: » the Dozens which appertain to each other" [3]. The origin of the cycle of Animals is shrouded in mystery and is a puzzle for Chinese authors, no trace of it being found in the Classics. Some have ascribed its use in China to the influence of intercourse with other nations, because it is in vogue among the Mongols, Coreans, Japanese, Siamese and other Asiatic peoples. Schlegel has tried to demonstrate on astronomical grounds that it must be of pure Chinese origin [4].

Returning now to our extract from the Annals of Wu and Yueh, we must give our readers some information about the eight Celestial Winds and the winds emitted by the mystic Gates shut upon the Effulgent Sunlight, in order that a better insight may be obtained into Fung-shui in its earliest stages. Those eight winds are mentioned by Liu Ngan in the following words: » The Directing Wind » comes forty-five days after the winter solstice (that is to say, about » the beginning of spring); forty-five days afterwards (at mid-spring) » the Wind of the Illumination of all Beings blows, and again just » as many days later (in the beginning of summer) the Winds of » Pure Brightness come, to be replaced by the Winds of Bright » Sunlight after a like number of days (*i. e.* at midsummer). Again

---

[1] 巳爲蛇象形.
[2] 十二禽.   [3] 十二相屬.
[4] Uranographie Chinoise, pp. 565 *sqq.*

64

» forty-five days afterwards (in the beginning of autumn) comes the
» Cool Breeze, and after another forty-five days (at mid-autumn)
» the Wind of the Gates that are shut upon the Effulgent Sun-
» light. The Wind of Imperfection then arrives after forty-five days
» (in the beginning of winter), and again so many days having
» elapsed (at mid-winter), the Wind of Devoidness of Extensive
» Power begins to blow" [1]. From this excerpt we see that those
winds simply denote the influences of Nature which operate during
the eight seasons respectively, regulating the weather and the tem-
perature. As the seasons were connected with the points of the compass (see pp. 962 *seq.*), the winds too were theoretically identified
therewith. We read in the Historical Records, in a chapter specially
devoted to natural science:

» The Wind of Imperfection occupies the North-west, thus
» presiding at the killing of life. The Wind of Devoidness of Ex-
» tensive Power occupies the North. 'Devoidness of extensive power'
» means that (in the North) the Yang has sunk away, without the
» Yin having so extensive and great an influence as to stand on a par
» with that of the Yang. The Directing Wind occupies the North-
» east and consequently has the upper hand in the first production
» of everything endowed with life. 'Directing' means to manage
» all living beings in such a wise that they are produced, and
» therefore this wind bears this appellation. The Wind of the Illu-
» mination of all Beings is settled in the East, and its name refers
» to the illumination of living nature which is entirely produced
» (when it blows). The Wind of Pure Brightness has its seat
» in the South-east, and it dominates over all living nature over
» which the winds blow. The Wind of Bright Sunlight abides in
» the South; this word 'bright' expresses the condition of the
» breath of the Yang at the zenith of its (annual) revolution.
» The Cool Breeze occupies the South-west. And the Wind of the
» Gates that are shut upon the Effulgent Sunlight is stationed
» in the West. The word 'effulgent' refers to the brightness and

---

[1] 冬至四十五日條風至、條風至四十五日明
庶風至、明庶風至四十五日清明風至、清明風
至四十五日景風至、景風至四十五日涼風至、
涼風至四十五日閶闔風至、閶闔風至四十五日
不周風至、不周風至四十五日廣莫風至. *Hung lieh
kiai*, ch. III.

» glory (of the sun); 'to shut the gates' means to conceal; and
» the name of this wind alludes to the shutting up in the earth
» of living nature produced by the operation of the Yang" [1].

Hoh Lü's attempt to establish his supremacy over the surrounding
kingdoms by building his city in such a wise that the influences
of the heavens and the earth were represented by it and consequently operated upon it, affords proof of the correctness of our
statement made on page 936, that the rise of Fung-shui coincides with that of Taoism, the philosophical-religious system which
taught people that man, living, as he does, under the absolute
sway of Nature, best ensures his felicity by adapting and conforming
himself to the influences of the Universe. The ancients even went
so far as to suffer the heavens themselves to decide about the location
of the graves and dwellings they intended to build. For this purpose
they availed themselves of the stalks of a certain plant, called
shi [2], which they believed to be imbued with an extraordinary
supply of vital force or so-called shen, composed of Yang substance (see page 952), and therefore more capable than anything
else of divulging the will and intentions of the heavens, the great
embodiment of the Yang. Those stalks were so manipulated as to
give the lineal figures or kwa, and these figures were subsequently
interpreted by the aid of sentences contained in the *Yih king* and
other books of a similar character.

In its section on the funeral ceremonies for ordinary officers and
their nearest relatives, the *I li* contains a very lucid account of the
way in which this peculiar method of consulting Nature took place
when a grave had to be made. It literally runs as follows:

» Consultation of the divining stalks about an abode for a defunct.
» The Officer for the Grave Mounds having measured out a spot for

---

[1] 不周風居西北、主殺生。廣莫風居北方、廣
莫者言陽氣在下、陰莫陽廣大也。條風居東北、
主出萬物、條之言條治萬物而出之、故曰條風。
明庶風居東方、明庶者明眾物盡出也。清明風
居東南、維主風吹萬物。景風居南方、景者言陽
氣道竟。涼風居西南。閶闔風居西方、閶者倡也、
闔者藏也、言陽氣道萬物闔黃泉也。Chapter 25.

[2] 蓍.

»the purpose, a hole is dug at each of the four corners and the earth
»placed outside the spot; a hole is dug also in the middle, and the earth
»put down on the southern side. The principal mourners having
»finished their wailing for the defunct in the morning, resort thither,
»and range themselves on the south side of that spot assigned by a
»tortoise-shell, with their faces to the north, without the mourning
»bands around their heads.

» A person who is to order the stalks to be consulted, stands
» on the right of the principal mourners. The diviner turns his face
» to the east, pulls off the upper part of the case which contains
» the stalks, and, holding both the case and stalks in his hands and
» turning his face to the south, receives (by mouth of the afore-
» said person) the order to begin the work, which order runs as
» follows: 'The distressed sons So-and-So for the sake of their father
» So-and-So wish to consult the stalks about his grave, lest the site
» for his dark abode, which has been duly assigned by the figures
» of a tortoise shell, should entail troubles on any of them in
» future'. The diviner answers that he will obey the order, but he
» does not repeat the same.

» Now turning round to the right, so that he stands with his
» face to the north, he stretches out his finger to the centre of the
» grave and manipulates the stalks. A man for the k w a stands on
» his left side. When the divination is finished, (this man writes
» out the k w a, and) the diviner takes it, to show it to the person
» who has ordered him to consult the stalks. This man receives
» the k w a, inspects it and gives it back to the diviner, who,
» turning his face eastward, examines it with the aid of his
» assistants; then he comes forward, to say to the man who has
» ordered him to divine, and to the chief mourners: 'We have
» examined it, and it portends that the project may be executed'.
» The chief mourners now put on their headbands and wail, but
» without stamping their feet. If the stalks declare that the plan
» must not be executed, they are consulted, with observance of the
» above rules, about some other spot which has been selected" [1].

---

[1] 筮宅。冢人營之、掘四隅、外其壤、掘中、南其
壤。既朝哭主人皆往、兆南北面、免絰。
　　命筮者在主人之右。筮者東面、抽上韇、兼執
之、南面受命、命曰、哀子某爲其父某甫筮宅、

This excerpt teaches us that the first indications about favourable burial sites used to be obtained by the consultation of tortoise shells. Tortoises, like the divining plant, being considered to be pervaded throughout with s h e n substance, their shells were scorched with hot instruments, for the purpose of deducing predictions from the lines and spots thus rendered visible. The *Cheu li* says: »On the decease of the sovereign, the Sub-Intendant of Religious Worship »finds out by means of a tortoise-shell the place where the sepulchre »is to be made, and this he repeats when they begin to dig the pit"[1]. Such of our readers as understand the written language of the Chinese will see that, in this passage, the place assigned by a tortoise-shell as fit for a grave is denoted by the same character which the *I li* uses in the above extract to by the same character which the *I li* uses in the above extract to express the same thing, viz. 兆, which Chinese etymologists say is a hieroglyphic representation of the lines and marks found on a tortoise-shell. So, also, in the description of the functions of the Officer for the Grave Mounds the *Cheu li* denotes burial sites by the term 兆 域, which means: »places (域) appointed by the lines and spots» on a tortoise-shell". In many other works of antiquity reference to what they generally style p u h t s a n g 卜 葬, »drawing prognostics about burial »places from tortoise-shells", is often enough made to justify the conclusion that this practice was then most commonly prevalent.

This method of the ancients of suffering the heavens themselves to assign their graves through the medium of tortoises and s h i stalks, has been adopted by subsequent dynasties and incorporated into their ceremonial institutions. The K h a i y u e n Ritual contains rescripts on this head which, in the main, are the same as those of the *I li*; but they declare that only for officers of the five highest degrees a tortoise-shell may be consulted, viz. at the same time as the stalks are being used. Moreover, they state that this double augura-

---

度茲幽宅兆基無有後艱。筮人許諾、不述命。
　右還、北面、指中封而筮。卦者在左。卒筮、執
卦以示命筮者。命筮者受視、反之、東面旅占、
卒進、告于命筮者與主人、占之、曰從。主人絰、
哭不踊。若不從、筮擇如初儀. Chapt. 28, ll. 50 *sqq.*
　[1] 小宗伯王崩卜葬兆、甫竁亦如. Chapter 19, l. 23.

tion shall be followed by a sacrifice to the God of Earth, and they give detailed rules for this ceremony. That the dynasty which enacted those rescripts also practised them at the demise of emperors, may be seen from the description of the ritual which was instituted for the burial of Tai Tsung in A. D. 780 [1]. The funeral rites prescribed by the Ming dynasty for the use of the official classes and laid down in the *Ta Ming hwui tien* [2], do not, however, make any reference to the ancient method of selecting graves.

The devotees of geomancy themselves are fully convinced that their art has been practised from the earliest times on record in literature. If asked for proofs in support of this belief, they unanimously appeal to a certain passage occurring in one of the Appendices of the *Yih king* (chapter 13, l. 12), which says: » By » looking up, in order to contemplate the heavenly bodies, and by » looking down to examine into the natural influences of the earth, » man may acquire a knowledge of the causes of darkness and » light" [3]. Yet this passage in itself is valueless for ascertaining the antiquity of the system, even apart from the fact that the Appendix containing it bears internal evidence of having been written after the time of Confucius, though native scholars pretend that it is a product of the sage's pen. Nor is the fact that the k w a, cycles, constellations etc., which play a prominent part in the system, have been used for chronologic, astrologic and horoscopic purposes since very early times, any argument for the antiquity of Fung-shui, the established opinion of its adepts and professors notwithstanding.

The early traces of geomantic superstition assume sharper outlines during the dynasties of Ts'in and Han. It has been already remarked that grave brooks and grave tanks were then indispensable appurtenances of royal sepulchres (p. 947); that Shi Hwang's mausoleum was adorned with stars, constellations and the configurations of the Earth; that coffins used to be painted with heavenly luminaries and figures of the four Celestial Animals (page 979), all which practices

---

1 Compare the » Record of the Ceremonies for the Yuen Mausoleum" 元陵 儀注, inserted in the *T'ung tien* of Tu Yiu, and reproduced in the *Ku kin t'u shu tsih ch'ing*, sect. 禮儀, chapter 56.

2 Chapter 92, l. 7.

3 仰以觀於天文、俯以察於地理、是故知幽明 之故. Section 繫辭傳, I.

had decidedly no other object than that of concentrating the influences of the Universe around the dead. Besides, many other data which mark the progress achieved by Fung shui during the Han dynasty, are supplied by the books. They teach us that already in the second century before our era China possessed a class of proficients in geomancy. The Historical Records [1] mention such a category of persons under the name of Khan-yü kia [2], »the Khan-yü Class" (comp. page 940), among sundry species of diviners whom the emperor Hiao Wu [3], who reigned from the year 140 to 86 B. C., one day consulted upon the question whether a certain date was suitable for consummating marriage, and from whom he received entirely different answers. The books show furthermore that, during the Han dynasty, there existed a Fung-shui literature. The »Memoir on Skilful Writings" [4] in the Official History of that epoch mentions, under the heading: »Authors on the Five Ele-ments" [5], thirty-one titles of works of divination, one of which, entitled: The Golden Khan-yü Thesaurus, in fourteen Chapters [6], leaves no room to doubt that it was devoted to geomancy. The same Memoir sums up also six works of »Authors on the Rules »concerning Forms, who treated on a wide scale of the configur-»ations in the nine subdivisions of the Empire and derived there-»from the shape of cities and dwellings; they also treated of »the dimensions and numbers in the osseous system of man and »the six domestic animals, and of the forms and capacity of »vessels and implements, thus fixing of everything the respective »sound and breath, the value or non-value, the auspicious or in-»auspicious operation" [7]. Among these six works one was probably more specially devoted to geomancy than the others, being entitled: On the Configurations of Grounds for Mansions and Houses, in twenty Chapters [8].

---

1 In an appendix to chapter 127, written by Ch'u Siao-sun 褚少孫 in the first century B. C.

2 堪輿家.　　　　　　3 孝武.

4 藝文志, the 30th. chapter of the Books of the Early Han Dynasty.

5 五行家.　　　　　6 堪輿金匱十四卷.

7 形法者大舉九州之埶、以立城郭室舍形、人及六畜骨法之度數、器物之形容、以求其聲氣貴賤吉凶. Books of the Early Han Dynasty, ch. 30, ll. 49.

8 宮宅地形二十卷.

That treatises on geomancy and divination were numerous during the Early Han dynasty, is evinced by the following passage relating to Wang King [1], a high official of great renown for his learning and attainments in hydraulics. »From the very first it had » been his conviction that, although the six Classics all contain » references to divination by means of tortoise-shells and stalks, so » that every undertaking or proceeding was decided upon by the » divining plant and the tortoise, yet all the books extant con- » tained erroneous and confused statements on this head, and the » notions about the auspicious or inauspicious character of augu- » ries subverted each other. Hence he compared and collocated the » existing treatises of every author on the art of making calcula- » tions, as also the notions about the matters that were disallowed » and to be avoided at grave-making and house-building, the factors » of geomancy, horoscopy etc.; and he compiled everything, for so » far as it was of any practical use, into a work entitled: The » fifty Original Groundstones" [2].

Under, or perhaps shortly after the Han dynasty, there existed a work, called: The Canon of Dwellings [3], which is generally consi- dered to be the oldest exponent of Fung-shui extant, as still practised at the present day. Its origin was ascribed to Hwang Ti [4], »the Yellow Emperor", a mythical sovereign of the 27th. century before our era, for ever famous as the father of civilisation and the art of govern- ment. We can scarcely suppose this ascription to have been an idle attempt to give the book a saintly odour of antiquity. We think it must be taken simply as an indication that the doctrines laid down in the book were based upon the pure, unalloyed orthodox conceptions which had been in vogue from the dawn of civilisation about the Universe and its influence upon the fate of man. A small treatise under the same name still exists; but it is far from certain whether it is not a production of more recent date [5].

---

[1] 王景.

[2] 初景以爲六經所載皆有卜筮、作事舉止質於著龜、而衆書錯糅、吉凶相反。乃參紀衆家數術文書、冢宅禁忌、堪輿、日相之屬、適於事用者集爲大衍立基云. Books of the Later Han Dynasty, chapter 106, l. 8.

[3] 宅經.   [4] 黃帝.

[5] A reprint of it is inserted in the *Ku kin t'u shu tsih ch'ing*, sect. 藝術, ch. 651.

It gives a great extension to geomantic speculation by distinguishing between buildings in which either the Yang or the Yin has the upper hand, and contains directions for planning out both categories in such a wise that they insure a maximum of glory and honour, wealth, prosperity and official dignities to the inhabitants and their still unborn offspring for many generations. It also dilates elaborately upon the laying out of graves, and gives many useful hints · as to the restoration and rebuilding of dwellings of the living and the dead. It is said that from the Han dynasty dates also a so-called Canon of Burials [1], the authorship of which is ascribed to a certain Master Blue Raven [2], whose real name, if it were ever known, has fallen into oblivion. A few poor fragments only have escaped the destroying hand of time and are re-printed in the *Ku kin t'u shu tsih ch'ing* [3]; they may be consulted with advantage by those who can afford to waste more time and labour upon a study of the development and growth of the Fung-shui vagaries than we can.

The development of Fung-shui and its literature during the Han dynasty naturally coincided with the revival of the studies of antiquity, which marked that epoch. Under imperial auspices, every written relic which had escaped the incendiary caprice of Shi Hwang, was eagerly collected, studied and expounded; the Classics were cast in their present shape; and during the revival of a general interest in literature, philosophers arose, who indulged in wild speculations on Nature and its Tao or unalterable course, speculations for which they found ample material in the Classics. Thus a literature was created, abounding in cosmogonic vagaries, astrology and alchemy, and ever supplying food for new speculation of the same kind, which, being only guided by the traditional notions borrowed from the ancients, was gradually consolidated into the Fung-shui system in force at the present day, a system destined, it would seem, to crush China under its weight during the existence of its petrified culture. As the fundamental ideas and practices of the system can be traced back to very ancient times, and their development is intimately bound up with the enlargement of the scope of early speculations on Nature, the history of Fung-shui becomes the history of Chinese philosophy in general.

---

1 葬書.

2 青烏先生. Comp. page 1016, note 2.

3 Section 藝術, chapt. 655.

The part which Fung-shui superstition played in grave-building
during the Han dynasty is elucidated by the two following episodes, said to have occurred respectively in the first and the second
century of our era. » When Yuen Ngan's father had died, his
» mother ordered him to seek for a place to bury him. On the
» road he met with three literary men, who asked him where he
» was going. He informed them of his purpose, whereupon they
» pointed out to him a certain spot, saying: 'Bury him there;
» that place must produce to some generations of your family the
» highest office in the state'. At the same moment they vanished.
» Ngan felt interested in the prediction, and forthwith he buried
» his father on the spot those men had discovered by augury. Sub-
» sequently his offspring were overloaded with fame and glory for
» several generations" [1].

» When Wu Hiung was a lad, his family was so poor that, on
» the death of his mother, he cast his eyes upon a plot of ground
» in which nobody made graves, and there he selected a place
» to bury her. The burial he performed with so much haste,
» without inquiring whether the hour or day were favourable,
» that the medicating spiritist mediums unanimously prophesied
» that it must entail the extermination of his clan. But Hiung took
» no notice of their talk, and three generations of his family, viz.
» himself, his son Yin and his grandson Kung, became Comman-
» ders of the Palace Guard, and signalized themselves as famous
» writers on legislation" [2].

From these episodes we learn that, in those times, geomancy
sharpened its wits more especially in the discovery of graves which
would insure to the offspring of the occupants promotion to high state-
offices. This cannot surprise us, since investment with official dignities has always signified in China the same thing as wealth, power,

---

[1] 初袁安父沒、母使安訪求葬地。道逢三書生、
問安何之。安爲言其故、生乃指一處、云、葬此
地、當世爲上公。須臾不見。安異之、於是遂葬
其所占之地, 故累世隆盛焉. Books of the Later Han Dynasty,
ch. 75, l. 5.

[2] 吳雄少時家貧、喪母營人所不封土者擇葬
其中。喪事趣辦、不問時日、醫巫皆言當族滅。
而雄不顧、及子訢孫恭三世廷尉、爲法名家. Books
of the Later Han Dynasty, ch. 76, l. 3.

honour and glory in this world and the next, in short, the perfect
realisation of every Chinaman's favourite dream. We lay stress on
this main feature of early geomancy, because it has characterized
Fung-shui throughout all ages, and is at this day its principal
feature still.

That graves could produce the highest offices to the descendants
of the persons buried therein, nay, even the imperial dignity, was
during the Han dynasty an orthodox article of faith, even among
the most learned. Lie Hiang (see note 7, p.148), though one of the most
celebrated authors the Middle Kingdom has produced, a man,
moreover, who occupied a foremost place among the scholars employed in the task of elucidating and expounding the ancient texts
and who held the highest offices of trust during several years —
this man believed in it as firmly as the most superstitious child
of his nation. This is evinced by a memorial he presented to the
Throne with the object of breaking the power and influence of
» a family Wang, twenty-three members of which drove about in
» decorated cars with vermilion wheels; a family counting its mem-
» bers wearing blue or red sable fur by numbers like unto swarms
» of locusts, and standing arrayed around the Throne within the
» imperial mansion like scales around a fish" [1]. Insinuating that
many of them, in spite of their high dignities, indulged in bad
behaviour and nefarious acts, he wrote:

» Under the Emperor Hiao Chao, a stone rose up of its own
» power on the hill Kwan on mount T'ai, and the same thing
» occurred in Shang-lin with a willow that had fallen to the ground
» — and thereupon the throne was occupied by the emperor Hiao
» Süen [2]. At present, a post of Rottlera wood on the ancestral
» tombs of the family Wang located in the Ts'i-nan country, produces
» branches and leaves; the foliage it bears spreads out over the
» houses, and its roots extend underneath the ground. Nothing
» whatever, not even the stone and the willow that rose of them-

---

[1] 王氏一姓乘朱輪華轂者二十三人、青紫貂
蟬克盈、幄內魚鱗左右. Books of the Early Han Dynasty,
chapter 36, l. 29.

2 According to Chapter 75 of the Books of the Early Han Dynasty, these mi-
racles, and a few more into the bargain, occurred in B. C. 78, and were interpreted
by wise men as portending the enthronement of an emperor of another branch of
the reigning family. Indeed, the next emperor, Hiao Süen, was not a descendant of
Hiao Chao, but his uncle's grandson.

» selves, has ever given a clearer warning. But the significance of
» the two cases is by no means equally great. Indeed, the family
» Wang is not of so high a position as the family Liu (to which
» Your Majesty belongs); moreover, the miracle with respect to the
» last-named family merely predicted, through mount T͏ͨai, a paci-
» fication, while that (which has now occurred on the tombs) of the
» first named portends a lurking danger resembling a pile of eggs" [1].
The tendency of this warning was clear enough: the zealous minister
insinuated that the wonderful graves were preparing the descendants
of the occupants for the imperial dignity. However, we do not
find it recorded whether the emperor turned a willing ear to this
hint to exterminate the whole family.

The third century of our era, signalized by the downfall of the
Han dynasty, is marked in the history of Fung-shui as having given
birth to the first prophet of geomancy who has ever remained
famous for his high attainments in this art, viz. Kwan Loh [2], one
of the greatest astrologers, soothsayers and fortune-tellers Far Cathay
has ever produced. The marvellous acuteness this man possessed is
clearly instanced by the following event, recorded in his biography in
the Standard History of the dynasty under which he lived. » While
» travelling to the west with a division of the army, he passed
» by the foot of the sepulchre of Wu Khiu-kien. Reclining against
» a tree, he began to hum a verse in a wailing tone of voice,
» quite out of spirits. Being asked what the matter was, he said:
» ‘The copse and trees here grow luxuriantly, but those configura-
» tions necessary to secure a long existence to the offspring of the
» buried man are wanting. There will be no descendants to guard
» the eulogy engraven on the epitaph-stone, however flattering it is.
» The Black Warrior (*i. e.* the Black Tortoise) conceals his head,
» the Azure Dragon has no feet, the White Tiger holds the corpse
» in its jaws, and the Vermilion Bird is wailing piteously; the
» grave being placed under the protection of four imminent dangers,

---

[1] 孝昭帝時冠石立於泰山、仆柳起於上林、而
孝宣帝卽位。今王氏先祖墳墓在濟南者其梓柱
生枝葉、扶疏上出屋、根垂地中。雖立石起柳
無以過此之明也。事執不兩大。王氏與劉氏亦
且不並立、如下有泰山之安、則上有累卵之危·
Op. et cap. cit., l. 30.

[2] 管輅·

» it must surely entail the extermination of the clan, and this
» will happen within two years'. This prophecy was literally ful-
» filled" [1].

Kwan Loh's fame, great though it is, is almost entirely eclipsed
by the halo surrounding the name of Kwoh Poh [2]. This man, who
lived from 276—324 A. D., was a scholar of high attainments,
and his name as such is inseparably connected with some works of
antiquity which he annotated and commented upon. Not only is he
ranked among the highest authorities on antiquarian subjects, but
all the proficients, professors and adapts of Fung-shui look up to
him as the great patriarch of their art, nay even as their patron
divinity. He was at the same time a first-rate soothsayer, the art
of fortune-telling being, as our readers know, intimately connected
with geomancy and practised with the aid of much the same factors
and cycles. His biography in the Standard History of the dynasty
under which he lived recounts that » there lodged in Ho-tung (his
» native place) a gentleman of the same surname as his own, who was
» very clever in drawing prognostics from tortoise shells and divining
» stalks; he followed that person, learned from him the secrets of
» the art, and having received from him a 'Book on the Contents
» of the Blue Bag', in nine chapters, he thoroughly understood
» the arts relating to the Five Elements, Astrology and Divination,
» knowing how to expel calamities, how to avert disasters, and how
» to bring complete succour in hopeless cases. Even King Fang [3]
» and Kwan Loh did not excel him" [4].

His geomantic skill savours of witchcraft, and the records repre-

---

[1] 輅隨軍西行、過毋丘儉墓下。倚樹哀吟、精
神不樂。人問其故、輅曰、林木雖茂、無形可久。
碑誄雖美、無後可守。玄武藏頭、蒼龍無足、白
虎銜尸、朱雀悲哭、四危以備、法當滅族、不過
二載其應至矣。卒如其言. Memoirs of the Three Kingdoms;
Memoirs of Wei, ch. 29, l. 24.

[2] 郭璞.

3 A famous man of letters in the first century B. C.

[4] 有郭公者客居河東、精於卜筮、璞從之、受
業。公以青囊中書九卷與之、由是遂洞五行、天
文、卜筮之術、攘災、轉禍、通致無方。雖京房管
輅不能過也. Books of the Tsin Dynasty, chapter 72, l. 1.

sent him in fact as a cunning magician. » Having lost his mother,
» he resigned his office, and with a tortoise shell sought out a
» burial place for her in Ki-yang. The spot being not farther from
» the borders of the water than some hundred paces, there was much
» gossip abroad about its being too near; but Poh declared that
» the water would soon become dry ground. Afterwards sand was
» flooded up over an area of several tens of miles from the grave,
» and entirely converted into orchards and fields" [1].

» When Poh had made a grave for a certain man, the emperor
» disguised himself and went out to see it. 'Why have you buried
» the corpse in the horn of the Dragon?' he asked the owner
» of the grave; 'this must cause the destruction of your clan'.
» 'Kwoh Poh has declared', the owner answered, 'that, whereas
» at this grave the ears of the Dragon are not visible, it must
» cause a Son of Heaven to come here before three years have
» elapsed'. 'Shall it produce a Son of Heaven?' asked the emperor.
» 'It possesses the faculty of causing a Son of Heaven to come
» hither to ask questions', was the reply. The emperor stood struck
» with amazement" [2]. The *finesse* of this geomantic *tour de force*
consists in this, that the Dragon is the emblem of the emperor,
so that, if it has no ears, the emperor hears nothing, and is obliged
to come out and ask for information.

» When Ch'ing, the great-grandfather of (Chang) Yü, had to
» bury his father, Kwoh Poh drew prognostics about some spots,
» and said: 'If you bury him in this place, you will live to be over
» a hundred years of age and attain one of the three highest official
» dignities, but you will then not have a numerous offspring. And
» if you inter him in that spot, your lifetime will only be half as
» long and your official career will be cut off on having attained
» the dignity of Director of a Court, but your issue be honoured
» and illustrious for a series of generations'. Ch'ing performed the

---

[1] 璞以母憂去職、卜葬地於暨陽。去水百步許、
人以近水爲言、璞曰、當即爲陸矣。其後沙漲去
墓數十里、皆爲桑田. *Op. et cap. cit.*, l. 11.

[2] 璞嘗爲人葬、帝微服往觀之。因問主人、何
以葬龍角、此法當滅族。主人曰、郭璞云、此葬
龍耳不出、三年當致天子也。帝曰、出天子邪。
答曰、能致天子問耳。帝甚異之. *Op. et loc. cit.*

» burial in the weaker spot, and thus he became Director of the
» Court of Imperial Entertainment and died at the age of sixty-
» four; but his children and grandchildren had a glorious career" [1].

It might be expected that a man of Kwoh Poh's skill would
first of all have selected for himself a grave so perfect as to raise
his offspring to the highest earthly glory. It is stated that » he
» never omitted to cut off and bury his nails and hair wherever
» he found an auspicious spot, in consequence of which graves of
» Kwoh Poh are to be found everywhere" [2]; and yet his biographer
only makes mention of one of his sons who was called to an
official dignity, viz. that of prefect of Lin-ho [3], in the present province
of Kwangsi. It does not, however, appear that this plain fact has
ever, to the present day, shaken the national belief in the efficacy
of Fung-shui.

The biographer of Kwoh Poh relates that » his disciple Chao Tsai
» stole the Book of the Blue Bag, and that it fell a prey to the flames
» before he could commence the study of it" [4]. It must not therefore be confounded with the work ascribed to Kwoh Poh, which
is current at this day under the title of » Canon of the Blue Bag
and the Corners of the Seas, revealed by the mysterious Virgins
of the nine Celestial Spheres" [5]. This title designates a treatise
on the heavens, which are indeed a sort of blue bag comprising
everything, and dealing, moreover, with the earth, girt at the
four points of the compass by oceans; it is, in short, a book on
natural philosophy, based upon revelations given in the good old
time by certain mystic beings about the evolution of the Universe

---

[1] 初［張］裕曾祖澄當葬爻、郭璞爲占墓地、曰、葬某處、年過百歲、位至三司、而子孫不蕃。某處、年幾減半、位裁卿校、而累世貴顯。澄乃葬其劣處、位光祿、年六十四而亡、其子孫遂昌云. History of the Southern Part of the Realm, ch. 34, l. 2.

[2] 凡遇吉地必剪爪髮葬之、故郭璞墓所在有之. *Tan yuen tsung luh*, quoted in the *Ku kin t'u shu tsih ch'ing*, sect. 坤 輿, ch.140.

[3] 臨賀.

[4] 璞門人趙載嘗竊青囊書、未及讀而爲火所焚. Books of the Tsin Dynasty, ch. 72, l. 1.

[5] 九天玄女青囊海角經. These Virgins have been mentioned already on page 105.

from chaos or primary nothingness. Starting from the origin of the Cosmos, it dilates upon the numerical proportions supposed to lie at the basis of the laws of Nature and to be expressed by the characters and cycles with which our readers are now acquainted. It places these formulæ in concentric circles, and combines these circles together in sundry ways, as is still done by geomancers nowadays. It expatiates largely upon the k w a, upon the influences which the twenty-eight stellar mansions exert on this earth, and upon all the other factors which we have passed in review, connecting the influences of the five Elements or planets with the outward forms of hills and mountains in the manner set forth by us on page 956.

Kwoh Poh is also the reputed author of a treatise which, under the title of The Book on Burial [1], takes rank among the products of Fung-shui literature as a standard work. There are, however, good reasons for doubting whether it really is from his hand. No work of that name is mentioned in his biography in the Books of the Tsin Dynasty, although it gives the titles of three other works he wrote, and of half a dozen books he commented upon and annotated. Nor does the Catalogue of classical and other works, contained in the Books of the Sui Dynasty [2], mention a Book on Burial; nor is it certain that the treatise occurring in the Catalogue in the two Official Histories of the House of Tᶜang [3] under the title of »Book on Burial and Canon on the Pulses of the Earth, in one Chapter" [4] is from Kwoh Poh's hand, as no author's name is appended to it. For the first time the work in question appears in the Catalogue of books in the History of the Sung Dynasty, under the explicit title: »Kwoh Poh's Book on Burial, in one Chapter" [5]. Probably this is the same treatise which is reprinted in the *Ku kin tᶜu shu tsih chᶜing*, under the title of »Kwoh Poh's Canon of Burial, based on Antiquity" [6].

Without doubt we may consider the age in which Kwoh Poh lived as the golden era of Fung-shui, as the epoch in which the ascendency of its power reached its apogee and its vagaries struck

---

1 葬書.   2 Chapters 32—35.

3 Old Books, ch 47, l. 16, and New Books, ch. 59, l. 28.

4 葬書地脈經一卷.

5 郭璞葬書一卷. Ch. 206, l. 22.

6 郭璞古本葬經. Sect. 藝術, chapt. 665.

ineradicable roots in all classes of society, involving them for good and all in its intricate net of error and delusion. In point of fact the Books of the Tsin Dynasty refer to Fung-shui matters far oftener than the Annals of earlier times, and certainly just as often as those of subsequent dynasties. The belief that even emperors and princes could be produced by the selection of proper graves, then waxed strong. We read, for instance, of the military grandee Yang Hu [1], who lived in the second half of the third century: »The » site of his grandfather's tomb was declared by a man who » was clever in observing the properties of graves, to possess a » breath which could produce emperors and kings, but the occu- » pant would remain without issue if it were hacked into. Hu there- » fore hacked into it, whereupon the other, on perceiving what he » had done, said it would now still produce a Minister of State » with a broken arm. Finally Hu fell from his horse and broke his » arm; and he became a minister, but begot no sons" [2].

From nothing does it appear that, since those times, the belief in the efficacy of Fung-shui has ever been seriously shaken in China. It has borne undisputed sway over the nation down to the present day. Nevertheless there have existed some minds which, though not disbelieving in the system, were far from placing implicit confidence in all that the proficients and experts dished up for the public as genuine geomancy. Yen Chi-t'ui, for instance, wrote in the sixth century: »The art of utilizing the two Breaths of Nature » having sprung up with Heaven and Earth themselves, confidence » must be placed in the indications of that art with respect to good » luck and ill, weal and woe. But a long time has elapsed since the » ancients lived. Therefore the writings on that art, transmitted from » one generation to another, are altogether the product of unsettled » popular notions, and contain gossip of a vulgar and superficial » kind; little therein is trustworthy, much is pure nonsense. » Yet, by contravening the art in question, by deviating from it, » or by refusing to utilize it, calamity might finally be incurred. » Infelicitous results cannot be always eluded by attending to it

---

[1] 羊祜·

[2] 有善相墓者言、祜祖墓所有帝王氣、若鑿之則無後。祜遂鑿之、相者見曰、猶出折臂三公。而祜竟墮馬折臂、位至公、而無子. Books of the Tsin Dynasty, ch. 34, l. 12.

» with anxious carefulness or by entirely relying upon it; but ad-
» vantage is just as little to be secured by sticking to it with very
» great anxiety" [1].

In the seventh century, the emperor T‘ai Tsung [2] of the T‘ang
dynasty appointed a commission of more than ten scholars, with
orders to sift, under the presidency of Lü Ts‘ai [3], a famous man
of letters, the existing literature on divination and geomancy, and
to glean from it everything orthodox and of real practical value.
The result of their labours was a work in one hundred chapters,
which was published by order of the emperor. They passed a sweeping
sentence on the then existing literature on the subjects in question, flatly condemning all such selection of auspicious graves and
lucky times for burial as is not sanctioned by antecedents from antiquity. An ample account of the way in which those scholars acquited
themselves of their task is given in the two Standard Histories of
the T‘ang dynasty [4].

This imperial effort to check the boundless expansion of un-
authentic geomantic theory and superstition was entirely without
effect, and the literature on the subject has continued to swell from
age to age. The Catalogue of literature in the Books of the Sui
Dynasty gives only some dozen titles of works and treatises; the
Catalogue in the Books of the T‘ang Dynasty contains a much
larger number [5], and in that of the History of the House of Sung
we count over a hundred [6]. It is unnecessary to say that under
every dynasty the books contain numerous names of geomancers
of renown, and sundry stories illustrating their capacities and marvellous attainments.

These authors and experts generally based their theories upon
the so-called hing shi [7], »influence or power of forms and outlines", that is to say, the influence and power of the Elements

---

[1] 凡陰陽之術與天地俱生、其吉凶德刑不可
不信。但去聖旣遠。世傳術書皆出流俗、言辭鄙
淺、驗少、妄多。至如反支不行、竟以遇害。歸忌
寄宿不免凶終、拘而多忌亦無益也. Domestic Instructions, § 19.

[2] 太宗.   [3] 呂才.

4 Old Books, ch. 79, ll. 12 sqq.; New Books, ch. 107, ll. 4 sqq.
5 Old Books, ch. 47, and New Books, ch. 59.
6 Chapter 206.   7 形勢.

or planets indicated by the shapes of mountains and hills. In the latter half of the ninth century, the most prominent figure in this School of Forms was Yang Yun-sung [1], a native of Teu-cheu [2], which is a part of the department of Yuh-lin [3], in Kwangsi. He is frequently mentioned by his other name Shuh-meu [4], and commonly known as »the Master who saved mankind from poverty" [5], probably for the reason of his high attainments in finding graves that never failed to render the offspring of the occupants wealthy and fortunate. Under the reign of Hi Tsung [6] (874—888) he held the office of Imperial Geomancer, and was even invested with the high dignity of Director of the Court of Imperial Entertainment [7]. The latter period of his life he spent as a geomancer in Kiangsi province, in the department of Kan-cheu [8], at that time called Khien-cheu [9]. Both from his wide-spread fame and the works he wrote, he has always been regarded as the great patriarch of the School of Forms, since denoted the »Kan-cheu Method" [10]. By him particularly stress was laid upon the shape of mountains and the direction of water-courses, or, in other words, upon the influences of the Dragon, (comp. p. 951), which imaginary animal plays a part in his system under various names and aspects. Hence the titles of three of his writings are: »Canon on the Means to set Dragons in Motion" [11], »Book of thirty-six Dragons" [12], »Canon for the Approximation of Dragons" [13]. His treatise entitled: »Method of the twelve Lines" [14] still holds the rank of a standard work for tracing out favourable spots in connection with the contours and configurations of high grounds and mountains.

Yang Yun-sung had many disciples, most of whom wrote geomantic works and treatises. The corypheus among them was Tseng Wen-ch‘wen [15], who composed a »Treatise on the art of searching for Dragons" [16], »Queries and Answers about the two Breaths of Nature" [17], etc. [18]

---

1 楊筠松· 2 竇州· 3 鬱林州·

4 叔茂· 5 救貧先生· 6 僖宗·

7 光祿大夫· 8 贛州府· 9 虔州·

10 贛州法· 11 撼龍經·

12 三十六龍書· 13 疑龍經· 14 十二杖法·

15 曾文遄· 16 尋龍記· 17 陰陽問答·

18 The above information is gleaned from the *Ku kin t‘u shu tsih ch‘ing*, sect. 藝術, ch. 679.

The Compass and Form Schools

Under the influence of the metaphysical speculations by which, during the Sung dynasty, a notorious school, of which Chu Hi was the principal leader, sought to elucidate on a broader scale than had ever been done before the principles of creation and re-production, and to expound the influence which the heavens are supposed to exercise upon terrestrial affairs, a second school of geomancy arose, which more particularly laid stress upon the k w a, the Branches and k a n, the Constellations, etc., assigning a place of minor importance to the configurations of the earth. It is generally called the »Method of Man (*i. e.* Fuhkien)" [1], the first chief representative of it being Wang Kih [2], also named Chao-khing [3] or Khung-chang [4], a native of Kan-cheu, who spent the latter period of his life in the north of Fuhkien, viz. in Sung-yuen [5], now called Sung-khi [6]. His »Canon of the Core or Centre" [7] and his »Disquisitions on the Queries and Answers" [8] were published by his pupil Yeh Shuh-liang [9]. The Fuhkien School is frequently styled »the Houses-and-Dwellings Method" [10]. It is more attached to the use of the compass than the Kan-cheu School, this latter using that instrument only as a secondary aid, viz. to sound the influences of the country around after its forms and contours have been pronounced to be favourable.

These two schools have shared the predominance in the Fung-shui system down to the present day. So far as we know, no other school of significance has risen up beside. It is hardly feasible to define the present status and relative position of each, together with their influence in the various parts of the Empire. Professors of geomancy unanimously assert that there still exists a distinct line of demarcation between the two schools, but that they are in so far fused together that no good expert in either ever neglects to practise the methods of the other school as well as his own. In the mountainous southern provinces, the School of Forms obviously predominates. Even in Fuhkien no geomancers are so highly esteemed as those who pretend to exercise their vocation in strict accordance with the Kiangsi method, and in every town of that province there are houses with sign-boards to decoy patrons

---

1 閩之法.   2 王伋.   3 肇卿.

4 孔彰.   5 松源.   6 松溪.

7 心經.   8 問答語錄.

9 葉叔亮.   10 屋宅之法.

by stating that the inmate is an adept of that school, or has improved his talents by the teaching of a genuine Kan-cheu professor. Many such accomplished experts are accustomed to introduce and recommend themselves to the public by means of placards stuck up in squares and at street-corners.

The Fung-shui literature is at present as rich as ever. Popular expositions of the theory and its practical application are on sale in every bookshop, mostly of considerable bulk, and illustrated with woodcuts. In general such products are subdivided into three main sections. The first deals with the »Rules concerning the Dragon" [1], that is to say (see page 951) the situation and configurations of mountains and the direction of water-courses. This section often commences with a dissertation on the doctrine, set forth by eminent expositors of the system, that the whole Empire has a Dragon which rules the fortunes of all its inhabitants, to wit, the immeasurable Kwun-lun [2], a range of mountains in the north-west, between Tartary and Tibet, the »progenitor of all the mountains of the world [3] and the centre of the Earth" [4], in which the great rivers that carry the beneficial influences of the Dragon to the south and south-east, take their rise. Often also this section contains dissertations, illustrated with maps, on the Fung-shui of every province as a whole, such as the »Authors on the Rules concerning Forms" had already written two thousand years ago (see page 995); further it generally gives astronomical maps elucidating the relations between certain parts of the canopy of heaven and their counterparts on earth (comp. page 954).

The second section dilates on the five Elements or Planets, and the art of discovering their presence or influence in the forms of hills, mountains and terrestrial objects. The third section is practically the most important, being devoted to a technical application of the doctrines expounded in the first and second sections; that is to say, it gives directions as to how a hüeh [5], *i. e.* a favourable site for a grave or building amidst good and bad surroundings of every sort and description, is to be found at any given place. Generally it is profusely illustrated, and gives illustrated instances of graves of great renown for their good Fung-shui; besides, it contains systematic enumerations of things that are detrimental or dangerous, and wise rules

---

1 龍法· 2 崑崙· 3 天下諸山之祖·
4 地之中· 5 穴·

established by professors and proficients of high repute. In many
books this section is subdivided into two parts, entitled »Rules
concerning Gravel or Sand (*i. e.* the ground)" [1], and »Rules concerning Water" [2], respectively teaching how to utilize for purposes of
all sorts every part of the configurations of mountains or hills and
lakes or water-courses.

It now remains for us to give some information about the Fung-
shui professors and the way in which they work among the people,
which will convey to our readers some idea as to the extent ot
the influence geomancy possesses over social life in China.

4. The Professors of Fung-shui. The Influence of Fung-shui on Practical Life.

As stated on pp. 938 *seq.*, every member of the educated class who,
by learning to read and write, has picked up a smattering ot
knowledge of the classical works and the principles of philosophy,
is in China, to some extent, a geomancer; nay, even men and
women with no literary education at all pretend to know much,
if not all, about Fung-shui. But the true professor of this art, who
earns his living by it, is distinguished from those dilettanti by
many characteristics.

He assumes all the airs of the literati and the gentry, dresses,
as they do, in a long gown, wears a pair of large spectacles,
though not short-sighted, and awes his patrons into admiration
and respect by scarcely ever opening his mouth, except to utter a
few wise words, or a classic phrase borrowed from the books.
Others on the contrary establish and keep up their reputation by
loquaciousness, overawing everybody by speaking a mystifying, learned
jargon, and by apocalyptic utterances of which the ordinary Chinaman
understand next to nothing. Many professors are very dignified in
their habits, wear a grave and haughty look, and strut about like
peacocks among the ignoble fowl around them. About all their
movements there is an air of classic decorum; and it is no wonder,
therefore, that the masses regard the geomancers as fountains of
wisdom, marvels of learning, capable of fathoming all the mysteries
of heaven and earth.

Yet, truth to say, scarcely any of them have acquired their skill

---

[1] 砂法.   [2] 水法.

by profound and serious studies of the books written by the sages and philosophers of the nation. A geomancer has, as a rule, learnt to read and to write at school; but, for the rest, he has picked up almost all his wisdom by strolling about in the open country for a few years at the heels of some professor who had adopted him as his disciple, catching from his lips a large supply of empty phrases about dragons, tigers, branches and other mysteries of the compass. Though he has the name and outward appearance of a literary man, yet he is, like Chinese scholars in general, quite ignorant of his national history and literature, nor does he possess the slightest knowledge of the history and literature of the art of which he calls himself an expert. At best he may have consulted one or two handbooks badly printed; but he seldom looks into these products a second time, finding it easier to rely upon his own inventiveness and eloquence, which both he himself and others are readily enough inclined to regard as wisdom and innate genius. But his ignorance casts no shadow upon his reputation. For, after all, he knows more about the art than the bulk of the people; moreover, he is extremely smart in bewildering his employers by bullying them, whenever he thinks fit, with a flood of technical expressions and hazy utterances about tigers and dragons, branches and k w a, elements, and spiritual influences of all sorts and descriptions.

Clever Fung-shui professors are accustomed to resort to other devices, in order to keep up the reputation of their calling and that of their own persons. The names of the ancient sages and sovereigns, revered by the whole nation as the holiest and most perfect of creatures the Universe ever produced, are constantly on their lips, especially those of the reputed inventors of the k w a and the authors of the *Yih king,* viz. king Wen, and the Prince of Cheu, his son; frequently also they appeal to the illustrious Chu Hi, the father of modern philosophy and an ardent votary of good, orthodox Fung-shui. Thus they ably contrive to get themselves associated by the people with great and famous names in history. They further enhance the general admiration of their wisdom by concluding each flow of words from their lips with this refrain: » Yet many other arguments could I adduce, were they not to numerous to be summed up".

The people are perfectly aware that geomancers are not only useful, but also dangerous. Indeed, these men can supply them with graves and dwellings which establish the prosperity of whole families;

but they have also the power of plunging families into woe and misery by undoing graves and houses of good Fung-shui by their cunning artifices. The professors themselves take good care to keep up this double reputation by steadily spreading tales and anecdotes which illustrate their twofold power, and by which the people are constantly reminded how advisible it is to cultivate their friendship and to propitiate their good will in all circumstances of life. They frequently relate that, once upon a time, there lived a family, which was rendered very rich and prosperous by the influence of a grave sought out for it by a geomancer of great renown. He, on discovering this priceless spot, had become aware that it would cost him his eyesight if anybody were buried in it; and yet he had not hesitated to assign it to that family, on condition they should lodge, clothe and feed him to the end of his days, and give him a decent burial after his death. So he lived with them, quite blind, but happy, and free from worldly care, leading an enviable life of leisure and idleness. One fine day it came to pass that a kid belonging to the family fell into an open privy and was suffocated. The Chinese are a thrifty people, and even the wealthy classes are averse to throwing useful things away. Hence the family, as none of them chose to eat of the kid, resolved to cook it for the professor, who, being blind and not aware of the circumstance, would certainly enjoy the savoury food. This was done; but, unfortunately, a loquacious matron of the family told him in secret how ignomiously the others had abused his helpless condition. Our readers can guess the end of the story: — the professor without mercy destroyed the good Fung-shui of the grave by giving wrong advice regarding it, and so he brought the family back to the same dire poverty from which he had extricated it. We are not, however, told whether he recovered from his blindness, after having thus avenged himself.

In spite of such professional tales, and numerous accounts about graves that have rendered their owners prosperous for many generations in succession, accounts which, whether or not illustrated by woodcut figures, are appended to many handbooks; — in spite, also, of the fact that many a geomancer is so sharp and clever as to be able to make out at a glance from the moss or weather-beaten spots on a grave stone whether the Fung-shui of the grave is good or bad — yet there are many persons bold enough to refuse implicit trust in all they say. Such sceptics are, perhaps, more numerous now than they were in times gone by. To none among them does it ever occur to doubt the perfectness of the principles of the system, these forming the chief corner stone of natural philosophy as expounded by the holiest and wisest men. But the bare fact that many who, in the hopes of buying a grave that must render them rich and prosperous, pour half their wealth into the lap of the professors, and yet become poor, while others, not wealthy enough to employ a professor, rise to wealth and distinction, acts as a great check upon the credulity of the public. Among the educated classes it is an open secret that the predictions of geomancers are all guess-work, and that all they have to dispose of is a little experience collected in the course of their practice. It is no wonder then that, in Amoy, people often make fun of their geomancers, and deride them in the following quatrain:

Tē-lí sien-sing koàn soat hong,
Tsí lám, tsí pok, tsí se tong;
San tiong dziók iú óng hộ tē,
Hó put sím lái tsōng nái ong [1].

» Professors of geomancy are accustomed to telling nonsense,
» They point to the south, north, west and east;
» But, if they can really find places in the mountains which pro-
   » duce princely dignities,
» Why then do not they immediately bury their own elders there?"

A Fung-shui professor would be a nonentity among his colleagues if he had not an amount of wise sophistry in store wherewith to counteract the popular prejudice. We, geomancers, thus he argues, can in reality thoroughly fathom, by profound study, the secrets of the Ti li or natural influences pervading the earth (see page 940), and thus we can discover means to lead human happiness into any desired channel. But these influences are in every respect dominated by those of the heavens, viz. the T'ien li [2], the earth being swayed by the supreme celestial powers embracing it. Hence it is that our calculations must necessarily fail, unless backed by two direct emanations from the heavens, which human power cannot control, viz. the happy destiny of the individual who invokes our

---

[1] 地理先生慣說謊、
指南指北指西東、
山中若有王侯地、
何不尋來葬乃翁.

[2] 天理.

services, and, secondly, the factor which, through the hand of heaven, bestows such a destiny upon him, to wit, a virtuous character, manifesting itself by meritorious deeds. Is it not set forth as a golden principle by all the authors of geomancy: » Nobody should neglect to cultivate secret virtues, the accumulation of virtuous deeds being the only firm base for all searching after felicitous grounds"?[1] Should a man without virtue acquire the most propitious graves for his dead, and the best possible dwellings for himself, their Fung-shui can profit him nothing, seeing it is doomed to impotence and inactivity because of the refusal of the T᷍ien li to co-operate in making him happy. From which we see that Fung-shui is not a *creator* of happiness, but merely the indispensable medium through which a happy fate, held in store by the heavens, is forwarded to its destination.

Of course it seldom occurs to anybody to investigate his own merits and inner qualifications before squandering away his possessions in search of spots for building or grave making. What man in this world ever entertains the least doubt of his own excellence? Who would presume to anticipate, even by a humble investigation of his own demerits and unworthiness, the decrees of the high heavens in respect to his destiny? Not until the working of a grave or dwelling has been watched for some time can it be decided whether the virtues, required to make it yield profit, are present or absent in the persons concerned. These theories, the logic of which no Chinaman ever contradicts, has the advantage of discharging the professor from all blame in case places selected by him bring no blessings. He can, moreover, make use of them to explain the fact that children sometimes rise to wealth and distinction who have buried their parents, for want of money to pay a professor, in a site decried as valueless from a geomantic point of view, or even in a bad spot from which others, by the advice of clever experts, have removed their dead. In such a case it is the T᷍ien li who, moved by the virtues of the persons in question, virtues which they themselves were probably unconscious of possessing, have compelled the Ti li to set to work in their favour with all their energy. Even the doctrine of the transmigration of souls is here brought to bear, as events such as the above are often declared to be rewards for deeds performed in some previous incarnation. But most generally they are ascribed to long forgotten merits of some an-

---

[1] 不可不修陰德、積德求地之本也.

cestor, it being a settled doctrine that good acts are not seldom requited in the offspring of the individual who performed them, just as his crimes and sins must be atoned for by them.

From the above our readers will perceive that the Fung-shui doctrines, when handled with dexterity and eloquence, can explain all the phenomena of human life and fate. Thanks to the sage and useful theory of the supremacy exerted by the Tʿien li over the Ti li, no smart professor can ever be brought to bay. When asked why he did not bury his own relations in the excellent graves he boasts of having found for others, he is humble enough to confess that they would be of no avail to him, his virtues being so few and insignificant, his natural fate consequently so bad, and his chance of prosperity in this world so small; neither have his ancestors laid up a store of merits large enough to enable him to reap the profits of his geomantic attainments himself. This shows that geomancers can also assume the airs of humility, when it serves their turn. Again, when asked how it is that former generations have not used up all the good grounds, they having produced so many myriads of perfect and virtuous men, the answer is: » The Tʿien li do not nowadays reward the virtuous any less than they did in bygone times. As in days of yore, they imbue on their behalf sundry parts of the earth with benignant influences, thus continuously creating anew favourable sites for building and burying purposes. It often occurs that entire valleys, quite devoid of good geomantic influence, are converted into inexhaustible mines of Fung-shui by the Tʿien li, when an alteration in the windings of a waterstream is made by a shower of rain, or by a small earth-slip, or the downfall of a rock through the action of the wind and rain. How then can there ever be a question of the exhaustion of the supply of burial sites?" — In the neighbourhood of every village and every town there are in fact numerous unknown spots, the favourite dreams of the inhabitants, which promise an income of ten thousand gold coins, and promotion to the very highest literary degree into the bargain, to whomsoever buries his father or mother there. But no professor, even were he the incarnation of Kwan Loh or Kwoh Poh, can detect those grounds, unless set to work by such men of virtue as are appointed by the Tʿien li for the enjoyment of so much bliss. Is it then to be wondered at that every man with common sense on the death of his parents applies to the best professor his purse can afford, in the hope that he may be among the number of the elect?

By so much verisimilar reasoning the popular scepticism in regard
to Fung-shui and its professors is not lulled to sleep. It is en-
couraged by many of the best authors, and even by the government.
Hardly sixty years ago, Wu Yung-kwang, (see note 8, p.148) wrote:
» Its poison (viz of Kwoh Poh's Book of the Blue Bag, see p. 1003) subse-
» quently deluged the whole Empire. T'ai Tsung of the T'ang dynasty
» ordered Lü Ts'ai to publish a treatise in which geomancy was
» subjected to profound criticism (comp. page 1006), but even this
» measure could not check its influence. Sons and grandsons,
» misled by the talk about felicity and mishap, invited the grave
» professors to search after propitious grounds, and these men
» then set themselves to work, hacking and hewing into the pulses
» of the earth, reasoning about forefronts and backs, and selecting
» auspicious years, months, days and hours. The poor could not
» afford to select any grounds at all; the rich selected them with
» too much precision; and the result was that grandfathers and
» fathers were cruelly left body and soul unburied under the open
» sky. There were men who performed no burial during their whole
» lives; nay, some people even neglected interring their dead for
» many generations in succession" [1].

In the » Memoirs concerning Amoy" we read:
» The poor among the inhabitants of Amoy Island are accustomed
» to bury their dead after ten or fourteen days, because their
» dwellings are narrow and small. The well-to-do class, however,
» have frequently an open ear for the adepts of the Blue-Raven
» School [2], and all of them, the wise as well as the stupid, are

---

[1] 其毒遂橫流於天下。唐太宗命呂才著論以
深闢之、竟不能止。爲人子若孫者怵於禍福之
說、延葬師求吉壤、剖析地脈、斟酌向背、諏選
年月日時。貧者不能擇地、富者擇之太詳、於是
祖父之體魄暴露中野。有終身不葬累世不葬者.
Wu hioh luh, ch. 19, ll. 8 *seq*.

2 According to tradition, there lived under the Ts'in dynasty and in the beginning of the reign of the House of Han, a sage whose name is unknown, but
who is generally styled: The Philosopher Blue Raven 青烏子. He is the reputed author of a geomantic treatise, entitled: The Blue Raven Canon 青烏經;
and as he is the oldest known author on Fung-shui matters, geomancy is sometimes
called: The School of the Blue Raven 青烏家. Perhaps he is a mythical

» deluded and led astray by these latter, placing full confidence
» in whatever they say. These men are vulgarly called Geomancers.
» The greatest confidence is placed in their indications and selec-
» tions, and, moreover, much importance is attached to auspicious
» years, months, days and hours; and as sundry branches of a
» family usually live in discord, and each puts its trust in its
» own professor, the one professor always vindicating whatever
» the other rejects, it frequently comes to pass that encoffined
» corpses are stored away and remain unburied. Though beginning
» with a mere desire to acquire auspicious burial sites, the end
» is that the interment is for many days postponed, during which
» the family is gradually ruined" [1].

Likewise by reason of its constantly preventing timely burial, a
very severe judgment is pronounced on Fung-shui and its professors by the present Code of Laws. That the high authorities for the
same reason sometimes caution their subjects officially against the
cobwebs of delusion, is shown by the proclamation, wherewith the T a o
T'a i at Amoy in 1882 interdicted any further postponement of burials
within his jurisdiction.

In spite of popular suspicion and official denunciation, parties of
men, headed by a geomancer, may be seen every day in the open
country, strolling about in search of favourable sites for burying
the dead. The geomancer is scarcely ever allowed to do this work
alone. For, as our readers know, every right principled man is
pretty familiar with Fung-shui matters, as filial duty prescribes
that for the sake of his parents he should be able to control
the professor in his choice (see pp. 938 seq.). If the family be
wealthy, such strolls are made several times; for, searching out a
grave which must secure the welfare and fortunes of a whole family
for many generations is certainly not a task to be performed in

---

personage, and his book, which seems to be still extant, a spurious production of
much later times. On page 997 we have stated that the authorship of the Canon
of Burials is ascribed to him.

1 厦島人貧者十日半月卽葬、房屋窄小故也。
富者往往聽靑烏家言、人無知愚惑而信之。俗
稱爲地師。聽其指擇、又拘年月日時、房分不齊、
又各信一地師、彼善此否、往往停柩不葬。始則
希圖吉穴、遷延日久、漸至門戶破落. Chapter XV.

a day, unless the family be too poor to pay the professor high wages. All the expenses entailed by such excursions have of course to be defrayed by the family. They must also procure palankeens and bearers for the professor and themselves, as walking is vulgar work, unbecoming people of distinction who possess the means of avoiding bodily fatigue (see note 9, p.148).

While wise discussions are being held on the contours of the country, and the hands are continuously moved up and down and in all the directions of the compass, the party keep themselves under the shade of umbrellas of paper or silk; for around most towns scarcely a tree or shrub affords a shelter against the scorching sun, all vegetation having in course of time been radically destroyed under the direction of geomancers. Now and then the professor brings forth his compass from a linen bag hanging from his shoulder, and lying full length, or creeping on the ground, he takes the bearings by placing over his instrument a so-called *hun-kim soà*[1], »thread for subtle measurement", which is a red cord, from each end of which dangles a copper coin to keep it stretched. His judgment with reference to every given spot he pronounces in a learned jargon; and though his decisions may sometimes be objected to by those who accompany him, yet they are, as a rule, received with respectful awe and superstitious dread.

At length, after the professor has pocketed many bountiful remunerations for his pains, a spot is discovered upon which good geomantic influences are concentrated to any extent, and which accordingly promises to realize the boldest wishes of the family. Many days are now lost in bargaining, through an agent or broker, with the owner of the ground. But in the end this man is prevailed upon to accept a small sum of earnest money, in exchange for which he allows the family to make an experiment as to the properties of the soil, and binds himself not to sell it to anybody else until they have declined the purchase. Without delay a small quantity of pig's bones are bought at the butcher's, and interred on the spot in a small box of wood or earthen jar. After about a year, the family exhume and examine them. If they come forth hard, dry and white, the soil is approved of, as showing that it possesses sufficient preservative power to keep the osseous remains of the dead in a good condition for a very long time to come

---

1 分金線. Hun-kim = *Fen Chin*, the 120 sub-division of the Lo P'an circle.

and, consequently, to attach his manes for good to the spot. A shorter experiment is to bury some duck's eggs and afterwards examine them, to see whether they dry up or rot away. Pieces of charcoal are also used, for, being hygroscopic, they soon tell whether the spot is dry enough to serve for burying purposes.

In Amoy, these proceedings are called *ìm khoàⁿ* [1], »hiding experiments", or *tᶜàm kᶜoàⁿ* [2], »sounding experiments". Should the soil be found to be bad, it is, in some cases, resolved to improve it by digging away the earth around the place where the coffin must lie, and supplying the void with earth of a better quality.

It is by no means rare that a family, after having made the experiments, consult a second professor, in order to verify the decisions of the first. In nine cases out of ten, this new marvel of wisdom with a flow of astute critical remarks contradicts everything his colleague has done, for, though Fung-shui professors are dignified in their demeanour, they are subject to the influences of professional jealousy just like the rest of mankind, and constitute by no means a mutual-admiration society. The new adviser of the family is not long in discovering, for instance, that there is a dangerous bed of stones or solid rock under the soil, through which it will be impossible for the Terrestrial Breath to break its way and reach the corpse; some diggers are set to work immediately, and no sooner do they find a couple of stones than . . . . everything has to be done over again from the beginning. The earnest money is lost; the outlays for the numerous excursions into the mountains have been made in vain; nor can either the payments made to the professor, or the advances he has obtained, be recovered. Even the expenses the family made to propitiate the dangerous man with dinner parties, now become a dead loss; indeed, they still bounteously regaled him many a time, for fear he should counteract their whole future destiny by putting them off with a grave entirely valueless from the geomantic point of view.

Now the new marvel in turn puts the family to expense. He borrows money of them whenever an opportunity presents itself, claims payment for every trifle of work he does, and is most likely to intrigue with the proprietor of each plot of ground he declares to answer the purposes of the family; for why should he despise his honest share in the purchase-money which he enables this man to squeeze out of the family? In short, there is probably not much

---

[1] 廕看.   [2] 探看.

exaggeration in the assertion of the Chinese themselves that many
well-to-do families, unable to restrain their passion for Fung-shui,
are either ruined, or brought to the brink of poverty by geomancers.

Pending the acquisition of an auspicious grave, the deceased
parent remains unburied, either in the house, or somewhere in a
shed or temple. Although public opinion decries long postponement of
burial as the height of unfilialness, and both law and government threaten
it with severe punishment, yet these three mighty factors combined stand
powerless in the matter, and regularly every year thousands of
dead are deprived of a timely burial because of the exigencies of
Fung-shui. Up to a certain point this phenomenon may be explained
from the circumstance that postponement of burial was a legal
custom in ancient China, based on the then prevailing ideas of a
resurrection, so that the Chinese cannot but regard it as perfectly defensible on the grounds of orthodoxy and fashion. It may
be also explained from the fact that the ancients used to depose
the dead for some time in their dwellings before conveying them
to their last resting place, and that this custom has been transmitted to posterity by so venerable a book as the *I li*, and sanctioned by many dynasties as a legal rite of the state religion.

Cases of long postponement of burial have undoubtedly been
numerous in China ever since Fung-shui bore sway there. Many
have been entailed by the acknowledged necessity of selecting
auspicious dates for burials, which custom, as our readers know,
is most closely connected with the Fung-shui doctrines. We read,
for instance, of Ho Siün[1], a statesman who lived in the third
and the beginning of the fourth century, that » when he was
» finally invested with the governorship of Wu-khang (a part of
» modern Chehkiang), it was very usual among the people to bury
» their dead at great expense, and there were also those who,
» entertaining a superstitious dread of years and months in which
» certain things ought not to be done, stored up their dead, not
» committing them to the earth. These practices were forbidden by
» Ho Siün once and forever"[2]. With the object, probably, of put-

---

[1] 賀循.

[2] 最後爲武康令、俗多厚葬、及有拘忌廻避歲
月、停喪不葬者。循皆禁焉. Books of the Tsin Dynasty, ch. 68, l. 15.

ting a check to the evil in question, several dynasties have formally excluded from the state-service those of their subjects who postponed the burial of their parents. It is stated that »under the » Wei dynasty and the House of Tsin, the only reason for ex- » cluding a man from an official post was the fact of the corpse » of his grandfather or father being kept uncoffined or unburied"[1]. This rule prevailed also during the Tᶜang dynasty, for we read in the biography of Yen-chen-khing[2], who lived in the eighth century: When he held a high post in the country of Ho-tung, »there was » living there one Ching Yen-tsu, who after his mother's death had » left her corpse unburied for twenty-nine years within the walls » of a Buddhist monastery. Chen-khing reported the case to the » Throne, with this result that the said man and his brothers were » not registered among the office-bearers for thirty years, and the » whole empire was alarmed and moved"[3]. Still later, in 952, during the short-lived Cheu dynasty, the emperor Tᶜai Tsu[4] issued a decree, stating that »henceforth, in each case of a paternal grand- » parent or parent not having been committed to the earth after his » demise, the elders of the family at the head of which he had » stood during his life, should not be entitled to solicit for official » dignity, nor would the officers already sprung from that family be » granted any promotion or transference to another post; but these » rescripts did not apply to the inferior or junior relations, nor to » the members of the family still lower in rank"[5].

Szĕ-ma Kwang, the famous statesman and ethical philosopher, stands foremost in the ranks of those who, during the Sung dynasty,

---

1 魏晉唯祖父不殮葬者獨不聽官. Books of the Tsin Dynasty, ch. 110, l. 8.

2 顏眞卿.

3 有鄭延祚者、母卒二十九年殯僧舍垣地。眞卿劾奏之、兄弟三十年不齒、天下聳動. Old Books of the Tᶜang Dynasty, ch. 128, l. 8; also the New Books, ch. 153, l. 8.

4 太祖.

5 今後有父母祖父母亡歿未經遷葬者其主家之長不得輒求仕進、所由司亦不得申舉解送、如是卑幼在下者不在此限. Old History of the Five Dynasties, ch. 112, l. 10.

turned their sharp pen against Fung-shui, because it deprived so many of the dead of a decent and timely burial. In A. D. 1084 he wrote: »The » people nowadays do not bury the dead more luxuriously than they did » anciently, but the importance attached to the prohibitions created by the » Yin-and-Yang system has become much greater! The treatise on burial » now in circulation investigate the influences of the forms of mountains » and water-courses, rocks and fields; they examine the Branches and » k a n which indicate the years, months, days and hours, considering » the low or high rank of the offspring in the social scale, their » wealth and poverty, late or early death, intelligence or stupidity » to be entirely bound up with those factors, so that burials can- » not be performed unless in such-and-such grounds and at such- » and-such times. The whole nation is bewildered by these theories » and places belief therein, in consequence of which it frequently occurs » that those who lose their parents postpone their burial for a con- » siderable time. If asked the reasons why they do so, they say: » 'Year and month are not yet propitious', or: 'We have not yet » found a felicitous plot of ground', or: 'Some of our family reside » far from here in the service of the State and have not yet found » an opportunity to come home', or: 'We are so poor that we » are not yet able to procure the requirements for the burial'. » These are the causes of there being people who do not perform one » single burial during their whole lives, nay, during many generations » in succession, in consequence of which encoffined corpses are aban- » doned and lost sight of, so that it becomes unknown where they » are. Oh! how is it possible that such things do not make a man » sigh and lament from the bottom of his heart![1].

» With a view to the life to come, a man sets great value upon » having posterity, that they may properly bury his remains. But » if his offspring act in the above way, a man is worse off than

---

[1] 今人葬不厚於古、而拘於陰陽禁忌則甚矣。今之葬書乃相山川岡畒之形勢、考歲月日時之支于、以爲子孫貴賤貧富壽夭賢愚皆繫焉、非此地非此時不可葬也。舉世惑而信之、於是喪親者往往久而不葬。問之、曰、歲月未利也、又曰、未有吉地也、又曰、遊宦遠方、未得歸也、又曰、貧、未能辦葬具也。至有終身累世而不葬、遂棄失尸柩、不知其處者。嗚呼、可不令人深歎愍哉。

» if he died on the road without leaving any son or grandson, for
» then some benevolent creature, on beholding him, would throw
» something over his remains to hide them from view [1].

» According to the ceremonial rules enacted by the ancient
» sovereigns, the period within which their burial must take place
» did not exceed seven months, and the present dynasty has or-
» dained that every one, from the Imperial princes downwards, shall
» be interred ere three months have elapsed. Those rules also demand
» that the children shall not make any change in their mourning
» dress before the burial, that they must eat gruel and live in sheds
» built against the wall, for grief that their parents are homeless,
» and that they shall gradually diminish their mourning after
» the interment. But people nowadays turn a deaf ear to these rules,
» and openly transgress the rescripts. They put off their mourning
» dress ere the burial is over, occupy official posts in any part of
» the realm, eat rice, dress in ornamented garments, drink spirits
» and make music. Can their hearts be at ease when they do so? [2]

» The social standing of any man, his wealth and the length of
» his life depend on the heavens, and his mental development on
» himself; but these matters stand in no connection whatever with
» burials, nor are they pre-influenced thereby. If nevertheless every-
» body follows the advice of burial professors, mankind must come
» to suffer under a concurrence of events entailing grief and misery.
» And how is it to be borne that people do not refrain from
» cruelly exposing their parents to wind and weather, merely for
» the purpose of establishing their own wealth and fortunes? [3]

» Formerly, when my own forefathers were buried, my family

---

[1] 人所貴於身後有子孫者、爲能藏其形骸也。
其所爲乃如是、曷若無子孫死於道路、猶有仁
者見而殣之耶。

[2] 先王制禮葬期遠不過七月、今世著令自王
公以下皆三月而葬。又禮未葬不變服、食粥、居
倚廬、哀親之未有所歸也、旣葬然後漸有除變。
今之人背禮違法。未葬而除喪、從宦四方、食稻、
衣錦、飲酒、作樂。其心安乎。

[3] 人之貴賤貧富壽夭繫於天、賢愚繫於人、固
無關預於葬。就使皆如葬師之言、爲人子者方

» were too poor to procure proper vaults and coffins, and they did
» not use these until one of them was raised to the dignity of
» Generalissimo. Not the slightest quantity of gold, silver, pearls
» or jade was ever placed in their graves. When the Generalissimo
» was to be buried, my clansmen unanimously said: 'A burial is
» an occurrence of great significance in a family; may we therefore
» abstain from consulting geomancy? Certainly not!' My elder
» brother Poh-khang was compelled to comply with their desires,
» and said: 'I assent to advising with geomancy; but where shall
» we find a good burial professor to consult?' Upon which a
» clansman replied: 'In the village close by there lives one Chang,
» a clever professor, employed by everybody in several districts'.
» My brother called this man and promised him twenty thousand
» copper coins. On hearing him mention such a sum, the geomancer
» was greatly delighted, for he was a simple rustic, and the geo-
» mancers being at that time looked down upon by the people as
» mere rustics, he had never received more than a thousand coppers
» for a burial. Still my brother said: 'I will entrust you with the
» burial on condition that you follow my instructions; otherwise I
» shall employ another professor'. 'I will do nothing else but what
» you order me', was the reply. [1]

» My brother himself now selected such a burial place as pleased
» himself best, fixed the month, year, day and hour of the inter-
» ment, the depth and dimensions of the grave, and the road along
» which the procession should pass, making everything agree in the

---

當哀窮之際。何忍不顧其親之暴露、乃欲自營
福利耶。

[1] 昔者吾諸祖之葬也家甚貧、不能具槨棺、自
太尉公而下始有棺槨。然金銀珠玉之物未嘗以
錙銖入於壙中。將葬太尉公、族人皆曰、葬者家
之大事、奈何不詢陰陽、此必不可。吾兄伯康無
如之何、乃曰、詢于陰陽則可矣、安得良葬師而
詢之。族人曰、近村有張生者、良師也、數縣皆
用之。兄乃召張生、許以錢二萬。張生野夫也、世
爲葬師爲野人、葬所得不過千錢、聞之大喜。兄
曰、汝能用吾言吾俾爾葬、不用吾言將求他師。
張師曰、唯命是聽。

» best way with the circumstances. He then ordered Mr. Chang to
» control his work with the help of his books of burial, and the
» man declared everything to be highly felicitous. Which, being
» communicated to the clansmen, filled them all with delight, none
» of them raising objections or expressing any other opinion [1].

» (In spite of all this), my brother is now seventy-nine years
» old, and his official career has raised him up to the dignity of
» Minister of State. And I am now sixty-six and, though unworthy
» of the honour, I am invested with the dignity of minister in
» immediate attendance upon the Emperor; moreover, twenty three
» clansmen of mine are office-bearers. And now behold how people
» who carefully employ the books of burial, are unable to surpass
» my family! Two years ago my wife died. No sooner was her
» coffin made than we placed her in it; no sooner were the
» preparatives finished than we carried her away; no sooner was
» her grave dug than we buried her, nor did we waste a single
» word in consulting an expert in Fung-shui matters. And yet,
» nothing infelicitous has up to the present befallen me, unless by
» other palpable causes. Geomancers have founded false systems with
» which they delude the multitude; they cause woe and misery
» to prevail for many generations in families which are visited by
» death. But still worse, the proposal lately made by me to the
» Throne in my capacity of a Censor, to the effect that the books of
» burial in the Empire should be forbidden, has not been agreed
» with by any of those who hold power under the government!
» This disquisition is made by me, in the hopes that sons and
» grandsons may in future bury their dead at the proper time. If
» they wish to learn that the requisites for burial need not be
» costly, let them consider what has found place with *my* forefathers;
» and if they desire a proof that the books of burial deserve no
» belief, show them what has occurred in *my* family!" [2]

---

[1] 於是兄自以已意處歲月日時、及壙之深淺
廣狹、道路所從出、皆取便於事者。使張生以葬
書緣飾之、曰大吉。以示族人、皆悅、無違異者。

[2] 今吾兄年七十九、以列卿致仕。吾年六十六、
忝備侍從、宗族之從仕者二十有三人。視他人
之謹用葬書未必勝吾家也。前年吾妻死。棺成
而斂、裝辦而行、壙成而葬、未嘗以一言詢陰陽

In another piece from his hand, Szĕ-ma Kwang laments over the
same subject in a somewhat different key. »The people, placing
» trust in the gossip of burial professors, are wont to seek for good
» influences from the forms and contours of mountains and water-
» courses even after they have selected felicitous years, months,
» days and hours for the burial, considering the wealth and social
» position of their sons and grandsons, their mental faculties and
» the length of their lives to depend thereon in all respects. But
» there prevails so much diversity of opinion among those proficients,
» and they confuse matters by their quarrelsome discussions to such
» an extent, that no decision can be arrived at with regard to a
» date for the burial, so that some people do not bury any of their
» dead during their whole lives, nay, during several generations.
» It also occurs that the offspring do not bury their dead because
» a decadence of their fortunes causes them to forget or lose sight of
» the place where they have cast away the remains. Supposing for a
» moment that burials could virtually render man happy and pros-
» perous, would it even then be tolerable that sons and grandsons
» should cruelly leave the decaying remains of their nearest relations
» exposed to the open sky, with the object of reaping profit for
» themselves? Such acts are the worst sins against the rites, the
» worst violations of human duty that can be.

» The sorrowful resentment a bereaved filial son bears in his
» heart is profound, and his grief extends far. Hence he fears
» that, if he does not bury the remains deep enough, others will
» exhume them, and that, if he places them too deep in the ground,
» they will become wet and moulder away quickly. Consequently,
» he certainly searches out a place where the earth lies thick and
» the water is deep beneath the ground, and there he buries the
» corpse; in this respect he must certainly select a proper place" [1].

家。迄今亦無他故吾嘗疾。陰陽家立邪說以惑
衆、爲世患於喪家。尤甚、頃爲諫官嘗奏乞禁天
下葬書、當時執政莫以爲意。今著茲論、庶俾後
之子孫葬必以時。欲知葬具之不必厚、視吾祖、
欲知葬書不足信、視吾家 *Ku kin t'u shu tsih ch'ing*, sect.
禮儀, ch. 97.

    [1] 世俗信葬師之說、旣擇年月日時又擇山水
形勢、以爲子孫貧富貴賤賢愚壽夭盡係於此。

When Szĕ-ma Kwang thus tried his wits upon improving the customs of the nation at a time when the ascendency of his authority and influence had reached its height, the ruling Son of Heaven was endeavouring to put a stop to the postponement of burials by sterner measures. »In the fifth year of the period Yuen fung » (1082) he decreed that those who did not bury their dead relations » without postponement, should be banished for two years, and » that those who retained such men in official employ should » incur punishment"[1]. About the same time, thus the Histories of that time recount, one Wang Tszĕ-shao[2], a functionary in Hunan of very high position, »was denounced by the censor Chang » Shang-ying for not having buried his parents, and he was dis-»missed from his office on account thereof"[3]. A few years later, » Liu Ping, who, while in charge of the government of Chʻen-»cheu, had with his younger brother Hwan been raised to the » dignity of Minister in immediate attendance on the Throne, was » deprived of this dignity as a punishment for not having buried his » deceased parents, and dismissed from his prefectship"[4].

The Ming dynasty likewise decreed that punishments should be

而其爲術又多不同、爭論紛紜、無時可決、至有終身不葬、累世不葬。或子孫衰替、忘失處所棄捐不葬者。正使殯葬實能致禍福、爲子孫者亦豈忍使其親臭腐暴露而自求其利耶。悖禮傷義莫甚於此。

然孝子之心慮患深遠。恐淺則爲人所掘、深則濕潤速朽。故必求土厚水深之地而葬之、所以不可不擇也. *Ku kin tʻu shu tsih chʻing*, sect. 禮儀, ch. 92 and 63.

[1] 元豐五年詔不卽隨葬者徒二年、因而行用者罪之. History of the Sung Dynasty, ch. 124, l. 15.

[2] 王子韶.

[3] 御史張商英劾其不葬父母、貶. History of the Sung Dynasty, ch. 329, l. 18.

[4] 劉昺知陳州、昺與弟煥皆侍從、而親喪不葬、坐奪職、罷郡. The same work, ch. 356, l. 8.

inflicted upon those who rendered themselves guilty of such exe-
crable deeds. »In the fifth year of the period H u n g w u (A. D.
» 1372) it was decreed by the emperor that, whereas there were
» often people who, led astray by Fung-shui, left encoffined corpses
» unburied for more than a year, not setting them at rest in a
» grave, the ministers in the departments of the central government
» should meet in council and draw up a law against this evil; this
» law should be everywhere promulgated and properly observed,
» and punishments be pronounced against those who should pre-
» sume to violate it" [1]. This decree was duly obeyed, for we find
an article in the Code of the Ming dynasty, threatening with
eighty blows with the long stick those who, led astray by Fung-
shui, kept a corpse unburied for longer than a year [2]. It is
worded exactly like that of the present Code of Laws.

Much time is lost in seeking a grave especially when the dead
man leaves many children. Our readers know from pp. 964 *seq.*
that six of the k w a are identified by the *Yih king* both with six
points of the compass and with sons and daughters. Consequently,
the fortunes of all the members of a family cannot be insured
by the grave of their father or mother unless the forms and contours of the surroundings are perfect on six sides thereof; and as
such a perfect sepulchre is hardly ever to be acquired, even by
the ablest professors, it follows that some of the children are
excluded from the benefits yielded by the grave. It is unnecessary
to say this gives rise to domestic discord, especially when the
children thereby prejudiced are the offspring of a jealous second wife
or of concubines, for these women instigate the dear fruits of their
loins not to stoop to such wrong, but rather to oppose it vigorously
to the end. Happily, family quarrels arising from such Fung-
shui questions are moderated to some extent by the fact that the
interests of the daughters are little attended to, they being destined
to enter another clan by marriage, after which their own fate

---

[1] 洪武五年詔、有惑於風水、停柩經年、不行
安葬、宜令中書省臣集議定制、頒行遵守、違者
論罪. History of the Ming Dynasty, ch. 60, l. 22. See also ch. 2, l. 9.
[2] See the *Ta Ming hwui tien*, chapter 129, l. 9.

and that of their children will be entirely bound up with the graves of their parents-in-law.

The theory that a grave can seldom send forth blessings to all the sons equally, is one of the grandest inventions of geomantic sages. It safeguards their system from some of the most dangerous attacks of scepticists, as it imposes immediate silence upon all those who might ask: »Showers of blessings descend upon my brother's house because, as the professors say, the position of our father's grave is extremely felicitous; why then am I, though likewise his son, overwhelmed by poverty and misfortune?" Remarks of this sort are readily disarmed also by the following argument: »That the one brother is poor and the other is rich, is simply a consequence of the latter's neglecting to give the former his fair share in the profits the grave produces him. To share those profits with his brother is his moral duty; but instead of fulfilling his duty, he keeps everything for himself, even at the risk of ruining his own fortunes, for he is thus stupidly amassing a store of demerit by which the indignation of the T‘ien li will be aroused in the end. They will inevitably punish him by withdrawing their protecting hands from the grave, and so cause its Fung-shui to flow away, which will render him poorer than he ever was before".

The doctrine that a grave may yield great profits to one member of a family without advantaging the others, is by no means a modern invention. Already in the histories of the emperor Wu [1] of the Liang dynasty we read:

»When the lady Ting, the emperor's concubine of the first »rank, had breathed her last, the heir-apparent (her son) had dele- »gated some men to find a propitious place to bury her in. When »they were about to cut away the plants and shrubs from that »spot, some individual who had a plot of ground for sale tried to »sell it through the medium of the eunuch Yü San-fu, promising »him one million if he managed to get three millions for it. »San-fu secretly applied to the emperor, telling him that the »ground the heir-apparent had secured could by no means ensure »the imperial felicity to the same degree as the plot he himself »had now found. The emperor who, being in the last years of his »life, entertained sundry superstitious fears, gave him orders to »purchase it.

»After the corpse had been buried in it, a Taoist priest, versed

---

[1] 武帝. A. D. 502—549.

» in the discovery of felicitous graves, declared: 'This grave shall
» not profit the heir-apparent, but the sphere of its good influences
» may perhaps be widened by certain repressive measures". So he
» made a goose of wax, and with some other things buried it at
» the side of the grave, at the point of the compass corresponding
» to the eldest son. (Ch'en, 震, due East, see page 964.)

» At that time there were two Palace Inspectors, Pao Moh-chi
» and Wei Ya, formerly in high favour with the heir-apparent. Moh-
» chi having espied what had happened, he apprized Ya of it, and
» privately told the emperor that this latter was the man who
» had thus suppressed the felicity of the spot on behalf of the heir-
» apparent. On this, the emperor secretly dispatched somebody to dig
» up the earth and see whether the affair was real, and the goose and
» the other things were actually found. Much frightened, the em-
» peror would have the matter thoroughly investigated; but Sü Mien
» firmly withheld him from any such measures, and the priest alone
» was put to death. To the heir-apparent the business was a cause
» of deep remorse to the end of his days, and the consequences
» were that his offspring never occupied the throne" [1].

We read also in the biography of a certain Wen Ta-ya [2], a
high statesman and the corypheus of filial conduct and fraternal
devotion who lived in the first part of the seventh century: » When
» he transferred the remains of his grandfather to another grave,
» a diviner who calculated the properties of the spot said: 'It

---

[1] 初丁貴嬪薨、太子遣人求得善墓地。將斬草、
有賣地者因閹人俞三副求市、若得三百萬許以
百萬與之。三副密啓武帝、言太子所得地不如
今所得地於帝吉。帝末年多忌、便命市之。
　葬畢、有道士善圖墓、云地不利長子、若厭伏
或可申延。乃爲蠟鵝及諸物埋墓側長子位。
　有宮監鮑邈之魏雅者二人、初並爲太子所
愛。邈之晩見、疎於雅、密啓武帝云雅爲太子厭
禱。帝密遣檢掘、果得鵝等物。大驚、將窮其事、
徐勉固諫得止、於是唯誅道士。由是太子迄終
以此慙慨、故其嗣不立. History of the Southern Part of the Realm,
ch. 53, ll. 6 seq.

[2] 溫大雅.

» will be felicitous for your younger brother, but of no advantage
» to yourself; what do you intend to do?' 'Should your prophecy
» be realised', was the reply, 'I will enter the ground with a smile
» on my lips'. After that year had elapsed, he died"[1].

From what has been adduced in the foregoing pages it is sufficiently
manifest that the possession of sons and money is not an unmitigated
blessing, for the consequences may be fatal to a Chinaman after his
death. Indeed, if each son is anxious to secure through his father's
grave his own fortunes in particular, and money enough has been
left them to provide what they believe to be a perfect Fung-shui, discord arises, whereby the burial of the old man is postponed for months
and years, to the prejudice of his manes. No wonder therefore that
many a well-to-do father, if blessed with numerous sons, endeavours
to elude this calamity by having his grave made during his lifetime, with the observation of all the rules of geomantic science.

This custom may be placed on a level with that of procuring,
during life, one's own grave clothes and coffin. It saves many a poor
soul from the gloomy fate of hovering about in the other world as a
homeless paria, an outcast without a shelter into which it can retire
from the evils and nuisances of the spirit world. Moreover, it is
considered very grand in this present life to possess one's own grave,
especially if it has been built by the care of the sons under the guise
of filial devotion.

A grave made during the life of the person who is to occupy it, is
called in Amoy a *siū hík*[2], »longevity region". This term owes its
origin to the same idea as »longevity garments" and »longevity
boards or longevity wood", which are terms respectively denoting
grave clothes and coffins made before death.

To prepare one's own grave during life is a custom of very ancient date. The emperor Shi Hwang started the works for his mausoleum shortly after this accession to the throne and the same line of
conduct was followed by the sovereigns of the Han dynasty, for which
reason their sepulchres are often denoted in the annals of their reign as
»longevity mausolea"[3].

---

[1] 改葬其祖、卜人占其地曰、弟則吉、不利於
君、若何。大雅曰、如子言我含笑入地矣。歲餘
卒. New Books of the Tʻang Dynasty, ch. 91, l. 1. Also the Old Books of that
House, ch. 61, l. 1.

[2] 壽域.   [3] 壽陵.

That the custom was then in vogue among the official class also, is proved by the Histories of that epoch, which relate that the grandee » Heu Lan, having on the death of his mother in the » second year of the period Kien ning (A. D. 169) returned » home and there built a large sepulchre, the Judge of the Circuit, » Chang Kien, impeached him in a memorial addressed to the Throne » of having prepared for himself a longevity sepulchre with a vault » of stone, a gate with two entrances, and high side buildings ot » a hundred feet" [1]. And of the minister Chao Khi [2] we read: » In » the sixth year of the period Kien ngan (A. D. 201) he died, » having previously built a longevity tomb for himself" [3]. Also after the Han dynasty instances of this same custom are regularly recorded. So, for instance, at a time corresponding to about the year 480 after the Christian era, a high office-bearer, named » Ch'en T'ien-fuh ordered his family to build a longevity tomb for him" [4].

Never have geomancers such a grand opportunity of showing off their ability and astuteness as when a *siū hik* is being made. There is then plenty of time for the family to consult any number of them and to admire that display of profound learning wherewith each of them can frustrate what the other has projected and executed. Of course in the end the one is chosen who manifests more erudition than all the others by uttering ambiguous nonsense and at the same time shows a good deal of deference to the views expressed by the male and female members of the family, who, indeed, feel sure they know all about the art. An experiment with pig's bones having produced good results, the grave is finished under the auspices of that wisest of the wise, the tumulus made, and an inscribed grave stone erected in front of it. If the *materfamilias* be still alive, a sepulchre is in general at the same time made for her on the right hand side, the left appertaining to her husband, as it is considered the place of honour, both in life and death.

---

1 侯覽建寧二年喪母還家、大起塋冢、督郵張儉因舉奏覽豫作壽冢石椁雙闕高廡百尺. Books of the Later Han Dynasty, ch. 108, l. 14.

2 趙岐.

3 建安六年卒、先自爲壽藏. The same work, ch. 94, l. 19.

4 陳天福令家人豫作壽冢 History of the South of the Realm, ch. 22, l. 17.

When the grave is ready, it is necessary to prevent it from emitting influences of untimely death over its future occupant. To this end, a piece of red paper is pasted over his name which is carved in the grave stone. This sheet need not be replaced by a new one after time and rain have destroyed it, the influences of the grave, geomancers say, having by that time blended harmoniously with those of the Universe and, so to say, become one with it, thereby losing their dangerous character. Now the old man feels perfectly at ease, and greatly enjoys the happy prospect of being committed to the earth with promptitude after his death. The sons too cheerfully await the future and the wealth and fortune it is sure to bring them. Still, in many cases, everything goes wrong. Unrelenting, insidious death may strike the old man in a year when the line in which his grave is made is not felicitous, thus enforcing a long delay of the burial; or — and this is much worse — the professor under whose auspices and directions the grave has been made, may in the mean time have departed this life or removed to another part of the country, and his colleague, whom the family intrust with the burial, will tell them the Fung-shui is not worth a brass farthing. Struck with consternation, the men give vent to their sorrowful resentment in hot discussions, the women by loud vociferations and utterances of wrath; but as this does not remedy the evil, the coffin is kept at home and another burial site sought for. The *siū hík*, so dearly paid for, is sold to others, or employed to bury a slave or unmarried daughter in, or a person who has no offspring desirous of deriving profit from his earthly resting place.

Of course not every *siū hík* turns out such an unlucky business; otherwise people would long ago have given up making them.

Fung-shui often preventing people from burying their parents with suitable promptitude, it becomes a great nuisance especially to those who cannot afford to buy coffins good and substantial enough to permit of their keeping them in the house without suffering from the nauseous smell. In the island of Amoy, such families, as also those who, desirous of escaping the blame of unfilialness, will not adjourn burials, but neither wish to give up their chances of deriving profit from the graves through the intermedium of Fung-shui, often have recourse to a provisory interment, which they call *tͨao tái* [1] or *tͨao tsōng* [2], »a stealthy or

---

[1] 偷埋.   [2] 偷葬.

clandestine burial". Under escort of a plain funeral cortege, they take the coffin into the mountains or into the open country, depose it somewhere on the ground and cover it with earth, without having the properties of the spot examined by a Fung-shui expert; neither do they erect a grave stone, thereby indicating that the coffin is not there in a definite grave, but is to be removed afterwards to a resting place under propitious geomantic influences. Now it may occur that, ere the new grave is found, the family begins to prosper. Such unexpected bliss can, of course, only be ascribed to the good Fung-shui of the provisory grave. They laugh in their sleeve because the great lot in the lottery of life has become theirs by pure accident or undreamt-of merits of their own or their ancestors; and now they are certain not to transfer the corpse, nor do they convert the spot into a sepulchre worthy of the dead man, for fear the Fung-shui, sensitive as it is, might be splintered asunder by a false blow with a hoe, or be dispelled for ever by one single brick applied in the wrong place. Thus the dead man is forced to live, like a pauper, in a miserable dwelling, unworthy of his rank and station. But this causes no qualms of conscience, for the blessings he bestows upon his family are strong proofs that he feels himself perfectly happy and comfortable where he is.

Though the poorer classes cannot, of course, afford great outlays for their dead, yet they seldom neglect consulting a Fung-shui expert when they have to bury their father or mother. This man does not take long to find a suitable site when he knows there is not much money to be made out of his patrons; and he has quite a stock of second-rate plots in store for them, which he constantly increases when in search of good burial places for the rich. The poor know very well that they can hope to buy but little Fung-shui for the small sums they are able to pay. Hence they are moderate in their demands, merely seeking graves that are screened from the worst æolian influences and located on a slope which is not unfavourably situated; and they employ a professor specially to insure the placing of the coffin in the grave in the felicitous line of the current year.

As hinted above, the Fung-shui of even the best grave or dwelling is considered to be a fragile combination of imaginary influences fitting into and acting upon each other like the different parts of a machine, the slightest defect in which may bring the whole to a standstill. It is no small boon to the professors that such ideas prevail. Indeed, Fung-shui being of such a delicate nature, no man, however economical or avaricious he be, is bold enough to dispense with the guidance of an expert; and this ensures them an everflowing source of income. Besides, Fung-shui being so easily disturbed, professors have always a ready excuse at hand if their prophecies are not realized: — the Fung-shui they say, was perfect at the outset, but it has been »wounded" by some accident, or by some malicious act of a bad neighbour.

Such wounds may be inflicted by a mere trifle. A stone carelessly thrown away, or set up somewhere in the neighbourhood by a person wishing to improve the Fung-shui of a grave of his; the erection of a stone boundary mark; the building of a hut or shed at some distance from the grave or on a visible mountain brow; in short, anything may prove fatal. But nothing is so perilous for a grave as the construction of another grave in the adjacent grounds. In general it is the professor who discovers the impending danger. He does not delay for a moment to open the eyes of the family to the sorrowful fact that the new grave will intercept the influences of a water-course, or that, being made higher up, just in the pulse through which the beneficial influences of the tail or leg of the Tiger or Dragon hitherto used to flow, it »cuts off their effective operation": c h a n l i n g [1]. At the same time he convinces the family that only prompt and severe measures can heal the wound, and that, if these be not at once taken, the beneficient Animal will bleed to death and the Fung-shui be for ever destroyed.

Therefore everybody sets to work immediately. Negotiations are opened with the owners of the murderous grave, but without any good result, as they zealously stick to their good right of retaining a spot obtained at the cost of much science and money: Geomantic measures satisfactory for both parties are hardly possible, for what is good for the one grave is generally pernicious to the other, and the learned combinations of factors to which both must answer almost inevitably collide. Hard coin may perhaps lead to a better result. But the suffering party as a rule rebounds from the high demands of the other, who is certain to demand an excessive sum, especially if any of them are graduates or rich and influential men who, being on good terms with the local mandarins, feel sure of gaining their cause if the offended party should invoke the intervention of these latter to redress the wrong. In such cases nothing remains for the family but to beat a humble

---

[1] 斬靈.

retreat. Making a virtue of necessity, they gulp down the wrong and let things remain as they were, resolving, however, to remove their grave as soon as any decadence in their fortunes reminds them they cannot expect any more blessings from the wounded Fung-shui.

But, should the two parties possess an equal, or nearly equal, amount of social influence, or have no influence at all, a complaint is soon lodged with the chief local magistrate. Our readers might doubtless suppose that this worthy will simply dismiss the case, written law and the Government, as we have stated on page 1017, having denounced modern Fung-shui in contemptuous terms as a farrago of nonsense, and its professors as a set of deluders. However, in respect of geomancy, theory and practice in China are two different things, for should a mandarin refuse to hear such cases, his secretaries, constables, policemen and other hangers-on would be deprived of many a nice opportunity of making money in an easy way. These underlings by leaving the accusation unattended to after it has been entered, compell the plaintiff, who is anxious to save his Fung-shui from impendent death by loss of blood, to bribe them to make haste; but however hard this may render his lot, that of the defendant is still harder. If he has any money to lose, he lives in constant fear of being taken into custody, for the common people, though ever so innocent, are always liable to immediate imprisonment if an accusation has been lodged against them with the authorities. And as the Yamen officials take good care to remind the defendant of this danger, he fees them liberally, and fees them over and over again. And yet all these fees are not always sufficient to secure him from a terrible dungeon, a very hell of cold, filth, starvation and torment.

Not until they have wrung the last penny out of their victims do these underlings arouse the magistrate from his lethargy. He is then carried in state to the graves in his official palankeen, escorted by his usual attendance of soldiers, retainers, and lictors. Arrived at the spot, maps of the locality, put in by the plaintiff, are unrolled and collated with the deeds of sale of the property; with a dignified air the mandarin surveys the country, and mostly he is in a few moments convinced that his subordinates were quite justified in persuading him that the party which paid them best is in the right. Otherwise judgment is usually given in favour of the plaintiff; but many mandarins obstinately refuse to do this when the distance between the two graves exceeds a certain number of paces beyond which they believe no serious damage to the Fung-shui of a grave is possible. Still, most of the magistrates are imbued with too much respect for the noble geomantic art to decide grave questions in such an off-hand easy way.

Such a »Fung-shui inspection" or *khàm hong-suí*[1], as the Amoy Chinese call it, has of course to be defrayed by the party on whose behalf it is made. A good sum is squeezed out of them for the men who have accompanied the magistrate and carried his sedan-chair. Furthermore, the same party have to offer refreshments and delicacies to the great man while making his inspection, and to spread a piece of red cloth over the top of his palankeen, in order to protect him from noxious influences, which cloth is retained. Last, but not least, they must send him a sum of money, together with a selection of costly presents, lest their ship should be wrecked, in sight of the harbour, by the mandarin ultimately changing his mind in favour of the other party.

It follows from the above that poor people, the Fung-shui of whose graves has been disturbed, have to gulp down the wrong in silence. The Amoy Chinese are quite right when they say:

Gé-mn̂g pat dzī khai,
Bó tsíⁿ m̄ sái lái[2],

which means: »Mandarins' offices stand open quite as wide as the character 八 (eight); but those who have no money need not enter".

The abuse of litigation by petty officials for money-extorting purposes is very common in China, and is systematically tolerated in all cases, both criminal and civil. We say systematically; for, whereas the Government, acts on the principle that each individual or family should have their affairs regulated by their own clan and not trouble the higher authorities with them, those who are imprudent enough to call for interference may expect to suffer, and chiefly in their pockets. This method is very practical in the moral education of the people, teaching them to be mild and forbearing, and to avoid litigation. Mandarins are sometimes honest enough to issue proclamations in which those evils entailed by litigation are depicted in striking colours, thus openly confessing that extortions by police-officers and clerks are as a matter of course inseparably connected with lawsuits.

---

1 勘風水.
2 衙門八字開、無錢無使來.

Much strife and contention about graves is created by the foul intrigues and frauds of certain brokers, who derive a livelihood from assisting people in acquiring suitable grave grounds. These men possess, or are deemed to possess, a thorough knowledge of the localities where eligible burial sites can be had, and they know better than anybody else who the owners are, and the conditions on which they are inclined to sell. At Amoy, the people denote them by the not very flattering terms of *soan-kúi* [1], »mountain spectres", and *soan ka-tsoáh* [2], »mountain cockroaches", in allusion to their haunting graves like ghosts, and ruminaging every spot and recess in the open country like cockroaches in a house. When such a grave broker is applied to by a client, the latter is taken out to see the merchandize; and the broker's chief business is to ask the highest possible price and to prevail upon the owners to sell cheap, quietly pocketing the difference. As is the custom with brokers generally in China, the mountain cockroach settles the transaction without allowing the buyer and vendor to see each other, or even to know each other's name. For the sake of his own purse he lives on very friendly terms with all the Fung-shui professors in the district, these worthies being able to assist him greatly in the sale of any grounds by declaring for a fee that the geomantic influences under which they are situated are good, nay, exquisite.

The cockroaches are generally represented by the people as a reckless set, little less delicate in their choice of means for making money than thieves and robbers. It is chiefly they who commit frauds like those which are provided for in the fourth and fifth supplementary articles of the Law on Burial (see Appendix 1). They seek their victims especially among those who have not money or influence enough to gain the ear of the magistrates, should they apply to them for a redress of grievances. One of their most common tricks is the following. Within the borders of a grave of such a family the broker stealthily makes a grave mound scarcely visible. When the family perceive it, they dare not remove it, for fear the wicked unknown who has made it should be cruel enough to denounce them as grave robbers and thus bring upon them all the woes which an accusation, whether false or not, generally entails. The family having now given proof of its lack of power and influence by

---

[1] 山鬼.   [2] 山 ◯ ◯.

not reporting the matter to the authorities, after a couple of years the broker sells the mock grave to a third party, telling them that it is his legal property, from which he has for some reason or other removed the bones. Up to this point all goes well. But no sooner do the purchasers proceed to burying their dead, than the real owners sally forth to interfere. A scene ensues such as we have described (see note 10, p.148); quarrels, contentions and litigation follow. In most cases, however, both parties have the good sense not to commence a suit, and the legal owners are prevailed upon to give up their claim to the disputed ground for a small sum paid to them by the broker, who, of course, is most interested in hushing the matter up as quickly as possible.

With a view to check practices of this sort, pious people, anxious to keep the moral condition of their countrymen up to the highest possible level, sometimes erect slabs or small columns of granite in the grounds where people are wont to bury their dead, engraven with this inscription: » If thou desirest to find the beneficial influences of the earth (Ti li), then first gain those of the heavens (T'ien li)" [1], which can only be done by the cultivation of virtues (p. 1013).

In many other ways mountain-cockroaches cause serious grave questions to arise. Such worthies, not considering it beneath their dignity to misappropriate other people's grave grounds and sell them, can, of course, have no qualms of conscience about selling grounds which, when converted into graves, entirely disturb the Fung-shui of other sepulchres. Neither will they shrink from misleading the buyers so as to cause them to build their omega-shaped fence over the grave of another, thus inflicting a mortal blow upon the Fung-shui of such a grave, or a dagger stroke which causes an incurable wound. This stirs up the indignation of the owners to the highest pitch. If they have not money or influence enough to place the matter in the hands of the magistrates, and their remonstrances and threats remain without effect, they cool their anger under the cover of night by knocking to pieces the inscribed stone of the grave belonging to the encroachers, which stone is considered the place in which the geomantic influences are chiefly concentrated, and, moreover, the seat of the manes of the occupant of the grave. The next night they find their own grave

---

[1] 要求地理、先求天理.

treated in a like manner, the tumulus damaged with hoes and spades, nay, the coffin opened and the corpse mutilated; and now everything is ripe for a feud, each party, backed by their clan, thirsting for revenge. In the country, such feuds generally entail the desecration of several more graves, open fights, destruction of crops and incendiarism. Men, women and children are waylaid and entrapped, captured and maltreated, or held as hostages, either to be redeemed for money or exchanged; in short, civil war, which is always smouldering in China, breaks out in the locality with all its disastrous consequences.

When matters have reached such a pitch, the mandarins sometimes resort to rigorous measures. Soldiers are quartered in both villages and soon restore order by extorting money and food from the inhabitants so mercilessly that within a few weeks not a bushel of rice, nor a handful of coppers is to be found in either of the villages. While everything of value is thus being eaten up, carried off or gambled away by the peacemakers, the magistrate paternally corrects those who have taken an active part in the desecration of the graves, by making a liberal use of sticks both long and short, punishing some, if he deems it fit, with the utmost rigour of the Burial Law.

Social life not having undergone any radical change in China since culture was established there, we have no reason to suppose that conflicts about graves necessitating the interference of the authorities are exclusively peculiar to modern times. The passage in the *Cheu li*, (see note 11, p.148) gives evidence that already in the pre-Christian epoch certain Great officers were appointed to attend to litigations of this kind and to settle them by a judicial decision. That they have sometimes assumed enormous porportions is proved by the History of the Sung Dynasty, according to which, in the thirteenth century, one »Lü »Hang in the capacity of prefect of Wu-cheu managed to settle by judicial » dicision a suit which had been pending about some fields for » forty-two years between Mr. Chu and a certain Chang, and also » a contention about graves which had lasted twenty-nine years » between two gentlemen of the surnames of Wu and Wang" [1].

Hostilities between clans or villages not seldom arise from a

---

[1] 呂沆通判婺州朱君章訟爭田四十有二年、吳王府爭墓二十有九年、沆皆決之. Chapter 407, l. 21.

disarrangement of the Fung-shui of an extensive tract of country. A slight alteration made in the course of a brook for agricultural or other purposes; the modification of the brow of a hill or the out-lines of a rock by the erection of a house or shed; in short, any little trifle may seriously disturb the Fung-shui of villages or valleys, which is usually evinced by a decadence of their prosperity, bad crops, calamities etc. Attacks upon the Fung-shui of a landscape are often made.for malignant purposes. There are instances on record of the whole male population of a village having worked hard for several days to destroy the felicity of a hated neighbour by digging away a knoll, levelling down an eminence, or amputating a limb from a Dragon or Tiger.

Quarrels and litigation arising from Fung-shui questions are of daily occurrence in towns. The repairing of a house, the building of a wall or dwelling, especially it it overtops its surroundings, the planting of a pole or cutting down of a tree, in short, any change in the ordinary position of objects may disturb the Fung-shui of the houses and temples in the vicinity and of the whole quarter, and cause the people to be visited by disasters, misery and death. Should any one suddenly fall ill or die, his kindred are immedi-ately ready to impute the cause to somebody who has ventured to make a change in the established order of things, or has made an improvement in his own property, which he had a perfect right to do. Instances are by no means rare of their having stormed his house, demolished his furniture, assailed his person; sometimes they place the corpse in his bed, with the object of extorting money and avenging themselves by introducing the influences of death into his house. No wonder Chinamen do not repair their houses until they are ready to fall and become uninhabitable.

Fortunately much animosity and contention is prevented from the circumstance that Fung-shui, when disturbed, can be restored in various ways. Professors, if consulted in time, are generally able to suggest some remedy. When a dwelling house is endangered, they usually order the erection of certain fences capable of keeping oft or absorbing the s h a h which are, they think, encroaching upon the good geomantic influences. Among such fences, slabs of granite inscribed with the sentence: » This stone dares bear them" [1], are considered the best, if placed at a proper spot on the premises,

---

[1] 石敢當.

or inserted in the outer-wall. Very efficacious are also broad boards with the eight k w a, painted around the figure which is the common representation of the Yang and the Yin constituting unitedly the Tᶜai Kih or first creative power in the Universe (see page 960); such a board should be placed like a screen in the pathway leading up to the house. Other devices are, to place in front of the house, or on the top of the roof, dragons or lion-like animals of stone or burnt clay; or to nail down over the main entrance, or at each corner on the outside of the house, a square board with a tiger or a tiger's head daubed thereon. But this is leading us into the domain of amulets and talismans, which will be treated of in our Second Book.

In a paper read in 1867 at the Missionary Quarterly Meeting in Shanghai, the Rev. Mr. Yates relates the following interesting instance of the correction of the Fung-shui of a mansion. » During » the time the rebels occupied the city of Shanghai, the Yamen of » the district magistrate was destroyed. A short time previous to » this a magistrate had died, and his death was attributed by the » Fung-shui professor to my church tower, which was due North » of the Yamen. It must be borne in mind that the influence of » Fung-shui, when undisturbed, proceeds in a line due North and » South. When the rebels left the city, and the local authorities » were about to resume their old positions, they sent to me a » deputation to consult in regard to pulling down my church tower, » stating as a reason that it had been the cause of one magistrate's » death, and consequently no one was willing to serve while thus » exposed. My proposition to discuss the matter with the mandarins » was declined. Application was then made to high authorities for » the privilege of moving the Yamen to some other part of the city. » This was not granted. Finding it must be rebuilt on the exposed » lot, they called many Fung-shui professors and priests to devise » some means of counteracting the evil to which the place was » exposed. All, at first view, pronounced the position bad.

  » After a few days consultation and feasting, one astute fellow » was able to exclaim, in language equivalent to 'eureka, eureka': » 'Nothing could be more simple; build the Yamen on the old » plot, but do not place it due North and South. Thus, as the » murderous spirit proceeds due South, when it passes the corner » of the wall, its course will diverge from the end wall, and no

» evil influence can possibly follow'. The suggestion was adopted,
» and the Yamen stands to this day in that position. No magistrate
» has died there since the Fung-shui was corrected".

Also when the Fung-shui of a village, town or valley has been
disturbed, there are many means of remedying the evil. We have
stated already on page 958 how the calamitous contours of rocks,
mountains or plains may be rectified by skilful manipulations, and
turned into instruments of blessing. If an elevation is not high
enough, it can be made higher; a calamitous water-course may be
given a favourable turn; groves may be planted at the back or on
the sides of villages and towns as fenders; tanks and ponds may
be dug to counteract obnoxious breaths by the aquatic influences
of which they are the depositories (pp. 946 and 958); pagodas may
be erected for the same purpose, or piles of stone be made to
represent such structures (pp. 941 and 958). Temples for the worship of mighty tutelary divinities and even large Buddhist convents
generally owe their existence to a desire of the people to confirm the
Fung-shui of the environs. The particulars on this head we reserve,
however, for other parts of this work, wherein such sanctuaries
will be described.

Curious incidents illustrating the ways in which the Chinese endeavour to rectify the Fung-shui of towns or large tracts of country,
have been recorded by European residents. Especially instructive are
the following, which were communicated by Mr. Yates at the above-
mentioned Missionary Conference:

» Local rebellions and other public calamities are often attributed
» to some object that has destroyed the good Fung-shui, and allowed
» the murderous spirit (shah) to enter. Take the case of Shanghai.
» A few years ago, when the rebels left the city, the Fung-shui
» professors were employed to discover the cause of the disturbance
» in Fung-shui, and consequently the cause of the local rebellion.
» Their attention was directed to a large new temple within the
» north gate, called the Kwang-Foh sze [1]. They found on en-
» quiry that the Kwangtung and Fuhkien men were mainly instru-
» mental in rebuilding the temple, and the largest donor was the
» keeper of a house of ill-fame. As such men are called in common
» parlance a tortoise [2], they made strict examination to see if the

---

1 廣福寺, which means: Temple of Kwang(tung) and Fuh(kien).

2 Viz. » black tortoise" 烏龜.

» temple and plot of ground had any resemblance to that disreput-
» able animal. To the astonishment of all, it was found to be a
» perfect representation of a tortoise travelling South. It was bounded
» on the four sides by a street and water, with a stone bridge at
» the four corners, representing the four feet of a tortoise. There
» was a stone bridge just in front of the temple door, representing
» his head, and two wells at the door, representing the animal's
» eyes, and a large tree in the rear, representing his tail turned
» up, while the temple itself represented the body of the odious
» thing. If any thing was wanting to confirm them in their suspi-
» cions that that temple, from its resemblance to the tortoise, was
» the cause of the local rebellion, its name Kwang-Foh szĕ
» was quite sufficient to remove all doubts; for the city was taken
» by Kwangtung and Fuhkien men, who entered at the North
» gate, just in the rear of the temple. Now as Kwang-Foh szĕ
» was found to be bad Fung-shui, something must be done to
» correct it. They dare not order it to be pulled down, for it was
» occupied by the gods. The Fung-shui professors had no difficulty
» in finding a remedy, both simple and effectual. They decided
» that to change the name of the temple and put out the eyes of
» the animal would be quite sufficient to render him incapable of
» doing further injury. The order was given, and the wells were
» filled up, and the name of the temple changed to The first Moun-
» tain of the City on the river Hu [1].

» Again, about twelve months ago, the merchants within the
» city of Shanghai became alarmed at the great falling off of busi-
» ness within the walls. The Fung-shui experts were consulted to
» ascertain the cause. The cause was soon discovered. As the Little
» North gate was simply a hole in the wall, without the ordinary
» fender and side entrance, the good influences from the South
» passed without obstruction into the foreign community, while the
» evil from the North flowed into the city. The order was given
» to build the circular wall with a side entrance, which we all
» know was done without any apparent reason, as there was no
» danger of an attack from that quarter, it being well defended
» by the foreign settlements. Unfortunately for the credit of Fung-
» shui, trade has not revived within the city.

---

[1] 滬城第一山. The Hu is a branch which flows into the Hwang-pu 黃浦 at Shanghai.

»Kü-yung [1], a city near Nanking, has a history in connection
» with Fung-shui, well known in the Northern and Central Pro-
» vinces. Early in the Ming dynasty, a Fung-shui professor discov-
» ered that that city would produce an emperor, and that all its
» population would be mandarins. The Emperor, alarmed at the
» prospect of being superseded by an appointment of this kind,
» took steps to have the Fung-shui of that city corrected. It was
» decreed that the North gate, at which the evil spirit entered,
» should be built up solid, and remain so, and that the people
» should devote themselves to other than literary pursuits. It is a
» well known fact that Fung-shui has kept the North gate of Kü-
» yung closed for a period of over four hundred years. The people
» were ordered to choose one of three callings — a barber, a corn
» cutter or a bamboo root shaver, each of which necessitated the
» use of sharp edged instruments. It is supposed that the shah
» spirit never comes near one who uses sharp edged instruments.
» In confirmation of the fact that such an order was issued, and
» that it was obeyed, we have ocular demonstration even at this
» day, seven tenths of the dressers of the dried bamboo shoots, an
» equally large proportion of the corn cutters in connection with
» the various bathing establishments, and the same proportion of
» the barbers of this city and of the many cities in the Central
» Provinces are known to be Kü-yung men. The monopoly of these
» trades is readily conceded to them, since it is known to be decreed
» that they should get their rice in this way.

»As every mandarin has the right to erect the official pole in
» front of his house, these people claimed it, and it was conceded
» in part. Each travelling barber was allowed to erect his official
» staff on his box. Any one who will notice a travelling barber
» going about the streets with his chest of drawers slung on either
» end of a stick on his shoulder, will observe a rod in front pro-
» jecting above the stick on his shoulder. This is his official pole,
» guaranteed to him for all time by the decrees of Fung-shui.
» Thus, by closing the North gate and dispersing the male popu-
» lation, Kü-yung has been prevented from producing an emperor,
» and the Empire has been saved".

It seems to us, however, that the above tale about the peculiar
vocations of the Kü-yung people savours too much of legend to
deserve implicit belief. We have never found anything about this

---

[1] 句容.

subject in Chinese books, and the custom of the street barbers of carrying an official pole in miniature on their wash-stand is often explained by the Chinese in quite another way [1].

In his work on The Folk-lore of China [2], Dennys reports the following incident, taken from a Shanghai newspaper:

» The general excitement caused in Hang-cheu, in common, ap-
» parently, with the rest of the province, was some weeks ago
» intensified by a development of the well known superstition of
» Fung-shui. A number of people having died in a certain part
» of the town, enquiries began to be made as to the cause of a
» mortality somewhat specially localised. But instead of looking to
» the physical conditions and environments of the district, the good
» folks of Hang-cheu called in the learning of the geomancers to
» explain the cause of the evil influence. These worthies were not
» long in pointing to a range of buildings belonging to one of the
» American missions, that stood on a hill overlooking the district
» where the abnormal mortality had prevailed. These buildings,
» though not high in themselves, were yet elevated by their site
» above all the surrounding buildings, and thus they interrupted
» the benign influences of the Fung-shui. The question then came
» to be, how the evil was to be remedied. The traditional mode
» of procedure would have been to organise a mob, raise a disturb-
» ance, and during its continuance contrive to pull down or burn
» the obnoxious premises. But, on the one hand, past experience
» of foreigners has convinced the authorities that this way of dealing
» with foreign property is sure to entail serious consequences;
» while, on the other, the satisfactory results of diplomatic action as
» illustrated at Peking has gradually inclined them to the *suaviter-in-*
» *modo* policy. Accordingly a number of the gentry were commis-
» sioned to proceed to Ningpo and put themselves in communication
» with the United States Consul on the subject. Arrived in Ningpo,
» they drew up a petition to that gentleman, setting forth the fears
» and anxieties which were excited among the common people of
» Hang-cheu by the disturbance of the Fung-shui occasioned by the
» mission premises in question, and setting forth the willingness of
» the authorities to grant them a site and erect buildings on some
» other site to be agreed on between them and the missionaries,
» or to pay the missionaries a money equivalent for the surrender

---

1 See »Les Fêtes annuellement célébrées à Emoui", in the »Annales du Musée Guimet", vol. XI, page 171.

2 Page 66.

» of their property. The missionaries, on being communicated with
» by Dr. Lord, signified their preference of the proposal to grant
» them an equally eligible site and erect suitable buildings else-
» where, in exchange for their existing property, and this arrange-
» ment is now in course of being carried out. No better instance
» of the difficulties which Fung-shui presents to foreign missionary
» and commercial enterprise could be adduced".

After this digression to return to the Fung-shui of the resting
places of the dead: — a wound inflicted on a grave does not necessarily entail the death of its Fung-shui. That of some graves is so
vigorous that it can sustain many an injury without being seriously
damaged, nay, even the amputation of a Dragon's or Tiger's
limb. Of others, on the contrary, the Fung-shui is so frail that the
slightest wound is sure to affect its working and bring the whole
machine to a standstill. Only professional experts are capable of
ascertaining whether the wound is dangerous, and whether a cure
is possible. They aver that, as in the case of the human body,
the gravity of the injury chiefly depends upon the part affected.
The stone, for instance, on which the grave inscription is carved,
and the tumulus, are especially vulnerable, they being, as stated
before, the chief seat of the manes of the occupant of the grave.
Whether a wound is mortal is inferred from its consequences.
Should the family be visited by sickness, mortality or a decline in
business, or sustain any considerable pecuniary losses, then, after
long consultation with one or more learned professors, the death
of the Fung-shui is taken for granted. It is then of no use to remove
the object which has caused the wound, or to repair the violated
tumulus, or to erect a new grave stone in the place of the one
that has been knocked to pieces. Indeed, so people argue, neither
the extraction of the dagger from the body of a murdered man, nor
the patching up of his wounds, can ever restore him to life.

When enough evil has befallen the family to convince them
that the wound, inflicted on their grave, is mortal, they generally
arrive at the conclusion that the best thing they can do is to
ask their professor to look out for another grave, and re-bury the
corpse. It not seldom occurs that a professor, eager for business
and gain, makes a family believe that one of their graves has
entirely lost its good Fung-shui, the corpse having fallen a prey
to termites, the skeleton being turned upside down, or the bones
lying out of order or topsy turvy in the coffin; he tells them it is
their duty to break the grave up and give the soul a better resting

place elsewhere. Still all his logic is powerless so long as the fortunes of the family take no unfavourable turn, for this is the most decisive proof that everything is all right with the Fung-shui. But no sooner does a disaster occur, than the professor's argument gains attention; and a few more mishaps suffice to make the family surrender themselves bound hand and foot into his power. When the grave is opened, fortunately for the credit of the Fung-shui and the professor, the correctness of the latter's statement is often verified by facts. In truth it is a very common occurence in China for termites to built their nests in coffins, or for foxes, rats or other beasts to nestle therein; besides, the stick of a mountain cockroach or of the professor himself can secretly disarrange the bones so as to insure the triumph of the latter. And even if everything in the grave should be in the best condition, and the bones dry and hard, and the coffin but little affected by decay, the professor has plenty of arguments to prove that the Fung-shui was thoroughly bad.

It is not necessary to dilate further on Fung-shui and its influence upon social life. The above pages will suffice to show what it really is: — the product of egotism under the guise of filial piety; a sure criterion that this highest among the national virtues of the Chinese, so often extolled to the skies by European authors, is much less sincere than is generally supposed; that it is not spontaneous, but calculating; not generous, but thoroughly selfish. Fung-shui is fetichism applied to the dead and their corporeal remains. It is a hybrid monster, born of the union of filial devotion in its vilest form with blind gropings after natural science. At the outset a benumbed viper, it has, carefully fostered by the nation, developed into a horrid hydra suffocating the whole Empire in its coils and deluging it with its venom throughout its length and breadth.

In fact, as we have stated, wielding its cruel scourge with vigour, it disturbs social peace and order, sowing endless discord among families, clans and villages, and giving rise to quarrels, litigation, contention, incendiarism and bloodshed. It causes the ruin of many families, wasting their fortunes under the pretext of creating fortunes. It constrains the people to keep their dead unburied for months, nay years, in spite of epidemics and contagious diseases, and to exhume them before the process of decay has done its work, thus increasing mortality. But further, Fung-shui interferes with industry and commercial enterprise, as being the ground for refusing many improvements which would be of the greatest advantage to the people. The cutting of a new road or canal, the construction of a new bridge, almost always entails the amputation of a limb of some Celestial Animal, intercepts good aquatic influences or affects the calculations of geomancers in some way or other, causing entire clans, wards, villages and towns to rise up as one man against the reckless individual whose enterprising spirit presumes to bring misfortune upon them all. » When", says Dr. Eitel [1], » it was proposed to erect a few telegraph poles, when the » construction of a railway was urged upon the Chinese Govern- » ment, when a mere tramway was suggested to utilize the coal- » mines of the interior, Chinese officials would invariably make a » polite bow and declare the thing impossible on account of Fung- » shui. When, thirty years ago, the leading merchants of the » Colony of Hongkong endeavoured to place the business part of » the town in the so-called Happy Valley, and to make that part » of the island the centre of the whole town, they ignominiously » failed on account of Fung-shui. When the Hongkong Govern- » ment cut a road, now known as the Gap, to the Happy Valley, » the Chinese community was thrown into a state of abject terror » and fright, on account of the disturbance which this amputation » of the Dragon's limbs would cause to the Fung-shui of Hong- » kong; and when many of the engineers, employed at the cutting, » died of Hongkong fever, and the foreign houses already built in » the Happy Valley had to be deserted on account of malaria, the » Chinese triumphantly declared, it was an act of retributory justice » on the part of Fung-shui. When Senhor Amaral, the Governor of » Macao, who combined with a great passion for constructing roads » an unlimited contempt for Fung-shui, interfered with the situation » and aspects of Chinese tombs, he was waylaid by Chinese, his » head cut off [2], and the Chinese called this dastardly deed the » revenge of Fung-shui".

As a matter of fact, all the books of geomancy re-echo the doctrine of Ch'ing I-ch'wen, that, in selecting graves, »one must not be » remiss in avoiding the five following evils: Care must be taken lest some » day or other roads are made there, or city walls, canals or ponds; or lest

---

1 Feng-shui, pp. 1 *seq.*
2 Comp. page 355.

» people of rank and influence appropriate the place to themselves,
» or agriculture be exercised thereupon"[1]. As a consequence hereof,
Fung-shui causes an immense waste of labour in China, for as it
prevents in most parts of the Empire the construction of good
canals and roads, ships, beasts of burden or carts can only be
employed in limited numbers, which necessitates a great use of
the human shoulder for the transport of persons and merchandise
along paths scarcely passable. Nor is it rare to see hundreds of
ships and vessels taking a wide roundabout and difficult circuit,
simply because Fung-shui has forbidden a bridge to be built high
enough to allow of their passing underneath.

The question will be asked, how is it possible that so large a
portion of the human race, though imbued since its childhood
with sacred awe for the mysteries of the Universe, has grown up
to manhood and hoary old age without arriving at even an elementary knowledge of the true laws of Nature? How is it the
Chinese never built up anything better than a speculative system
based upon ancient formulæ and mystic diagrams, and amount-
ing to little more than a mechanical play of idle abstractions,
a system so unscientific, so puerile, that it can only move us to
a smile?

The answer must in the first place be sought in the educational
system of the nation. This has always been grounded upon an
unbounded reverence for everything which could claim an ancient
origin. Whatever the ancients thought, taught and wrought always
was in everybody's eyes the highest truth, sacred and inviolable;
beyond it no other truth ever existed. Thus the classical books,
transmitting the ideas and actions of the ancients to posterity,
naturally became the exclusive starting point of instruction, both
public and private. And the Government being recruited, regularly
and systematically, from the classes thus educated, it never could
do otherwise than disparage, nay, formally forbid any doctrines and
studies arising from other principles; on the other hand, it never
occurred to any one among the people to pursue another line of
study, because only the old method opened up any prospect of
being admitted into the ranks of the ruling party, which is the
highest ambition of every true Chinaman.

---

[1] 五患不可不謹、使他日不爲道路、不爲城郭、
不爲溝池、不爲貴勢所奪、不爲耕犁所及. Domestic
Rituals, ch. VI.

So nobody in China has ever thought of studying Nature in that independent matter-of-fact way which alone can reveal to man the secrets of the Universe; nor have the Chinese tried to make instruments to aid them in the contemplation of the canopy of heaven, the study of the atmosphere, the laws of gravity and hydrostatics. Instead thereof, they have blunted their wits upon conjectural theories, evolving an entire system of natural science from their religious superstitions with respect to the dead in connection with a few rough guesses at Nature occurring in the Classics; the product being a monstrous medley of religion, superstition, ignorance and philosophy, more strange than was ever hatched by the human brain. It seems never to have occurred to any one, not even to the wisest of the wise, that methodical, independent research might be a better groundwork for big books than the ignorance of the ancients. Chinese sages, by spinning out the dogmatic formulæ of ancient tradition to an infinite length, have succeeded in proving that oceans of wisdom lie hidden in those formulæ. Thus the position of the ancients has been strengthened, so as to render it impregnable, but in the mountains of reasonings not a single grain of common sense is to be found; and though these sages have obtained places of worship for themselves in the Government temples dedicated to Confucius and the great disciples of his school of learning, thus gaining the highest laurels ever conferred in their country on the human intellect, not one of them has ever enriched the Empire with the simplest rudiment of real, useful knowledge.

Even at present the educational system of China is based, as firmly as ever, upon the principle that the Classics are the sole depositories of true science; and everything which is not built upon the principles laid down therein, is ignored, or stigmatized as heterodox. And the Government is in the hands of the learned class, as it has always been. Hence Fung-shui is still in the apogee of its power, bearing sway in the mansions of emperors and princes just as in the cabins of the poor. The palace-grounds in the Metropolis and the gorgeous mausolea of the Imperial Family as well as the graves of the lowest class are laid out in accordance with its rescripts. That Fung-shui has a legal status we have seen from the fact that the authorities entertain the claim and give judgment when complaints about the disturbance of the Fung-shui are placed before them.

Fung-shui has even a political status. » When a rebellion breaks » out in any one of the eighteen provinces, the first step taken by

» the Government is not to raise troops, but invariably to dispatch
» messengers instructed to find out the ancestral tombs of the several
» leaders of the rebellion, to open the tombs, scatter their contents
» to the winds and desecrate the graves in every possible way. For
» this is supposed to be the surest means of injuring the prospects
» and marring the possible success of the rebels" [1]. The books make
mention of emperors having, no doubt for similar reasons, destroyed
the graves of the dynasties they had dethroned. Chwang Tsung,
for instance, the first sovereign of the short-lived posterior T͟'ang
dynasty, »having destroyed the House of Liang, desired to dig up
» the grave of T͟'ai Tsu, (the founder) of that House, and to hack
» up his coffin and mutilate the corpse. But (Chang) Ts͟'üen-i gave
» it as his opinion that, though that family had been in overt
» enmity (with the present emperor), enough retributive justice had
» been done it by its slaughter and destruction, and that the
» cutting-up of a coffin and the mutilation of the corpse was not
» a sublime measure for a sovereign to take as a warning example
» to the world. Chwang Tsung opined he was right, and merely
» demolished the gate of the tomb" [2]. There is little doubt that it
was not merely rapacity which inspired insurgents to destroy, in
the course of centuries, so many imperial tombs, but also a desire
to weaken the Throne by depriving it of the indispensable protection
of its ancestors. To minimize such dangers, walled cities have, since the
Han dynasty, been built in the neighbourhood of the imperial mausolea,
and the latter are walled and garrisoned down to the present day. Should
European armies have for a second time to march on Peking, it will be
worth while trying whether the campaign cannot be shortened and loss of
life spared by a military occupation of the burial grounds of the Imperial
Family. Indeed, should the Court receive the ultimatum that these tombs
will be successively destroyed by barbarian explosives, its belief in Fung-
shui will without a doubt force it to submit implicitly to the foreign
demands.

---

1 Eitel, *op. cit.*, page 80.

2 初莊宗滅梁、欲掘梁太祖墓、斲棺戮尸。〔張〕
全義以謂梁雖讐敵、今已屠滅其家足以報怨、
剖棺之戮非王者以大度示天下也。莊宗以爲
然、鏟去墓闕而已・History of the Five Dynasties, ch. 45, l. 3.

By thus making use of the Fung-shui doctrines to harm their ene-
mies, the foreign powers would merely be wielding the same weapon
which Chinese statesmen have so frequently and cunningly used against
them in times of peace. » When land had to be ceded to the hated
» foreigner along the coast of China, as a so-called foreign conces-
» sion, the Chinese Government invariably selected ground condemned
» by the best experts in Fung-shui as combining a deadly breath
» with all those indications of the compass which imply dire ca-
» lamity to all who settle upon it, even to their children's children.
» If the spot had not had to be ceded by treaty, it would have been
» pointed out to the unsuspecting foreigner as the only one open
» for sale, and anyhow the ignorant barbarian sceptic would be made
» the supposed dupe and laughing-stock of the astute Chinaman.
» Witness, for instance, the views held by intelligent Chinese in
» regard to the island of Sha-meen, the foreign concession of Canton.
» It was originally a mud flat in the Canton river in the very worst
» position known to Fung-shui. It was conceded to the imperious
» demands of the foreign powers as the best available place of
» residence for foreigners; and when it was found that the Canton
» trade, once so important, would not revive, would not flourish
» there, in spite of all the efforts of its supporters — when it was
» discovered that every house built on Sha-meen was overrun with
» white ants as soon as built, boldly defying coal tar, carbolic acid
» and all other foreign appliances — when it was noticed that the
» English Consul, though a special residence was built for him
» there, preferred to live two miles off under the protecting shadow
» of a Pagoda, — this was a clear triumph of Fung-shui and of
» Chinese statesmanship" [1].

Afterwards, when the barbarians had been settled long enough
in the several ports for the Chinese to witness the rise of flourishing
mercantile houses, surrounded by buildings and villas which must
appear to them to be palaces when compared with their own
huts and houses, then a decided change in their ideas as to the
stupidity of foreigners in Fung-shui matters came about. Did not
the fact that there were never any paupers to be found among them,
and that most of them became rich enough to pay to their humblest
clerks salaries which, if earned by a Chinaman, would stamp
him as a man of wealth, sufficiently prove that they knew all about
that noble art? In Amoy many professors have not words enough

---

[1] Eitel, op. cit., pp. 80—81.

wherewith to extol the Fung-shui of the foreign houses in the island
of Kulangsu. Nearly all of them, they say, are placed under the
protection of excellent Tigers and Dragons, and the gardens too
are laid out in a way which native experts could hardly improve
upon, the groves and trees serving as perfect fenders against obnoxious shah. The Fung-shui of those dwellings is so solid that
the inmates need no such cabalistic amulets and talismans as the
natives are forced to affix to their own walls and to wear about
their bodies in considerable numbers; they may even regularly
clean their houses without fear, whilst the cleansing of a Chinese
dwelling would inevitably expulse therefrom the tsᶜai khi [1]
or »wealth-producing breath", and so cause the ruin of the inmates [2]. Last, though not least, it is the good Fung-shui of their
buildings which exempts foreigners from the trouble of selecting
auspicious days and hours for their enterprises. They never consult
a day professor, nor cast a look into an almanac, and yet,
even in the hottest summer months when hosts of obnoxious
spirits and dangerous breaths innumerable decimate the natives
by cholera and other diseases, they look hale and healthy; and
though they recklessly spoil the Fung-shui of many Chinese graves
by erecting buildings for trading purposes, dwellings and amuse-
ments, they are wonderfully exempt from the disasters sent down
by the irritate spirits. How is it then to be believed that foreigners
do not know more about Fung-shui than they are willing to tell?

However firmly the foreigners maintain that they are quite
ignorant of the art and only characterize it as ridiculous, the Chinese
are astute enough to understand that they do so simply to
rid themselves of importune questioners anxious to ferret out their
valuable secrets. If they know nothing of Fung-shui, it is asked,
why do they lay out the graves of all their dead in one plot in
Kulangsu, a plot carefully selected on the slope of that marvellous Dragon-head Hill (p. 949) which commands the Fung-shui
of the whole island, the town and the harbour? Why do they
place the graves there in uniform straight lines, and surround

---

[1] 財氣.

[2] As a matter of fact the Chinese of Amoy assimilate the filth in their houses
with their family fortunes. This no doubt is the explanation of their well known
sordidness, in which they are surpassed by no people on earth. In subsequent parts
of this work we shall have to mention curious customs and habits illustrating this
assimilation.

them with trees and bamboo groves? Why have they, just in the centre of that ground, a queer tower-like building exhibiting lines and contours both mysterious and marvellous? Why have they walled that cemetery on three sides, thus screening it at the back and the sides from obnoxious s h a h and leaving open the frontside with the iron railing, exactly as if it were a good Chinese grave? Why have they laid it out in such a wise that at the back there are gently shelving terraces, and in front a large pond in which water-courses converge from the four chief bluffs of the island, everything in strict accordance with Fung-shui? In short, they ask, how can foreigners pretend to know nothing of Fung-shui, when we ourselves see how anxious they are to accumulate their dead in that mysterious, narrow plot which combines everything required for a perfect Fung-shui, thus giving us the clearest evidence that they regard it as the chief palladium of their fortunes?

Fung-shui being most deeply rooted in the minds of the people and firmly entwined with their religious system, in so far as this consists in the worship of ancestors, divinities and saints as exercised at graves, domestic altars and in temples, we cannot expect that it will be eradicated as long as the people remain so totally ignorant of the exact sciences as they have done up to the present. The only power capable of overthrowing it, or weakening its all-pervading influence, is sound natural science. Seeing, however, that neither the ruling classes, nor the people have ever manifested the slightest inclination to make a study of Nature by an experimental and critical survey of its laws, and that a national stagnation has kept their mental culture down at such a low level, it seems hopeless to expect that sound views of natural science will ever be acquired by the Chinese on their own initiative. Perhaps the foreigners may be able to shed some rays of the light of their science upon the Middle Kingdom. But where are the men to be found, willing and able to take upon themselves the Herculean task of educating such a nation, and capable of writing clear and popular explanations of the laws of Nature in that idiomatic, attractive Chinese style which alone finds favour in the eyes of the educated? And even were such men to be found, their attempts would most likely suffer shipwreck from the national ignorance of the written language, for, owing to the fact that this language is extremely difficult to learn, only very few men in every hundred or, more correctly speaking, in every thousand, are able to understand a book. And thus, even though it were granted that the Chinese race is not stamped for ever with the total incapacity to rise to a higher level of mental culture, a complete overthrow and re-organisation of its religion, philosophy, literature, customs and social forms would be required to uproot Fung-shui. In other words: Fung-shui will bear the supreme sway in China as long as China is China, and the Chinese are Chinese.

APPENDIX 1

大　清　律　例　卷　二　十　五
刑　律。賊　盜　下
發塚

CHAPTER XXV OF THE LAWS OF THE GREAT TSᶜING DYNASTY.
CRIMINAL LAWS. — REBELLION, ROBBERY AND THEFT, III.
ON OPENING GRAVES

First Fundamental Article

凡發掘他人墳塚見棺槨者杖一百流三千里。
已開棺槨見屍者絞監候。發而未至棺槨者杖一
百徒三年。招魂而葬亦是。爲從減一等。
　若年遠塚先穿陷及未殯埋而盜屍柩者杖九
十徒二年半。開棺槨見屍者亦絞。
　其盜取器物磚石者計贜准凡盜論、免刺。

» Every person who opens a grave belonging to others and renders
the coffin or the vault visible, shall receive one hundred blows with
the long stick and be deported for life to a distance of 3000 miles.
Should he have opened the coffin or the vault and rendered the
corpse visible, he shall be strangled, after previously being kept in
jail to await (the confirmation of his sentence by the higher authorities). And he who has opened a grave without reaching the coffin or
the vault, shall be punished with one hundred blows with the long
stick and three years' banishment. — The same punishments shall
be inflicted if only an evoked soul were buried in the grave [1]. —
Accessories to the crime shall be liable to a punishment one degree
less severe.

» If a coffin containing a corpse be stolen out of a grave of old
date which has become open or has caved in, or if such a coffin
be stolen before provisory burial or burial for good, the perpetrat-

---

1 This clause is interesting, as it shows that the law for the protection of the
dead is chiefly intended to protect the soul, which cannot subsist without the body.

ors shall receive ninety blows with the long stick and be banished for two years and a half. Should they have opened the coffin and rendered the corpse visible, they shall also be strangled.

» In case of theft of implements and objects, bricks and stones (from a grave), the culprits must be punished as in ordinary cases of theft, according to the value of the things appropriated [1]; but they need not be branded [2].

Fourth Supplementary Article

貪人吉壤將遠年之墳盜發者、子孫告發、審有確據、將盜發之人以開棺見尸律擬絞監候。

如非其子孫、又非實有確據之前人古塚、但因有土墩見人埋葬輒稱伊遠祖墳墓、勾引匪類夥告夥証、陷害無辜、審明、將爲首者照誣告人死罪未決律杖一百流三千里。爲從各照誣告爲從律科斷。

若實係本人遠祖之墳被人發掘盜葬、因將所盜葬之棺發掘拋棄者、照祖父母父母被殺子孫不告官司而擅殺行兇人律杖六十。

若盜葬者並無發掘等情、止在切近墳旁盜葬、而本家輒行發掘者、應照地界內有死人不報官司而輒移他處律科斷。如有毀棄屍骸、照地界內有死人而移尸毀棄律科斷。

若非係墳地、止在田地場園內盜葬、而地主發掘開棺見屍、仍照律擬絞。其不開棺見尸者各照本律減一等治罪。

如兩造本係親屬、其所侵損之墳塚棺槨屍骸與本身皆有服制者各照律內服制科斷。

» If some one, coveting another's burial ground which brings good luck (to the offspring), has fraudulently dug up a grave of ancient date, and the descendants of that dead person lodge a complaint against him with the magistrates, who, on investigating the case, find incontestable proofs of the crime, the perpetrator thereof shall be condemned to strangulation in accordance with the fundamental law against opening coffins and rendering visible the corpses therein contained, and be imprisoned until his sentence has been confirmed by the higher authorities (See the first fundamental article).

»Should there, however, be no offspring of that dead person, or no incontestable proofs exist that the old grave is really that of some person of former times, and it should appear that people, on seeing a burial performed in a place where there was a heap of earth, have pretended without good reasons that it was a grave of a remote ancestor of theirs, bringing with them bad folks of the same sort as themselves to lodge a complaint in concert with them and to bear witness with them, for the purpose of plunging innocent folks into grief and trouble — in such a case, after the truth has been properly ascertained, the chief culprits shall be sentenced according to the law which provides for cases of false accusation against others when the sentence of death has not yet been executed, that is to say, they shall be punished with one hundred blows with the long stick and transportation for life to a distance of 3000 miles [1]. And their accomplices shall each be sentenced in accordance with the law which contains provisos against accomplices in false complaints.

»But, if the grave be really that of a remote ancestor of the party concerned, and this ancestor has been dug up by others and another corpse fraudulently buried in his place, — it then this second coffin be dug up (by the original owners of the grave) and cast away, they shall be punished with sixty blows with the long stick, in accordance with the law against sons or grandsons who, should their grandparents or parents be killed, do not enter a complaint with the authorities, but, taking the law into their own hands, slay the murderer.

»Should the parties who have buried the corpse in a fraudulent manner not have unearthed the old corpse or done any damage to the same, but simply performed the burial in the immediate proximity of the tumulus, then the original owners shall, if they have dug out the second corpse without authorisation, be sentenced according to the fundamental law which provides against those who, when a person is found dead within the precincts of a place, do not inform the magistrates thereof, but arbitrarily transfer the corpse to another spot (sixth fundamental art.). And if thereafter the corpse

---

1 Comp. Chapter 30 of the Code, § 誣 告.

or the skeleton be mutilated (by others), or cast away, they shall be sentenced according to the fundamental law which provides against those who, when a person is found dead within the precincts of a place, transfer the corpse to another spot, in consequence of which it is mutilated or cast away (see the sixth fundamental art.).

» If the fraudulent burial has not been performed in a burial ground, but simply in a field, meadow or garden, and the owner of this ground has dug up the grave, opened the coffin, and rendered the corpse visible, he shall be condemned to strangulation, in accordance with the fundamental law (art. I). But if he has not opened the coffin or rendered the corpse visible, his sentence shall be reduced by one degree of punishment, likewise in accordance with the fundamental law (art. I).

» If both parties are relations by consanguinity or affinity, so that there exist mourning ties between the corpse in the damaged grave or coffin and the perpetrators, each one of the latter shall be sentenced in accordance with the gradations of mourning as fixed by law.

Fifth Supplementary Article

民人、除無故宪焚已葬屍棺者仍照例治罪外、其因爭墳阻葬開棺易罐埋藏占葬者亦照開棺見屍殘毀死屍各本律治罪。

若以他骨暗埋豫立封堆、僞說蔭基、審係恃強占葬者照強占官民山場律治罪。

審係私自偷埋者照於有主墳地內偷葬律治罪。其侵犯他人墳塚者照發掘他人墳塚律治罪。

如果審係地師教誘、將教誘之地師均照詐教誘人犯法律分別治罪。若地方官隱諱寬縱、不實力查究、照例參處。

» If — apart from the case when people, without valid reasons, take a buried coffin out of a grave and burn it, which is a crime that must be punished in accordance with the supplementary articles — it should occur that obstacles are laid in the way of a burial because the ground is in dispute, and yet such burial be arrogantly performed in those grounds after the parties have opened a coffin therein buried, placed the remains in an urn and interred them, they shall also be punished according to the (first and second) fundamental articles which contain provisos against opening coffins, rendering corpses visible and mutilating them.

» Should any person secretly bury other bones under a tumulus which he has thrown up for that purpose, and then falsely pretend that the spot is a patrimonial possession of his, it shall be inquired into whether this burial has taken place by an abuse of authority, and the culprit in this case shall be punished according to the fundamental law which provides against forcible appropriation of grounds reserved by the Government or belonging to the people [1].

» If, however, the enquiry brings to light that the deed was done in an underhand, clandestine manner, the culprit shall be punished according to the (fifth) fundamental article which provides against burying corpses stealthily in the burial grounds of others. And if he has thus encroached upon a grave of the other party, he shall be punished according to the (first) fundamental article which provides against digging up other people's graves.

» In case it is discovered that the culprit has been seduced by geomancers to commit the act, they shall be punished according to the fundamental law which provides against inducing people by bad suggestions to transgress the laws [2]. The local authorities also shall, according to the supplementary articles, be included in the case and punished, should they have hushed up, evaded or connived at such a crime, or neglected to investigate it with promptitude.

---

1 To be found in chapter 9 of the Code, § 盜賣田宅. It stipulates one hundred blows with the long stick, followed by lifelong banishment in a country three thousand miles away.

2 This law, contained in chapter 32 of the Code, stipulates the same punishment for the man who has induced another to a crime, as for the perpetrator himself.

APPENDIX 2

Coffins representing the Heavens

Many a time we have had occasion to state, that in China it is considered a matter of extreme importance to place the dead in graves which are situated under the beneficial influences of the Cosmos, that they may feel happy and comfortable there in every respect and thus be found willing and able to bestow from thence blessings upon their offspring. We have also seen that the ancient Chinese, wishing to facilitate the resurrection of their dead, surrounded them with jade, gold, pearls, timber and other things imbued with influences emitted by the heavens, or, in other words, with such objects as are pervaded with vital energy derived from the Y a n g matter of which the heavens are the principal depository. Now combining these conceptions and practices, the reader will have no difficulty in understanding why they used to paint their coffins in such a way as to make them represent the Universe in miniature. To this custom we must now call the reader's attention for a few moments.

The narrative of Tung Hien's tragic end has shown that it was an established custom with the ruling classes during the Han dynasty to decorate their coffins with ›› the colours of the four seasons". No doubt these colours were blue, red, white, and black, these having always been identified by Chinese philosophy respectively with the Spring or the East, the Summer or the South, the Autumn or the West, and the Winter or the North. The same narrative further informs us, that the coffins of grandees in those times displayed ›› a blue dragon on the left side, a white tiger on the right, a golden sun and a silver moon on the top"; moreover, the Books of the Later Han Dynasty state that the imperial coffins ›› used to be decorated and painted with a sun, a moon a bird, a tortoise, a dragon and a tiger"[1]. These four animals denoted in ancient China the four quarters of the celestial sphere, the eastern quarter being called the Azure Dragon[2],

---

[1] 文畫日月鳥龜龍虎. Ch. 16, leaf 2.　　　　[2] 蒼龍.

the southern the Red or Vermilion Bird[1], the western the White Tiger[2], and the northern the Black Tortoise[3]. For the sake of convenience we may draw up all the above cosmogonal elements in a table as follows:

East	. . . Spring	. . . Blue	. . . . Dragon
South	. . . Summer	. . Red	. . . Bird
West . . .	Autumn	. . White	. . . Tiger
North . . .	Winter . .	. Black	. . . Tortoise

Likewise during the Thang dynasty the imperial coffins ›› displayed a ›› sun, a moon, stars and asterisms, a dragon, a tortoise, and their ›› appendages, painted on the lid"[4].

The modern Chinese still embroider dragons and a tiger on the drapery of their catafalques, on top and the two opposite sides.

This partiality for surrounding the dead in their subterranean dwelling with the Universe in miniature explains the custom of stretching them in their coffins on a board with seven holes or circles arranged in the same order as the stars of the Great Bear. In China, this asterism — called the Northern Bushel[5] on account of its shape — anciently held a prominent place among the ruling powers of Nature. The *Shi ki* says: ›› The seven ›› stars of the Bushel, which are styled the Revolving Pearls or the ›› Balance of Jasper, are arrayed so as to form a body of seven rulers. The ›› Bushel is the chariot of the Emperor (*i.e.* of Heaven). Revolving ›› around the pole, it descends to rule the four quarters of the sphere and ›› to separate the Yin and Yang; by so doing it fixes the four seasons; ›› upholds the equilibrium between the five elements, moves forward ›› the subdivisions of the sphere, and establishes all order in the Universe. ›› All these functions have devolved upon the Bushel"[6]. It is clear that this passage means this much: — the Great Bear turning around the pole of the heavens once a year, it stands at the same hour of the night, in each of the four seasons in a different quarter of the sphere, and thus marks out

---

1 朱鳥.　　　2 白虎.　　　3 玄龜.

4 畫日月星辰龍龜之屬施於蓋. *Ku kin thu shu tsih ch'ing*, sect. 禮儀, ch. 56.　　　5 北斗.

6 北斗七星所謂旋璣玉衡以齊七政...斗爲帝車.運于中央、臨制四鄉、分陰陽、建四時、均五行、移節度、定諸紀。皆繫於斗. Ch. 27, leaf 2 *seq.*

on this the seasons, just as the hand on a clock indicates the hours; nay, it even compels the whole sphere to move round with it, thus *producing* the four seasons, the rotation of which *is* actually the course of Nature. Now then, it is quite natural that a people which was in the habit of depicting the heavens and the seasons on their coffins, should add thereto a representation of the power which, as they believed, brought their rotation and was thus the real creator of all life and all the blessings of Nature.

So far as we are aware, the pre-Christian literature of China does not contain any clear reference to the boards of the seven stars. In the *Tso ch'wen* it is stated that Yuen, a feudal lord of the state of Sung, in 515 B.C. said to his ministers: ›› If by your energetic help I save my head and ›› neck till I die a natural death, I pray you, do not then let the flat piece of ›› wood, which will serve to support my body, equal that used for the ›› former rulers"[1]. Though this passage unmistakably shows that this piece of wood was an object of great solicitude, yet there are no means of ascertaining whether it was a seven stars' board or not. For the first time we meet with the name in Yen Chi-thui's Domestic Instructions, written in the sixth century. In his *post-mortem* dispositions recorded in this book, the author prescribed as follows: ›› I must have a coffin of pine wood, two ›› inches thick, and on the spot where my body is to lie, nothing may be ›› placed but a seven stars' board"[2]. Among the rescripts concerning the obsequies of Tai Tsung[3], an emperor of the Thang dynasty who died in the year 779, we read: ›› A seven stars' board was placed inside the ›› Rottlera structure (*i.e.* the coffin), and the things which were to be ›› arranged collectively underneath were all placed below it first"[4]. The *Kai li* also prescribes the use of this board, and so does the *Ta Ts'ing thung li*, in its precepts regulating the funeral rites of the sundry classes of officers and of the common people.

---

[1] 寡人若以群子之靈獲保首領以歿、唯是楄柎所以藉幹者請無及先君. Twenty-fifth Year of the Ruler Ch'ao.

[2] 吾當松棺二寸、床上唯施七星板. Sect. 20.

[3] 代宗.

[4] 加七星板於梓宮內、其合施於版下者並先置之. *Ku kin thu shu tsih ch'ing*, sect. 禮儀, ch. 56.

Notes to Appendix 2

1. Although de Groot says that Dragons and Tigers are embroidered on the catafalque cloths, my experience has been that the Tiger is frequently replaced by the Phoenix (see Plate 3, p.211). The explanation given to me was that the White Tiger is believed to devour the souls of the dead.

2. The 'seven stars' board described in this passage from the *Shi Chi* is actually a much more fascinating artefact than de Groot could have guessed. Recent archaeological discoveries in China have shown that it was not uncommon for 'Divining Boards' to be included among the offerings placed in tombs with the deceased. The Divining Board was a kind of rudimentary planisphere used in astronomical and astrological calculations, and therefore regarded as a map of the heavens for the souls of the deceased to find their way to the abodes of the blessed. As can be seen in the illustration, the 'Heaven Plate' was marked with the seven stars of the Plough, known to the Chinese as the 'Northern Ladle.' Even the most cursory glance at the illustration on page 196 will reveal the Divining Board to be the immediate precursor of the *Lo P'an*.

Short Notes

1 In conclusion, it remains to be said that many families in Amoy carefully wait for the flood-tide to then encoffin their dead. This custom also prevails at Ningpo, as may be seen from the 'Records of the General Conference of the Protestant Missionaries of China, held at Shanghai in 1877' (page 404.) . . .

It is interesting to see, many people in Amoy render themselves independent of the flood by placing in the hall a couple of jars or buckets filled with seawater taken at the last high tide; they can then shut the coffin at any moment they choose, being convinced that the influences of the high tide over the dead and his offspring are likewise perfectly insured by this proceeding.

2 Thanks to the clouds and to the dragons which produce the same in their quality of water-gods, the greatest blessings which the Universe can bestow, viz. fertilising rains causing crops to grow and so giving food, raiment and wealth, surround the dead, and he may avail himself of those blessings for dissemination among his descendants from out the tomb. The unicorn enables the dead man to cause famous persons to be born into the family, for since this fabulous animal made its appearance at the birth of Confucius, its image can bring about the birth of sages, and of men destined to everlasting renown. And as to the tiger, its portrait keeps evil spirits away from the coffin, all Chinamen being convinced that ghosts and demons fear nothing so much as this monster.

3 ' . . . Yang, embracing light, warmth, life; the other Yin, or the principle of darkness, cold, and death. The former is more especially identified with the heavens, from which of course all light, warmth and life emanate; the Yin, on the other hand, with the earth. . . .'

'Souls in general, constituting the vital principle of men, are in the main composed of material derived from Yang, the great source of all life in nature. . . .'

'Yang' houses are houses for the living, 'Yin' houses, tombs of the dead.

4 Kuan Chang, or Kuan I Wu, died 645BC.

5 The Almanac.

Each annual edition of this useful book declares in which points of the compass the lucky direction lies for building, burying, etc for the current year; and if it says for instance: 'Great advantage lies in the line from east to west, and non luck is in the north', the family is compelled to postpone the interment till the next year if the tomb happens to have been placed, in accordance with the profound calculations of the geomancers, in another line, or if it faces the north.

6 Minister of the Kingdom of Wu in the sixth century BC.

7 Liu Hsiang who lived in the first century before our era, in 'Traditions on the Lives of the Immortals' *Lieh hsien ch'wen.*

8 Wu Yung Kuang, Governor General of Hukuang Province, in Wu Hsüeh Lu *'Record of My Studies'*

9 As a matter of course, the . . . 'officer who taps with his axe' must receive compensation for his trouble . . . So, the family afterwards send him a roll of dollars or a parcel of broken silver, with a couple of gilt flowers, a piece of red silk and occasionally other presents besides.

10 It is by no means a matter of rare occurrence that, as a coffin is about to be lowered into the grave, some individuals suddenly turn up to protest against the interment and even to forcibly prevent it, pretending that the soil is their property, or that the grave will completely spoil the auspicious situation of a tomb in the neighbourhood belonging to them. Noisy quarrels and vociferous discussions immediately ensue . . . meanwhile, the auspicious hour assigned for the interment elapses, the end being that the mourners have either to take the coffin to a temple in the vicinity, or leave it on or near the spot . . . Custom severely forbids taking a coffin homewards again.

11 The Great Officer for the graves has charge of the burial grounds of the whole State. He maps them out, sees that the inhabitants of the capital are buried on the same spot where members of their own clan sleep, maintains the prohibitions enacted in regard of such clan grounds, assigns the localities where they shall be laid out, determines the dimensions (of the graves) and the number (of trees to be planted thereon) and arranges that every clan has a cemetery of its own. Whenever people contend for a burial ground, he hears the cause (and delivers judgement). At the head of the officials attached to his person, he makes tours of inspection around the borders of the burial grounds; and he dwells in a mansion situated between the grounds, in order to watch over them. *Book of Rites of the Chou.* Chapter 21, lines 49-50.

The Commentaries

Commentary 1
The Chinese *Lo P'an*

Commentary to pages 959-976

The 'geomancer's compass' referred to here is actually only the upper part, or Heaven Plate, of an instrument more commonly known as the *Lo P'an*, which means 'net plate', from the pattern of the divisions on the surface, and the general shape of the instrument. The reason for the Heaven Plate being bevelled, like a tea-plate, is that it is meant to rest in the circular recess of an 'Earth Plate' which is neither illustrated nor described in de Groot's text. The Earth Plate, however, is little more than a plain wooden case in which the Heaven Plate rotates, save that it holds two cross-threads (invariably red) which traverse the Heaven Plate directly over the central pivot.

De Groot says that geomancers' compasses are generally painted yellow, although personally, I have never seen one of that particular colour. The examples I have encountered have been made in a variety of materials: a recent model from Kuangsi in southern China, for example, was made of wood covered with printed paper and varnished; those in the Horniman Museum, London, are made of lacquered wood; while other common materials are papier mâché, and baked clay. The range of *Lo P'an* models from Taiwan, which are now found throughout South-East Asia, are made of enamelled brass and set in a heavy resin Earth Plate.

In operation, the Earth Plate is placed according to the general direction of the terrain, or in alignment with the walls of the existing structure (see Plate 4, p.212). The Heaven Plate is then rotated until the compass needle lies over the North–South line engraved on the base of the needle-housing. The Heaven Plate will then be in the correct position with 子, 卯, 午', 酉 [Branches I, IV, VII, X) at the North, East, South and West points respectively. Auspices are read from the Heaven Plate by noting which signs lie under the red cross-threads.

A fuller analysis of the *Lo P'an* rings is given in Commentary 11.

Commentary 2
The Eight Trigrams

Commentary to pages 960-961

The mathematical implications of the broken and unbroken lines were first realised by a Jesuit missionary, Father Joachim Bouvet, about twenty years after Gottfried Leibniz had published his principles of binary or 'dyadic' arithmetic in 1679. Today, of course, the binary system forms the foundation of computer language, but two hundred years ago it was little more than a philosophical tool.

Both Leibniz and Bouvet credited the ancient Chinese with the invention of the binary system, as revealed by the diagrams of the *I Ching*. By allocating a value 0 to a broken line, and 1 to a full line, the eight *kwa* or trigrams, when arranged in a binary sequence, would follow the order given below. But neither the 'Former Heaven' sequence, which gives three full lines to the south and three broken lines to the north, nor the 'Later Heaven' sequence, which bases its sequence on passages in the *I Ching*, follow this mathematically logical order. It seems that there is no evidence to suppose that the original compilers of the *I Ching*, or even later commentators, had ever considered the binary sequence.

Curiously, though the order of the trigrams given by de Groot also follows a logical pattern, it appears that he is unaware that the lines of the *I Ching* diagrams are always reckoned from the bottom upwards! If his sequence is compared with the mathematical sequence below, it will be seen that he has listed them upside-down, and in reverse order.

THE EIGHT TRIGRAMS

The following Table gives the order of the eight trigrams arranged according to the binary sequence, together with the number of each trigram in binary notation.

The first line of compass directions gives the compass point associated with each trigram according to the Former Heaven Sequence, and the second line to the more usual arrangement, known as the Later Heaven Sequence. The Chinese names (*K'un, Chen, K'an,* etc) always refer to that particular arrangement of lines, whatever the compass direction.

Binary Sequence

K'un	Chen	K'an	Tui	Ken	Li	Sun	Ch'ien
000	001	010	011	100	101	110	111
0	1	2	3	4	5	6	7

Former Heaven Sequence

N	NE	W	SE	NW	E	SW	S

Later Heaven Sequence

SW	E	N	W	NE	S	SE	NW

Upper → trigram
Lower ↓ trigram

TABLE OF HEXAGRAMS FROM THE *I CHING*

		1	2	3	4	6	7	8	9
		K'un	Sun	Li	Tui	Ken	K'an	Chen	Ch'ien
1	K'un	2	20	35	45	23	8	16	12
2	Sun	46	57	50	28	18	48	32	44
3	Li	36	37	30	49	22	63	55	13
4	Tui	19	61	38	58	41	60	54	10
6	Ken	15	53	56	31	52	39	62	33
7	K'an	7	59	64	47	4	29	40	6
8	Chen	24	42	21	17	27	3	51	25
9	Ch'ien	11	9	14	43	26	5	34	1

Commentary 3
The Solar Fortnights

Commentary to page 968

The twenty-four periods which de Groot here calls 'seasons' were of critical importance to Chinese astronomers. Because the Chinese year, being determined by the Moon, is of irregular length, it was important to have some means of identifying fixed dates on which the stars would be at the same positions at a given time. As is well known, the true astronomical year is virtually 365¼ days long, and in the West, the ordinary calendar year, is sufficiently accurate for most purposes, although it falls out of step by a quarter of a day each year, until corrected by the extra day added during leap years. The Chinese calendar of twenty-four solar periods, however, is actually an astronomical one, its length being the time between two successive winter solstices. The twenty-four periods into which it is divided are reckoned precisely to the hour, not just the day. The first period, the Beginning of Spring, usually falls on the 4th or 5th of February, depending on the exact time of the Winter Solstice which preceded it.

The solar terms are known in Chinese as *Ch'i*, this, coincidentally, being the same word used for the beneficial currents of *Feng Shui*. As each *Ch'i* is just over fifteen days long, it is convenient to adopt the term 'solar fortnight' to avoid confusion with other meanings of *Ch'i*, as well as other measurements of time. One of these is the *Chieh*, or Festival, which being equal to two *Ch'i*, might likewise be called the solar month.

Now it happens that western astronomers also divide the astronomical year into twelve equal periods, familiarly known by the names of the signs of the zodiac. There is one significant difference, however; each Chinese solar month begins with the latter half of one zodiacal sign, and the first half of the next. As a direct result, the equinoxes and solstices, which mark the *commencement* of the zodiacal signs Aries, Cancer, Libra, and Capricorn, mark the *mid-points* of the second, fifth, eighth, and eleventh solar months.

One further point regarding the solar months might be mentioned. I am grateful to Mr Osman Chung for drawing my attention to the fact that tradition holds that Chinese calendar years which begin after the 'Beginning of Spring' are regarded as 'blind' and therefore unlucky, while corresponding auspices are made for those years which end with the Beginning of Spring, and those years are fortunate enough to include a Beginning of Spring both at the commencement and the end of the year.

THE TWENTY-FOUR SOLAR FORTNIGHTS

The twenty-four solar fortnights approximate to the following dates. Though they vary from year to year depending on astronomical factors, the discrepancy is rarely more than a day. A complete list of actual dates for this century is given in the author's *Chinese Astrology*, Appendix I. The four solar divisions are denoted by an asterisk.

1.	4 Feb	Beginning of Spring	Aquarius 2
2.	19 Feb	Rain Water	Pisces 1
3.	5 Mar	Insects waken	Pisces 2
4.	20 Mar	*Spring Equinox	Aries 1
5.	4 Apr	Clear and Bright	Aries 2
6.	20 Apr	Grain Rain	Taurus 1
7.	5 May	Beginning of Summer	Taurus 2
8.	21 May	Grain swells	Gemini 1
9.	7 June	Grain in ear	Gemini 2
10.	22 June	*Summer Solstice	Cancer 1
11.	7 July	Little Heat	Cancer 2
12.	23 July	Great Heat	Leo 1
13.	7 Aug	Beginning of Autumn	Leo 2
14.	23 Aug	End of Heat	Virgo 1
15.	8 Sept	White Dew	Virgo 2
16.	23 Sept	*Autumn Equinox	Libra 1
17.	7 Oct	Cold Dew	Libra 2
18.	22 Oct	Frost descends	Scorpio 1
19.	7 Nov	Beginning of Winter	Scorpio 2
20.	21 Nov	Little Snow	Sagit. 1
21.	7 Dec	Great Snow	Sagit. 2
22.	22 Dec	*Winter Solstice	Capricorn 1
23.	6 Jan	Little Cold	Capricorn 2
24.	21 Jan	Great Cold	Aquarius 1

Commentary 4
Animal Names

Commentary to page 989

The twelve animal names, used in popular parlance for the Twelve Branches (see page 158), came into circulation during the ninth century at the very earliest; the first examples to which definite dates can be ascribed are eighth-century stone tomb guardians from Silla, Korea, and mirrors and divining boards of the T'ang dynasty (620-900). As de Groot says, there is no mention of them in the classics, and the reference in the *Shuo Wen* dictionary is one of many misleading coincidences which plague research. To begin with, the snake is the only one of the twelve animals to be mentioned. Secondly, there are two other Chinese characters which are very easily confused with Ssu, one of them being Chi, the sixth Stem. The reference to the snake in the *Shuo Wen* is therefore nothing more than a helpful means of differentiating it from the other two characters.

Another odd fact, again merely a coincidence, is sometimes produced as evidence of an entirely contradictory theory which proposes that the animal names were borrowed from, or had the same origin as the western zodiac. As evidence in support of this, it is pointed out that the second sign of the Chinese 'zodiac', the Ox, coincides with the second western zodiacal sign. Again, it has to be stressed that this is the only emblem common to both systems, and that furthermore, whereas Taurus corresponds to April-May, the Chinese 'Ox' month corresponds to January.

There is, however, another factor to swing the pendulum back to the other side, and as this argument might be proposed by adherents of the 'common-origin' theory, it ought to be stated. Although the Chinese year begins January-February, with the second New Moon after the Winter Solstice, and the months counted accordingly [that is to say, the First Month begins in January-February] it is always allocated the third Branch. Textbooks invariably state in the Chou dynasty (about two thousand years ago) the year begin with the second Branch, and before that, with the first Branch, and that the adjustments were made in order to bring the calendar into line with observation of the seasons (because of the precession of the equinoxes). Now of course, if the original calendar did begin with the first Branch, then Taurus and the Ox-month would in fact coincide. But look at the maze of confusion which results if this were the case. To begin with, the Chinese calendar should now be readjusted once more, two thousand years being equivalent to the astronomical discrepancy due to the precession of the equinoxes, while in fact, the western zodiacal calendar has never been adjusted. Secondly, the animal names were only introduced in the seventh century at the earliest, which, if the Chinese textbooks are to be believed, would be four thousand years after the invention of the Chinese calendar.

Commentary 5
Stems and Branches

The Stems and Branches are part of the essential terminology of *Feng Shui*. They are more properly known as the Ten Heavenly Stems and the Twelve Earthly Branches. Although they are used principally for the reckoning of time, they can also function much in the same way that algebraic symbols indicate unknowns in mathematics, or as letters of the alphabet might be used to refer to people anonymously, or the parts of a diagram, as we might say 'Mr X' or 'Figure A'.

The Ten Heavenly Stems were originally used to enumerate the days of an ancient Chinese ten-day 'week'; as the Chinese word for 'Heaven' is also used to mean 'day' it is easy to see how 'ten daily stems' came to be interpreted as 'ten Heavenly stems.'

They are each associated with one of the Five Elements, while additionally the odd stems are classified as *Yang*, and the even stems as *Yin*. The usual convention is to refer to the Ten Heavenly Stems by the figures 1 to 10, and the Twelve Early Branches by the roman numerals I to XII.

甲	1	*Chia*	Wood	*Yang*
乙	2	*I*	Wood	*Yin*
丙	3	*Ping*	Fire	*Yang*
丁	4	*Ting*	Fire	*Yin*
戊	5	*Mou*	Earth	*Yang*
己	6	*Chi*	Earth	*Yin*
庚	7	*Keng*	Metal	*Yang*
辛	8	*Hsin*	Metal	*Yin*
壬	9	*Jen*	Water	*Yang*
癸	10	*Kuei*	Water	*Yin*

The Branches are used to enumerate all time periods counted in twelves: the twelve double-hours of the day, the twelve months of the year, and the twelve years of the Great Year. Outside China, the twelve years of the Great Year were known by the now familiar animal names although these did not achieve popularity in China until they had been firmly established in the countries on China's borders, from Japan to Turkey. The adjective 'Earthly' was probably coined analagously to the Heavenly Stems.

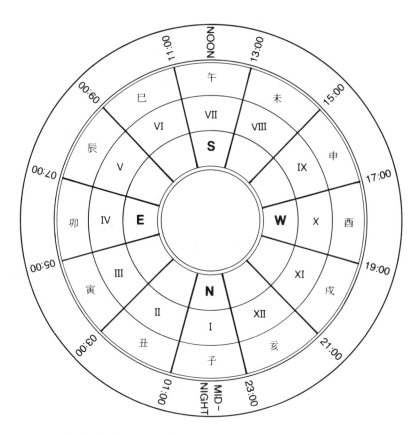

The Twelve Branches, Cardinal Points, and times of the day

The Twelve Branches, and their corresponding animal names, are as follows:

子	I	*Tzu*	Rat
丑	II	*Chou*	Ox
寅	III	*Yin*	Tiger
卯	IV	*Mao*	Hare
辰	V	*Ch'en*	Dragon
巳	VI	*Ssu*	Snake
午	VII	*Wu*	Horse
未	VIII	*Wei*	Sheep
申	IX	*Shen*	Monkey
酉	X	*Yu*	Rooster
戌	XI	*Shu*	Dog
亥	XII	*Hai*	Pig

The Earthly Branches stand at the 'hour' positions of the clock-face, representing the double-hours, but there are some important differences. Chinese time-markers almost invariably mark the mid-point of a period, not its beginning. Consequently, the precise moments of midnight and noon mark the mid-points of the first and seventh double-hours, not their beginnings. It then follows that if midnight is the mid-point of the first double hour, then the first double hour begins at 11pm, the previous evening.

As will become clear later, the midnight double-hour is associated with the direction North, and as on Chinese compasses North is depicted at the bottom of maps, in this volume, when depicting the Twelve Branches I to XII as round a clockface, Branch I will be placed at the bottom: this is therefore the position that they would occupy on a Chinese compass dial:

THE SIXTY SEXAGENARY PAIRS

Although the following remarks have no immediate application to *Feng Shui*, since their use is mainly calendrical, familiarity with the sixty Stem and Branch combinations is certainly desirable. As the choosing of an auspicious date is part of the process of the burial rituals, it is important to understand the way Stems and Branches are combined to form a cycle of sixty sexagenary pairs. Larger examples of *Lo P'an* depict the sexagenary pairs in various positions.

Stem and Branch pairs, used to identify particular days, have been found inscribed on oracle bones of the Early Bronze Age, but their use for reckoning years was not introduced until the time of the Emperor Wang Mang, in 13AD. The sequence is simple enough, but tedious to explain: and a glance at the table below will reveal that the two series of Stems and Branches proceed in parallel, forming a double sequence beginning (1) 1-I, (2) 2-II, (3) 3-III . . . through (10) 10-X, (11) 1-XI, (12) 2-(XII), (13) 3-I . . . and finishing (58) 8-X, (59) 9-XI, (60) 10-XII.

Notice that odd numbered Stems are always paired with odd-numbered Branches, and even Stems with even Branches, so accounting for the number of possible permutations being 60, and not 120.

According to this system, 1924, 1984, and 2044 are each Year 1. In the Mongolian and Tibetan calendars, which substitute animal names for the Branches and element-types for the Stems, these years would each be known as Wood-Rat years.

The complete sequence of Stem and Branch pairs is shown in the following table.

TABLE OF SIXTY
STEM AND BRANCH COMBINATIONS

Year	Number	Romanization	Chinese	Element-Animal
1924, 1984	(1) 1-I	*Chia Tzu*	甲子	Wood-Rat
1925, 1985	(2) 2-II	*I Chou*	乙丑	Wood-Ox
1926, 1986	(3) 3-III	*Ping Yin*	丙寅	Fire-Tiger
1927, 1987	(4) 4-IV	*Ting Mao*	丁卯	Fire-Hare
1928, 1988	(5) 5-V	*Mou Ch'en*	戊辰	Earth-Dragon
1929, 1989	(6) 6-VI	*Chi Ssu*	己巳	Earth-Snake
1930, 1990	(7) 7-VII	*Keng Wu*	庚午	Metal-Horse
1931, 1991	(8) 8-VIII	*Hsin Wei*	辛未	Metal-Sheep
1932, 1992	(9) 9-IX	*Jen Shen*	壬申	Water-Monkey
1933, 1993	(10) 10-X	*Kuei Yu*	癸酉	Water-Rooster
1934, 1994	(11) 1-XI	*Chia Shu*	甲戌	Wood-Dog
1935, 1995	(12) 2-XII	*I Hai*	乙亥	Wood-Pig
1936, 1996	(13) 3-I	*Ping Tzu*	丙子	Fire-Rat
1937, 1997	(14) 4-II	*Ting Chou*	丁丑	Fire-Ox
1938, 1998	(15) 5-111	*Mou Yin*	戊寅	Earth-Tiger
1939, 1999	(16) 6-IV	*Chi Mao*	己卯	Earth-Hare
1940, 2000	(17) 7-V	*Keng Ch'en*	庚辰	Metal-Dragon
1941, 2001	(18) 8-VI	*Hsin Ssu*	辛巳	Metal-Snake
1942, 2002	(19) 9-VII	*Jen Wu*	壬午	Water-Horse
1943, 2003	(20) 10-VIII	*Kuei Wei*	癸未	Water-Sheep
1944, 2004	(21) 1-IX	*Chia Shen*	甲申	Wood-Monkey
1945, 2005	(22) 2-X	*I Yu*	乙酉	Wood-Rooster
1946, 2006	(23) 3-XI	*Ping Shu*	丙戌	Fire-Dog
1947, 2007	(24) 4-XII	*Ting Hai*	丁亥	Fire-Pig
1948, 2008	(25) 5-I	*Mou Tzu*	戊子	Earth-Rat
1949, 2009	(26) 6-II	*Chi Chou*	己丑	Earth-Ox
1950, 2010	(27) 7-III	*Keng Yin*	庚寅	Metal-Tiger
1951, 2011	(28) 8-IV	*Hsin Mao*	辛卯	Metal-Hare
1952, 2012	(29) 9-V	*Jen Ch'en*	壬辰	Water-Dragon
1953, 2013	(30) 10-VI	*Kuei Ssu*	癸巳	Water-Snake
1954, 2014	(31) 1-VII	*Chia Wu*	甲午	Wood-Horse
1955, 2015	(32) 2-VIII	*I Wei*	乙未	Wood-Sheep
1956, 2016	(33) 3-IX	*Ping Shen*	丙申	Fire-Monkey
1957, 2017	(34) 4-X	*Ting Yu*	丁酉	Fire-Rooster
1958, 2018	(35) 4-XI	*Mou Shu*	戊戌	Earth-Dog
1959, 2019	(36) 6-XII	*Chi Hai*	己亥	Earth-Pig
1960, 2020	(37) 7-I	*Keng Tzu*	庚子	Metal-Rat
1961, 2021	(38) 8-II	*Hsin Chou*	辛丑	Metal-Ox
1962, 2022	(39) 9-III	*Jen Yin*	壬寅	Water-Tiger
1963, 2023	(40) 10-IV	*Kuei Mao*	癸卯	Water-Hare

1964, 2024	(41) 1-V	*Chia Ch'en*	甲辰	Wood-Dragon
1965, 2025	(42) 2-VI	*I Ssu*	乙巳	Wood-Snake
1966, 2026	(43) 3-VII	*Ping Wu*	丙午	Fire-Horse
1967, 2027	(44) 4-VIII	*Ting Wei*	丁未	Fire-Sheep
1968, 2028	(45) 5-IX	*Mou Shen*	戊申	Earth-Monkey
1969, 2029	(46) 6-X	*Chi Yu*	己酉	Earth-Rooster
1970, 2030	(47) 7-XI	*Keng Shu*	庚戌	Metal-Dog
1971, 2031	(48) 8-XII	*Hsin Hai*	辛亥	Metal-Pig
1972, 2032	(49) 9-I	*Jen Tzu*	壬子	Water-Rat
1973, 2033	(50) 10-II	*Kuei Chou*	癸丑	Water-Ox
1974, 2034	(51) 1-III	*Chia Yin*	甲寅	Wood-Tiger
1975, 2035	(52) 2-IV	*I Mao*	乙卯	Wood-Hare
1976, 2036	(53) 3-V	*Ping Ch'en*	丙辰	Fire-Dragon
1977, 2037	(54) 4-VI	*Ting Ssu*	丁巳	Fire-Snake
1978, 2038	(55) 5-VII	*Mou Wu*	戊午	Earth-Horse
1979, 2039	(56) 6-VIII	*Chi Wei*	己未	Earth-Sheep
1980, 2040	(57) 7-IX	*Keng-Shen*	庚申	Metal-Monkey
1981, 2041	(58) 8-X	*Hsin Yu*	辛酉	Metal-Rooster
1982, 2042	(59) 9-XI	*Jen Shu*	壬戌	Water-Dog
1983, 2043	(60) 10-XII	*Kuei Hai*	癸亥	Water-Pig

ELEMENTAL INTERPLAY OF THE STEMS AND BRANCHES

While it is a simple matter to identify the Five Elements with the Ten Heavenly Stems, unfortunately, as the number of Branches, 12, is not divisible by 5, the association of the Branches with the Five Elements is more complex.

It may be done *via* the cardinal points, and their associated seasons and months. In this case, the branches associated with the Wood element will be those associated with the East and the Spring: Branches III, IV and V, 寅, 卯, and 辰. By this reckoning, the Twelve Branches are considered to belong to four of the Five Elements, but Earth is omitted, as it is associated with the Centre, which has no season. There are two further systems whereby the Five Elements are reconciled with the seasons of the year, without omitting the Earth element. One method, expounded in the *Huai Nan Tzu*, the *Book of the Prince of Huai Nan*, is to divide the year equally into five periods of seventy-two days, although this system falls out of step with the solar calendar. In the second system, detailed in the *Book of Rites*, the final twelve days or so of each of the four traditional seasons is regarded as the Earth season. By analogy, the second Branch and every third Branch thereafter is considered to belong to the element Earth. Thus, Branches XII and I pertain to the element Water, Branch II to Earth; Branches III and IV to Wood, and V to Earth; Branches VI and VII to Fire and VIII to Earth; Branches IX and X to Metal and XI to Earth. For comparison, here the two systems are shown together.

子	I	Water	Water
丑	II	Water	*Earth*
寅	III	Wood	Wood
卯	IV	Wood	Wood
辰	V	Wood	*Earth*
巳	VI	Fire	Fire
午	VII	Fire	Fire
未	VIII	Fire	*Earth*
申	IX	Metal	Metal
酉	X	Metal	Metal
戌	XI	Metal	*Earth*
亥	XII	Water	Water

Whichever system is favoured, every sexagenary number will consist of two elements, one for the Stem, and the other for the Branch. The Stem and Branch elements must either be the same, or stand in either the productive or destructive sequence, as shown diagrammatically on page 36. For example, the Stem and Branch may have the same element, as 1-III (Wood); or Stem and Branch have elements which stand in the productive order, as 1-I (Wood, the element of Stem 1, is produced by Water, the element of Branch I); or 1-IX (the element of the Stem is destroyed by Metal, the element of the Branch).

Each of the resultant element factors can then be set against the influences of the elements pertaining to the cardinal points, so producing a resultant element which is the product of several factors. The larger examples of *Lo P'an* show the final auspices as a series of divisions, marked in red for lucky and black for unlucky, or sometimes black for neutral and black with a cross for unlucky.

Commentary 6
Magic Squares

The *Lo Shu*, or (River) Lo Book, is the name given by Chinese mystics to the mathematical arrangement of the numbers 1 to 9 to form a Magic Square, thus:

4	9	2
3	5	7
8	1	6

According to legend, the sequence was discovered in the markings of the shell of a sacred tortoise emerging from the River Lo. (The word *Lo* here has no connection with the word *Lo* of *Lo P'an*).

The arrangement of numbers is not only held to have mystical significance, it is also the key to the interpretation of the auspices of the Eight Directions.

The arrangement given above may be called the Primary position of the Lo Shu; in this arrangement (remember that south is depicted at the top), the Eight Directions are associated with the following numbers:

North	1
North-east	8
East	3
South-east	4
Centre	5
South	9
South-west	2
West	7
North-west	6

It will be noticed that the cardinal points are all associated with odd, or *yang* numbers, and the inter-mediary or 'corner' points with even, or *yin* numbers.

The table shown above may now be extended to show the Trigrams associated with the Eight Directions in the Later Heaven sequence, the one usually found on Chinese mariners' compasses.

North	1	*K'an*	
North-east	8	*Ken*	
East	3	*Chen*	
South-east	4	*Sun*	
Centre	5	–	
South	9	*Li*	
South-west	2	*K'un*	
West	7	*Tui*	
North-west	6	*Ch'ien*	

The relationships between the directions and the trigrams may be more easily discernable by referring to the Chart of Correspondences below.

Chart of Correspondences

8 Directions	9 Lo Shu Numbers
8 Trigrams	12 Months of Book of Rites

The Chinese classic, the *Book of Rites* specifies the palace rooms where the Emperor should be quartered, according to whether the direction would be appropriate to the season of the year. By extension, *Feng Shui* suggests that certain directions are more felicitous than others, according to the room's function, the nature of the occupier, and the season of the year, and principally, the direction the main building faces.

THE MAIN DIRECTION AND SUBSIDIARY ORIENTATIONS

In the Primary Arrangements of the Lo Shu, shown above, the position of the Nine Numbers applies if the grave-site or building faces the south. But if the horoscope of the individual directs that the grave-site should face some other direction, then the positions of the Nine Numbers migrate. This means that the trigrams associated with the eight compass points may enhance or conflict with those trigrams which pertain to the now migrated numbers of the Lo Shu. This results in eight different arrangements of auspices, according to the direction the site faces.

Consequently, as de Groot relates, this can often lead to dissension and disputes, as the placing of one grave-site may affect the auspices of another. Furthermore, as members of the family are themselves each associated with one of the trigrams (see de Groot's text, page 964) it follows that the orientation of the grave-site will enhance the fortunes of certain members of the family, but adversely affect others, again often leading to acrimonious dispute. Fortunately, adverse *Feng Shui* influences might be broken by the suitable disposition of trees, water courses, or man-made constructions.

The auspices pertaining to each direction are given in the diagrams on page 166. Notice that the eight auspices do not follow the compass directions, but change their positions according to the migration of numbers in the Lo Shu.

THE EIGHT ORIENTATIONS

Diagrams showing the auspices pertaining to each direction, according to the orientation of the grave-site (Yin dwelling) or building (Yang dwelling). The direction faced by the entrance is shown at the foot of each diagram.

Key

(1) Inner ring – the Eight Orientations

a	Direction faced			
b	*Nien Yen*	年延	Lengthened years	* *
c	*Sheng Ch'i*	生氣	Generating breath	* *
d	*Hai Huo*	害禍	Accident and mishap	†
e	*Chüeh Ming*	絕命	Severed Fate	† †
f	*Wu Kuei*	五鬼	Five Ghosts	† †
g	*T'ien I*	天乙	Celestial Monad	*
h	*Liu Sha*	六殺	Six Curses	† †

(* Favourable † Unfavourable)

(2) Middle ring – Twenty-four *Feng Shui* Stars (see page 177).

(3) Outer ring: Eight compass directions.

Charts of the Eight Orientations of a Site

Letters a-h: auspices ('a' is the direction of the entrance).
Figures 1-24 show the twenty-four stellar positions explained in Commentary 7.

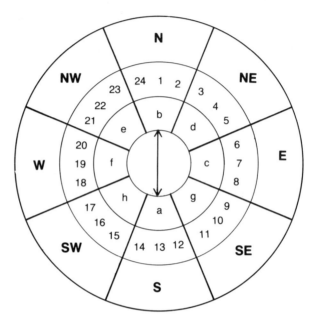

1   離 Li – South

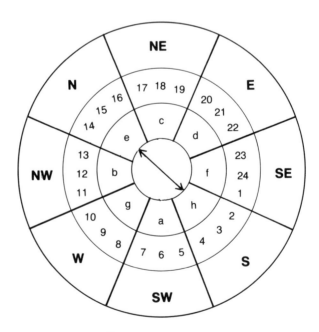

2   坤 Kun – South-West

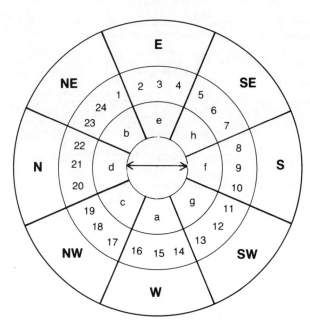

3   兌 Tui – West

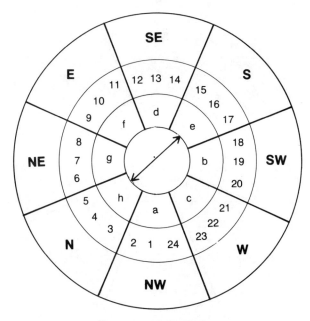

4   乾 Ch'ien – North-West

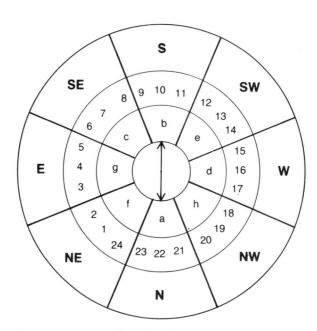

5 　　　　　　坎　K'an – North

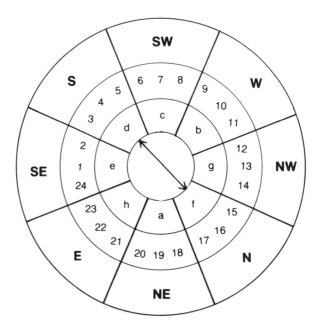

6 　　　　　　艮　Ken – North-East

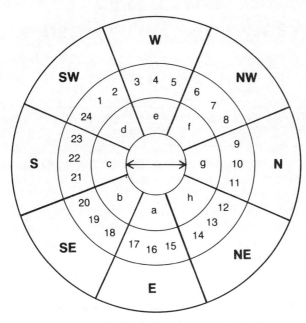

7   震 Chen – East

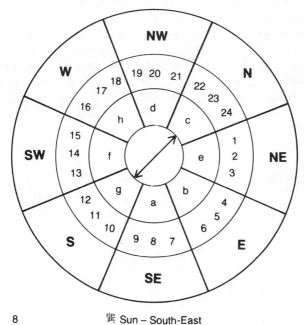

8   巽 Sun – South-East

Commentary 7
Twenty-Four Stellar Positions

Commentary to page 954

1 The reference in de Groot's text to 'other groups of stars' is a reference to *Feng Shui* Dial Plate Terms, which take their names from certain fixed stars, some regarded as having a benign influence, and others an unfavourable one. The position of these stars is affected by the orientation of the site, but the manner by which the stars are allocated to their places is extremely complex.

A list of twenty-four *Feng Shui* stars, and their positions for each of the eight orientations of a site, is given on page 171. The position of some Dial Plate Terms, however, is determined by the calendar; a representative list is given on pages 276-282 of the present author's *Chinese Astrology.* (See Bibliography).

2 In addition to the migration of the eight directional auspices, the change of orientation of a grave-site or building affects the location of another twenty-four geomantic 'stars'. These twenty-four stars always follow each other round the compass in regular order, but their initial positioning is determined as the result of complex reasoning based on the interaction of the two sequences of trigrams (the Former Heaven and the Later Heaven). For example, in the primary position, when the entrance faces southwards, due north is occupied by the first star in the following list, and due south by the thirteenth. But changing the orientation to south-west (a move of three points of the Chinese compass) does not, as might be imagined if the sequence of stars were to move three positions, bring either the tenth nor the sixteenth stars to the due south position, but the third star. The erratic progress of the stellar positions can be seen in the following table, which indicates the *Feng Shui* star occupying Chinese compass position 13 (due south), and the position it occupied in the primary (southern) orientation (North being 1).

THE STAR OCCUPYING THE SOUTH POSITION
FOR EACH ORIENTATION

Direction faced		Feng Shui Star	
South	13	Prosperity and wealth	*Wang Ts'ai*
South-west	3	Peace and happiness	*An lu*
West	9	Debauchery	*Ch'ang Yin*
North-west	16	Entering wealth	*Chin Ts'ai*
North	10	Relatives in marriage	*Ch'in Yin*
North-east	4	Land and dwelling	*T'ien Ch'ai*
East	22	Commencing a scroll	*Fa Chan*
South-east	11	Joyous pleasure	*Huan Lo*

THE TWENTY-FOUR STELLAR POSITIONS

1.	*Tien K'uang*	顛狂	Insanity
2.	*K'o She*	口舌	Mouth and tongue
3.	*An Lu*	安祿	Peace and happiness
4.	*T'ien Ch'ai*	田宅	Land and dwelling
5.	*K'u Ch'i*	哭泣	Weeping and wailing
6.	*Ku Kua*	孤寡	Orphan
7.	*Yung Fu*	榮福	Glory and prosperity
8.	*K'u Chüen*	苦絕	Sorrowful parting
9.	*Ch'ang Yin*	娼淫	Debauchery
10.	*Ch'in Yin*	親姻	Relatives in marriage
11.	*Huan Lo*	歡樂	Joyous pleasure
12.	*Pai Chüeh*	敗絕	Disruption
13.	*Wang Ts'ai*	旺財	Prosperity and wealth
14.	*Fu Teh*	福德	Happiness and virtue
15.	*Chi E*	疾厄	Sickness and distress
16.	*Chin Ts'ai*	進財	Entering wealth
17.	*Ch'ang Ping*	長病	Lengthy illness
18.	*Hsin Chao*	訴詔	Joyous proclamation
19.	*Kuan Wang*	官旺	Official of Prosperity
20.	*Kuan Kuei*	官貴	Official of Honours
21.	*P'o Ts'ai*	破財	Breaker of wealth
22.	*Fa Chan*	發展	Commencing a scroll
23.	*Yü Fu*	與福	Granting happiness
24.	*Fa Ch'ang*	法場	Execution ground

Chinese Charts of the Twenty-Four Stellar Positions

西四宅

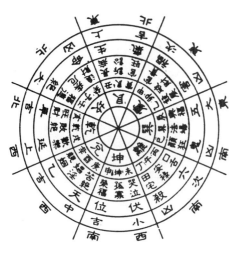

坤命八宅盤

South-west

艮命八宅盤

North-east

乾命八宅盤

North-west

兌命八宅盤

West

東四宅

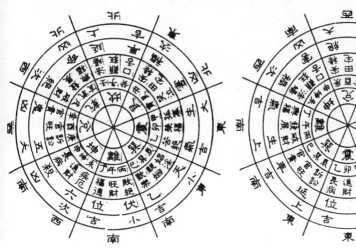

離命八宅盤

South

震命八宅盤

East

坎命八宅盤

North

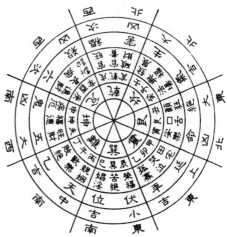

巽命八宅盤

South-east

Commentary 8
Magnetism

Commentary to page 967

In the commentary on the twenty-eight mansions, it is explained that the makers of geomantic compasses sometimes continued an established tradition of equating the positions of the lunar mansions in the outer-most ring of the *Lo P'an*, while other instruments took into account the shift in the heavens due to the precession of the equinoxes.

One very important aspect has vexed enquirers into the history of the magnetic compass, which is: 'Did the *Lo P'an* take into account the shift in the earth's magnetic field?'

When I enquired from professional geomancers in Kaohsiung, Taiwan, whether one should give greater attention to true north, or to magnetic north, the answer was unequivocal: the magnetic needle has to be observed, as it is this which is sensitive to *Feng Shui* currents. The celestial and terrestial correspondences shown on the *Lo P'an* Heaven Plate reveal the correlations between those forces on a universal scale, but for the site under examination, observations must be made of the prevailing magnetic field, including any local variations which might be present because of the geology of the region. Indeed, one of the geomancers used (and demonstrated, see Plate 5, p.212) a curious device known as a 'magnetic inductor' which, it was claimed, enhanced and so revealed the presence of secondary *Feng Shui* currents undetectable by the normal magnetic compass; I am afraid, however, that I am unable to vouch for the authenticity of its scientific foundation.

There does not appear to be any evidence of examples of *Lo P'an* being calibrated to take into account local or temporal variations in the earth's magnetic field which might have resulted in adjustments being made in order to accommodate the magnetic cardinal points with the more stable signposts of the celestial mansions. Until such examples have been found, and the relevant data examined, variations in the earth's magnetic field cannot be regarded as being a factor in the development of the *Lo P'an*.

SEAM AND CENTRAL NEEDLES

There is one other aspect of the *Lo P'an* which some writers have considered to be evidence that the Chinese were aware of fluctuations in the earth's magnetic field, in consequence, making adjustments to the calibration of the *Lo P'an* to compensate for the changes. (See Joseph

Needham, *Science and Civilisation in China*, Vol IV).

On all but the smallest examples of *Lo P'an*, the twenty-four compass points are repeated twice, one ring displaced $7\frac{1}{2}°$ clockwise, known as the 'seam needle' and the other $7\frac{1}{2}°$ anticlockwise, referred to somewhat incongruously as the 'middle needle.' The original ring from which the other two are derived is called the 'true needle'. It is said that the seam needle was introduced by Yang Yün Sung, inventor of the Kuangsi or Form School of *Feng Shui*, and that the middle needle was added later in the twelfth century by adherents of the Fukien Compass School. The twelfth century date agrees with the date pertaining to one of the versions of the *Lo P'an* calibrations, and it may well be that a new form of *Lo P'an* was introduced at this date. On the other hand, it does seem instinctive to presume that the Chinese predilection for symmetry would have led to both the seam and middle needles being introduced simultaneously.

The purpose of the seam and central needles is more prosaic and becomes immediately obvious when *Feng Shui* manuals, which frequently catalogue all the possible permutations of site and direction, are examined. Each of the twenty-four compass points is associated with one of the eight trigrams, and its stars, auspices, and *Lo Shu* numbers. Thus, although each Chinese compass direction occupies only 15° of the circle, its influence is manifested over 45°, the breadth of the corresponding trigram.

As a result of the interaction of overlapping directional influences with the introduction of associated *Feng Shui* forces such as the twenty-eight lunar mansions, or the twenty-four solar fortnights, secondary ripples of *Feng Shui* current are created, which are shown in the subsequent rings of larger models of the *Lo P'an*.

On the larger examples of *Lo P'an*, secondary rings attached to the compass rings are also repeated. These secondary rings depict the stems in regular sequence, the odd or *Yang* stems followed by five even or *Yin* stems. (In passing, it should be mentioned that the characters which de Groot speaks of are the stems 4 and 8, and 3 and 7; the 'occult reason' which de Groot supposes is behind the regular repetition of these four particular characters is simply convenience. To have inscribed all ten of the stems in the confined space available would have rendered them illegible.)

Each group of repeated rings is technically known as a 'plate' (*P'an*, as in *Lo P'an*).

The rings associated with the basic compass plate, or 'true' needle, are collectively known as the 'Earth Plate'; those with the 'middle' needle (the anticlockwise displacement) as the 'Mankind Plate'; and those attached to the clockwise displacement, or 'seam' needle, as the 'Heaven Plate.' Thus, the terms 'Earth Plate' and 'Heaven Plate' have two meanings: referring either to the lower and upper plates of the *Lo P'an* itself, or, in larger models of the instrument, to bands of two or three rings on the upper, circular plate of the *Lo P'an* itself.

Commentary 9
Twenty-Eight Lunar Mansions

Commentary to page 971

As in the west, Chinese astronomers identified the position of the Sun, Moon, and planets by reference to the constellation which was their backdrop.

Unlike astronomers in the west, however, the Chinese divided the celestial sphere into twenty-eight divisions, curiously and spectacularly irregular in size. The reason for the wide variation of these divisions (that of the largest being thirty-three times the width of the smallest, according to some authorities) is probably historical, due to the fact that the system of the twenty-eight 'lunar mansions' (as they are sometimes known) was not invented spontaneously, but was developed over several years, if not centuries.

One of the practical uses of the system of twenty-eight mansions was to determine the position of the Sun, and thus, primarily to enable corrections to be made to the calendar, and secondarily, for the calculation of eclipses. As stars cannot be seen during the day, the position of the Sun has to be inferred from the position of the Full Moon, which is always on the opposite side of the heavens to the Sun. Consequently, the time of the year could then be ascertained by reference to the twenty-four Solar Fortnights (see page 153), in turn associated with one of the twenty-four divisions of the Chinese compass (see page 180). This would be the original and practical purpose for the *Lo P'an* being inscribed with the twenty-eight mansions, as well as the twenty-four solar fortnights.

Adding to the difficulties created by the widths of the mansions being extremely irregular, is the imprecision of the boundaries of each division. Both in standard Chinese reference works, as well as actual examples of astronomical instruments there are discrepancies in the size and positioning of the twenty-eight lunar mansions. Variations can therefore be found in the alignment of the mansions with the twenty-four compass points, and also the number of degrees allotted to each mansion. Such discrepancies, however, are not due to inaccuracy on the part of Chinese practitioners, but rather, the converse, and is a direct result of the fact that *Feng Shui* is foremost an empirical science, involving considerable practical observation. Whereas the western astrologer no longer bothers to study the heavens, because professionally prepared ephemerides have a far greater precision than the amateur astronomer could hope to prepare, the Chinese geomancer customarily begins an assignment by taking careful measurements of distances and angles on site.

As a result of this need for daily observation and continuous systematic recording of terrestial and celestial data, the gradual misalignment of the mansions (due to the precession of the equinoxes) with landmarks having known compass directions would gradually have become apparent. It is likely, therefore, that certain influential and highly respected geomancers would adjust their instruments accordingly, while other traditionalists would prefer to use instruments calibrated to the system in which were trained. This is exactly what has happened, and today, manufacturers of geomantic instruments cater for the diverse philosophies by providing a range of Lo P'an calibrated to the different systems.

An examination of different examples of Lo P'an in my possession, and a comparison with the model illustrated by de Groot, reveals some interesting details. Each model stated the number of degrees occupied by each mansion, except in the cases of the very narrow mansions where there was insufficient space for this to be inscribed. Curiously, however, the stated number of degrees did not always tally with the actual number of degrees taken up by the division.

If a particular reference point of the Lo P'an compass is taken, and the corresponding point on the scale of lunar mansions measured, the variations in alignment can easily be demonstrated. If next, the theoretical alignment of the four cardinal points with the four central mansions of each group is compared with the examples of Lo P'an described below, an astonishing fact emerges. The differences between the theoretical correspondence, and the actual correspondence shown in the various Lo P'an models are 7°, 16°, and 24°. Taking the movement for the precession to be one degree every 71 years or so, then these variations represent periods of about 700, 1500, and 2150 years. These figures are highly significant. Allowing for the fact that a misreading or inaccurate marking of less than a degree represents fifty years, if the latest date is considered to be the mid-twentieth century, the calibrations of the other instruments correspond to AD1150, AD500 (the time of Wang Wei, reputed author of The Yellow Emperor's Classic of Dwellings), and 200BC, about the beginning of the former Han dynasty, the date ascribed to the divining board described on page 195.

One further remark: the Chinese formerly divided the circle into 365¼ degrees, one degree for every day of the Sun's progress through the heavens, thus revealing that their original interest in geometry lay in its application to astronomy or navigation. Old examples of the Lo P'an are measured in Chinese degrees, but modern versions including the five examples described here, adopt the standard 360° for convenience of reference. To add to the complexity, while the lunar mansions are reckoned in an anti-clockwise direction, the degrees themselves are numbered clockwise, beginning at the mid-point of 子, due-north.

COMPARISONS OF THE LUNAR MANSION DIVISIONS MARKED ON VARIOUS MODELS OF *LO P'AN*

The five *Lo P'an* described below comprise:

(a) The de Groot example, shown on page 189.

(b) An example from Kaohsiung known as the *San Yuan* (Three Primes) *Lo P'an*.

The *Lo P'an* is machine-made of enamelled brass, and sits in a resin Earth Plate.

(c) A second example from Kaohsiung, of similar construction, known as the *San Ho* (Three Harmonies) *Lo P'an* (see page 188).

(d) A wooden *Lo P'an* of unknown origin, but probably of recent manufacture, purchased in Hong Kong. All the divisions and lines have been marked by hand with a scribing tool, and all inscriptions written in ink. There are no division markings between the lunar mansions, however, and no significance should be attached to their inclusion, which are probably more decorative than practical.

(e) A modern *Lo P'an* from Fo Shan, purchased in Yang Chou in Kuangsi. This cheaply constructed *Lo P'an* is made of wood, covered with a printed paper and finished with a red-stained varnish, which soon flaked. Some markings have been added later in ink by hand.

TABLE SHOWING NUMBER OF DEGREES ALLOCATED TO EACH MANSION

The perimeters of each of the examples of *Lo P'an* are inscribed with the names of most of the twenty-eight mansions, together with their equatorial extensions (i.e., the number of degrees of the celestial circle which they occupy). But examination of the instruments shows that this number is not always the actual number of degrees shown on the instrument. In the following table, figures in brackets give the number of stated degrees, when these differ from the actual figure. Example (d) is curious in that there are degree markings, but no actual indications of where the mansions begin and end, while mansions 23 Ghosts, 24 Willow, and 25 Star, are missing altogether, particularly as the Star mansion is the celestial market for the south.

Example (e) is omitted as it is virtually identical to (b), apart from very minor differences of detail: the ninth mansion (Ox-boy) is allotted 8° of the circle, as the Kaohsiung example, but 7° are stated; conversely, while only 11° are claimed for mansion 21 (Orion), it actually extends for 12°. This discrepancy is balanced by the omission of the smallest mansion, 20, the Beak.

In example (f), the correspondence of the north cardinal mid-point 子 with the central point of the theoretically northernmost mansion, shown by divining boards of the Han dynasty (described in later paragraphs), has been included for comparison.

Lunar Mansion		Lo P'an			
		(a)	(b)	(c)	(d)
Eastern Quarter					
1.	*Ch'io* (Horn)	12 (13)	11	13 (12)	12
2.	*K'ang* (Neck)	9	11	9	9
3.	*Ti* (Base)	16	18	16	11
4.	*Fang* (Room)	6 (5)	5	6 (5)	5
5.	*Hsin* (Heart)	– (6)	8	6	6
6.	*Wei* (Tail)	18	15	18	18
7.	*Chi* (Basket)	9	9	9	9
Northern Quarter					
8.	*Tou* (Ladle)	22	24	22	22
9.	*Niu* (Ox-boy)	7	8	7	7
10.	*Nü* (Maiden)	11	11	11	11
11.	*Hsü* (Void)	9	10	9	9
12.	*Wei* (Rooftop)	16	20	17 (16)	16
13.	*Shih* (House)	18	16	18	18
14.	*Pi* (Wall)	9	13	9	9
Western Quarter					
15.	*K'uei* (Astride)	18	11	18	18
16.	*Lou* (Mound)	12	13	12	12
17.	*Wei* (Stomach)	15	12	15	15
18.	*Mao* (Pleiades)	11	9	11	12
19.	*Pi* (Net)	16	15	16	12
20.	*Tsui* (Beak)	– (1)	1	1	2
21.	*Shen* (Orion)	9	11	9	9
Southern Quarter					
22.	*Ching* (Well)	30	31	30	30
23.	*Kuei* (Ghosts)	3	5	3	. . .
24.	*Liu* (Willow)	14 (13)	17	13	. . . .
25.	*Hsing* (Star)	6	8	6	. . .
26.	*Chang* (Bow)	18 (17)	18	17	17
27.	*I* (Wings)	20	17	20	20
28.	*Chen* (Carriage)	19 (18)	13	19 (18)	18

The table below shows the alignment between the points of the compass, and reference points in the Ring of Lunar Mansions.

		Position of Due North 子	Chio 0°	Variation	Historical origin
de Groot	(a)	*Wei*, Rooftop 12 mansion 8°	133°	30°	AD1950
San Yuan	(b)	*Nü*, (Maiden) 10th mansion 4°	113°	10°	AD500
San Ho	(c)	*Wei*, (Rooftop) 12th mansion 0°	124°	21°	AD1150
Hong Kong	(d)	*Chen*, (Carriage Board) mansion 1°			
Div. Plate	(f)	*Hsü*, (Void) 11th mansion 4°	102°	0°	200BC

Commentary 10
The Compass Points

Commentary to page 965, last paragraph

The core of the *Lo P'an* is the compass ring, of twenty-four points. There is an essential difference between the western compass and the Chinese one, which de Groot misses. The western compass divides the four quadrants successively into two, producing thirty-two points, only eight of which coincide with the Chinese compass points: the four cardinal points, and their immediate sub-divisions, north-east, south-east, south-west, and north-west, which the Chinese conveniently call the four 'corners'. It is therefore inaccurate to try and identify the other Chinese points of the compass with western compass points, as de Groot does.

The composition of the Chinese compass can be seen in the diagram on page 181.

The Twelve Branches stand at the positions described on page 158, with 子 Tzu I, 卯 Mao IV, 午 Wu VII, and 酉 Yu X, at the cardinal points north, east, south, and west respectively.

The Branches, however, do not indicate the four 'corners', and these are represented by four of the eight trigrams.

For the remaining eight positions, the names of eight of the ten Stems are used. 1 and 2, associated with Wood, and therefore the east, stand either side of east; similarly 3 and 4, representing Fire, are allocated either side of the south point, 7 and 8, representing Metal, are placed in the vacant places alongside west, and 9 and 10, associated with Water and the north, occupy the appropriate positions. Stems 5 and 6, belong to the Earth, represented by the Centre, and therefore, not belonging to any direction, are therefore omitted. So goes the traditional explanation. A more prosaic reason may be that the character for Stem 5 is easily confused with that for Branch I, as are the characters for Stem 6 and Branch VI, and therefore these signs are omitted.

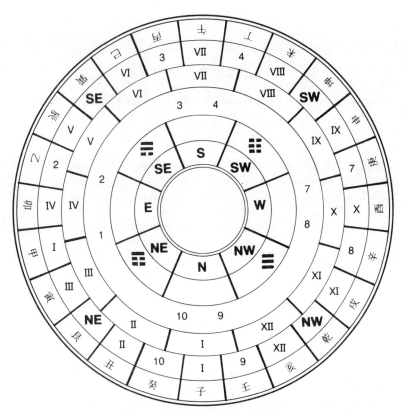

Evolution of the Lo P'an Rings
(1) The Basic Compass

Key to Diagram

From the centre:

Ring 1,   The Eight Directions
Ring 2,   Four of the Eight Trigrams
Ring 3,   Eight of the Ten Stems
Ring 4,   The Twelve Branches
Ring 5,   Composite of rings 2, 3 and 4
Ring 6,   As 5, in Chinese characters.

Commentary 11
The *Lo P'an* Rings

The *Lo P'an* has three functions: as a powerful talisman to ward off malignant spirits, as a table of correspondences between various aspects of Chinese philosophy, and as a compass to show the relationship of the twenty-four Chinese compass points with magnetic north. The *Lo P'an* appears in a number of sizes, and obviously, the talismanic power of the largest is regarded to be superior to that of the smaller versions. As a table of correspondences, the larger and more expensive instruments are able to indicate finer divisions of the compass ring; as a magnetic compass, however, the needle points south in the same direction no matter what the size of the *Lo P'an* is.

The following analysis of a large modern *Lo P'an* known as the Three Primes, serves as a useful reference point for comparison with the smaller *Lo P'an* illustrated by de Groot.

Two other analyses are also shown, one of a *Lo P'an* of thirty-three rings, which combines the functions of Three Primes and Three Harmonies (for an explanation of the fundamental difference, see page 178) and a much smaller *Lo P'an* with only five rings.

The Three Primes *Lo P'an* has thirty clearly defined rings, a few of which are compound, with more than one function. Those rings which appear on the de Groot *Lo P'an* will be described more fully in the appropriate commentaries. The remaining rings apply to other divination systems.

0. The central magnetic compass housing is known as the 'Heaven Pool.' A line is engraved on the base of the Heaven Pool, so that the upper plate of the *Lo P'an* may be turned and adjusted until the magnetic needle corresponds with the base line. The *Lo P'an* is rotated so that the needle points southwards – not northwards as in western compasses.

1. The Eight Trigrams in the Former Heaven Sequence.

This is actually a compound ring of three rings in one, comprising (a) the Eight Trigrams, (b) Stems or Branches associated with them, and (c) numbers from the *Lo Shu*.

In this example, the eight trigrams are inscribed as diagrams of three lines, but on some examples of *Lo P'an*, such as the de Groot example, the names of the trigrams are given instead.

The *Lo Shu* numbers are here given as Chinese numerals, but frequently the numbers are shown as groups of dots, joined by lines in the manner of constellation patterns. (The figure 1 being represented as one dot, with a curling line at each side.)

2. Earthly Branches matched with the Twelve Spirits.

3. Positions of the Twenty-four Heavenly Path Stars.

4. Nine Stars of Divination (The 'Greedy Wolf' sequence; see page 190ff).

5. Robber of Glory Curse.

6. Correct Needle (Earth Plate) Twenty-four directions. (The basic twenty-four directions; see page 181.)

7. Twenty-four Heavenly Stars.

8. Three Primes Water Shapes Dragon Gate in Eight Positions (for evaluating the auspices of Water Dragons, or water confluence patterns. See page 206.)

9. Piercing Mountains Seventy-two Dragons (for evaluating the auspices of contours of the horizon.)

10. Correct Needle, 120 *fen chin* (sub-divisions). (Alternate divisions marked by sexagenary numbers.)

11. Great Yang Enumeration of Directions of the Twenty-four Solar Fortnights, Favourable Palaces, Opposing Degrees (see page 153).

12. Twenty-four directions (Middle Needle or Mankind Plate) (see page 175.)

13. Twenty-four Solar Fortnights Great Yang Enumeration of Directions of Opposing Palaces and Favourable Degrees (references as rings 11 and 12.)

14. Former Heaven Sequence Sixty-four positions of Trigram Star Cycle Numbers (based on the *Lo Shu*.)

15. The above numbers revealed as the corresponding Trigrams.

16. The names of the Sixty-four Hexagrams, the upper three lines of the hexagram corresponding to the trigram above.

17. Hexagram cycle numbers. (The numbers do not refer to the corres-

ponding lower trigram, as might be expected from rings 14 and 15, but are the *Lo Shu* numbers for the whole hexagram.)

18. The Nine 'Greedy Wolf' Hexagram Stars. Positions of the Greedy Wolf stars determined by the 64 hexagrams. See page 181.

19. Father, Mother, Sons and Posterity matched with the Hexagrams, Five Elements, and *Lo Shu* numbers. A compound ring, comprising the Hexagram on the right, the element upper left, and the *Lo Shu* number lower left.

20. Three Primes, Third Plate Symbols
Divisions giving positions for Mother, Father, Heaven's Prime, Earth's Prime, and Mankind's Prime.

21. South-North Third Plate Symbols
Regions favourable for each particular direction, given as north, south (or other directions) of the Yangtse river.

22. Former Heaven Sequence Sixty-four Hexagram lines, in fortunate sequence, showing Star Rotation Numbers.

23. Heaven's Degrees, Lucky and Unlucky Spaces for the Avoidance of Errors. (That is, for greater accuracy. The auspices for each degree have been calculated on the basis of the direction, the associated lunar mansion, and other factors. See page 179.)

24. Former, Heaven Sequence Sixty-four Trigrams Uniting the Site and Subduing Correspondence. The divisions contain the Stem and Branch numbers pertaining to the hexagram in ring 16.

25. Twenty-four directions of the Heaven Plate or Seam Needle. The twenty-four Seam Needle compass points (see page 175) with associated Stem and Branch pairs.

26. Celestial Degrees, First Stem and Branch, Five Elements. Each division contains a stem in the sequence 1, 3, 5, 7, 9, 2, 4, 6, 8, 10 which is understood to be combined with a branch in the sexagenary sequence. The element in the compartment is the one associated with the Stem and Branch combination.

27. The Degrees of the Twenty-eight Lunar Mansions. (See page 179ff for the reference to this and the remaining rings.)

28. The Elements associated with each degree of the Twenty-eight Lunar Mansions.

Proceeding anti-clockwise, the degrees are given in western numerals.

29. The Twenty-eight Lunar Mansions
Together with their extensions in degrees, and the elements associated with each constellation.

30. Degrees of the Circle.

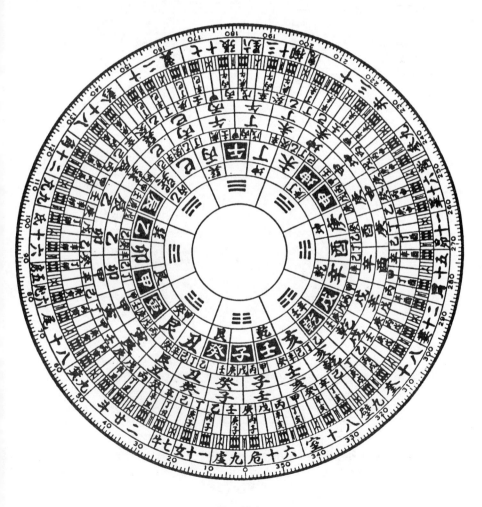

'San Ho'
'Three Harmonies' *Lo P'an*

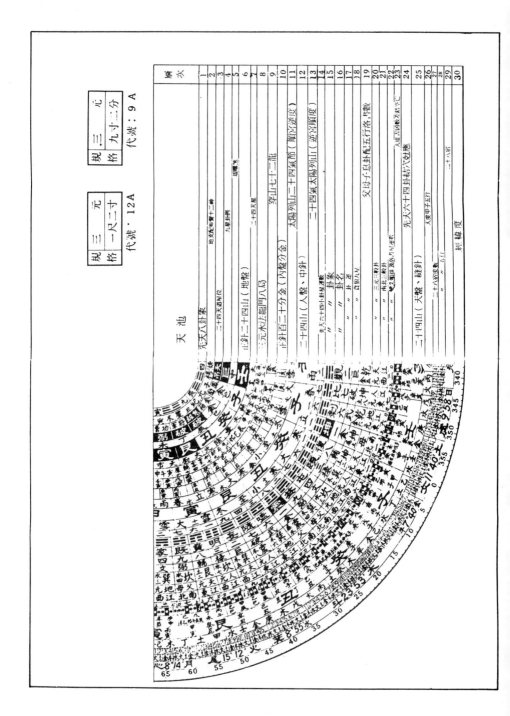

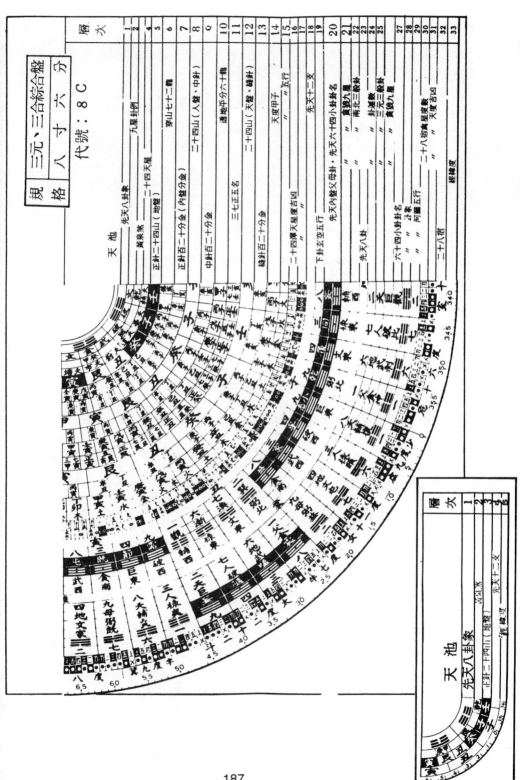

層次		
1	先天八卦象	天池
2		
4	九星卦例	
5	二十四天星	黃泉煞
6	正針二十四山（地盤）	
7	穿山七十二龍	正針百二十分金（內盤分金）
8	二十四山（人盤‧中針）	中針百二十分金
9		
10	透地平分六十龍	三七正五名
11	二十四山（天盤‧縫針）	
12		縫針百二十分金
13		
14	天度甲子	二十四禪天星度吉凶
15	" 五行	
16		
17		
18	先天六十四爻	下卦玄空五行
19		
20	先天內盤父母卦‧先天六十四小卦卦名	先天八卦
21	黃泉九星	
22	" 南北三般卦	
23	" 卦運數	六十四小卦卦名
24	" 三元三般卦	計數
25	" 黃泉九星	河圖五行
27		二十八宿貪狼度數
28	二十八宿	天度吉凶
29		
30		
31	經緯度	
32		
33		

規格　三元、三合綜合盤
　　　八　寸　六　分
代號：8 C

層次		
1	先天八卦象	天池
2		
3	黃泉煞	
4	正針二十四山（地盤）	
5	先天十二爻	羅經度

RINGS OF THE *LO P'AN* ILLUSTRATED BY DE GROOT

Ring numbers in brackets refer to the rings described in the Three Primes *Lo P'an.*

0. Heaven Pool (Ring 0 as above).

1. Chinese characters for the Eight Trigrams in the Former Heaven Sequence (Ring 1).

2. Stems and branches allocated to the twenty-four compass points, in an irregular sequence. This is possibly due to artistic licence, as a number of inconsistencies have been noticed. See the reference to Ring 8, below.

3. The twenty-four compass points in the Correct Sequence (Ring 6).

4. Stems associated with the compass points, the Branches being understood.

5. *Feng Shui* elements associated with the Correct Sequence.

6. The twenty-four compass points in the Middle or Mankind Sequence (Ring 12).

7. Stems associated with the Middle Sequence.

8. The twenty-four compass points in the Earth or Seam Needle Sequence (Ring 25). De Groot's text says that the *Lo P'an*'s eighth ring lists the twenty-four seasons, which is an important function of the instrument. (See page 153). The fact that de Groot specifically mentions this, but that the illustration does not, suggests that de Groot's unknown artist did not make an accurate representation of the compass in de Groot's possession.

9. Stems associated elements with the Seam Needle Sequence (Ring 26).

10. A further sequence of stems.

11. The sixty Stems and Branches, in a repeated pattern.

12. The five elements, in sixty-one sectors of unequal breadth, the products of calculations based upon the element of the direction and the element of the associated lunar mansion. See page 179. There is no corresponding ring on the Three Primes compass, although the twenty-eight mansions ring (29) has the associated element which the de Groot compass does not.

13. Finer divisions showing lucky and unlucky degrees (Ring 23).

14. Another enumeration of lucky and unlucky degrees.

15. The twenty-eight lunar mansions (Ring 29, but without their associated elements) .

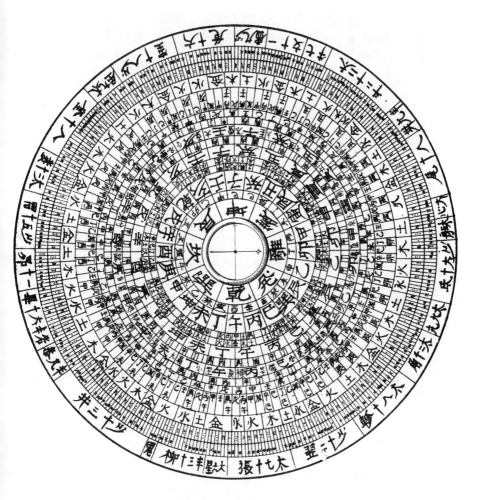

A Geomancer's Compass.

Commentary 12
Nine Stars of the Greedy Wolf

Commentary to page 956

The five basic element shapes described on page [956], and illustrated again on page 192 are not the only shapes which are recognised in *Feng Shui*. There is a further series of compound shapes associated with the Eight Directions (see the paragraphs on the Nine Stars, page 165), while from the traditions and theories of the Form School of *Feng Shui*, shapes of mountains which resemble objects, animals, plants or even Chinese characters are considered to be omens of good or unfavourable import. De Groot makes a number of references to such *Feng Shui* shapes, (see, for example, the anecdotes related on pages [977ff].) Examples of additional Form School shapes are illustrated on page 193.

NINE STARS OF THE GREEDY WOLF

The Nine Stars of the Greedy Wolf figure prominently in the writings of both the Compass School and Form School theorists. The natural contours of the terrain are classified into nine basic shapes, supposedly named after the seven stars of the Plough (known to the Chinese as the Northern Ladle) plus two other stars which are the markers for the Pole Star.

The names of the topographic shapes, (illustrated on page 193), are frequently known as the Greedy Wolf Stars, as the Greedy Wolf is usually given as the first of the series. In the list below, however, a different order is used, as this helps to reveal the pattern behind their movement in *Feng Shui* calculations.

NAMES OF THE NINE STELLAR GENII

(a)	*Tso Fu*	左輔	Left Supporter
(b)	*P'o Chün*	破軍	Destroyer of Armies
(c)	*T'an Lang*	貪狼	Greedy Wolf
(d)	*Lu Ts'un*	祿存	Preserver of Rank
(e)	*Wu Ch'u*	武曲	Military Pursuits
(f)	*Lien Chen*	廉眞	Purity and Truth
(g)	*Chü Men*	巨門	Officer of the Gate
(h)	*Wen Ch'u*	文曲	Literary Pursuits
	Yu Pi	右弼	Right Supporter

(The Right Supporter does not figure in the calculation of the star positions, as it represents an expanse of water, and cannot therefore function as a site.)

In passing, it should be mentioned that these particular stars have a much more significant role in the symbolism of Chinese astrology than any of the fixed stars have in western astrology. One of the reasons is the important function of the Northern Ladle in acting as a celestial signpost, for its handle (or tail) points, via the extremely bright star Arcturus, to the first lunar mansion, Chio. As it happens, however, Chinese astronomical charts do not use the *Feng Shui* names for any of the nine stars, nor are these names to be found in the famous astronomical treatise by Ssu Ma Ch'ien, writing in the second to first centuries BC. Though they are certainly ancient, they are not so much the names of particular stars, as the names of genii believed to inhabit those celestial realms.

When a *Feng Shui* site is ideal, the Nine Stars will be in their appropriate positions, depending on the orientation of the site; these are shown on the table below.

POSITION OF STAR

Orientation of Site

	S	SE	SW	W	NW	NE	N	E
S	a	b	c	d	e	f	g	h
SE	b	a	d	c	f	e	h	g
SW	c	d	a	b	g	h	e	f
W	d	c	b	a	h	g	f	e
NW	e	f	g	h	a	b	c	d
NE	f	e	h	g	b	a	d	c
N	g	h	e	f	c	d	a	b
E	h	g	f	e	d	c	b	a

The geomancer, having found a promontory corresponding to one of the basic shapes, then aligns the *Lo P'an* to see what the auspices are for the remaining stars in their respective positions, by reference to the Nine Star ring of the instrument.

Nine Stars of the Greedy Wolf, South Position

Five Element Shapes

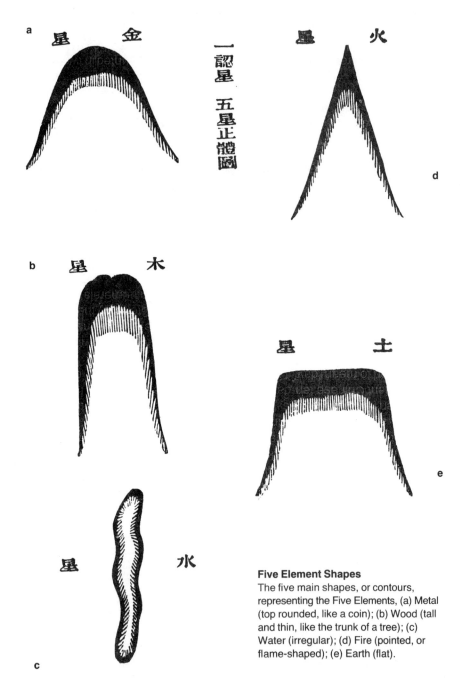

Five Element Shapes
The five main shapes, or contours,
representing the Five Elements, (a) Metal
(top rounded, like a coin); (b) Wood (tall
and thin, like the trunk of a tree); (c)
Water (irregular); (d) Fire (pointed, or
flame-shaped); (e) Earth (flat).

Pure Patterns

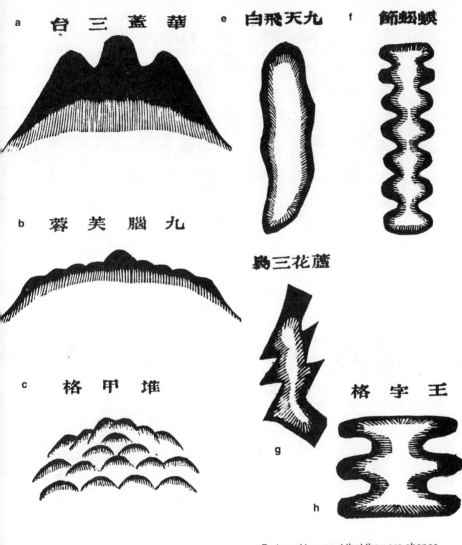

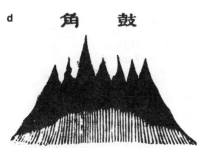

By 'pure' is meant that they are shapes, purely and simply, and have no other astrological or geomantic symbolism.

(a) Flowery Cover of Three Terraces; (b) Nine Fairy Flower Heads; (c) Overlapping Scales; (d) Drum of Points; (e) Nine Heavens Flying White (a brush stroke); (f) Jointed Centipede; (g) Three Spikes of Bullrush Flowers; (h) King Pattern (the Chinese character 王 means 'king').

Nine Star Varied Forms

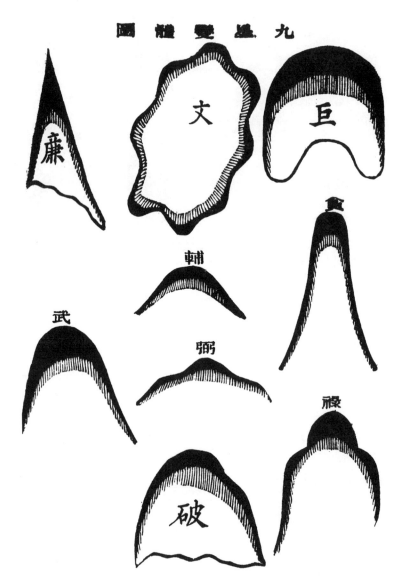

Contour shapes of the Nine Star or Greedy Wolf System.

Top row, left to right: Purity and Truth; Literary Pursuits; Officer of the Gate.

Second row: (centre) Left Supporter; (right) Greedy Wolf.

Third row: (left) Military Pursuits;

(centre) Right Supporter.

Bottom row: (centre) Destroyer of Armies; (right) Preserver of Rank.

The shapes of these contour forms should be compared with those of the Five Element shapes on page 192.

Commentary 13
The Han Divining Board

Recent archaeological discoveries have produced startling evidence for the antiquity of *Feng Shui*. The illustrations overleaf show how the 'star boards' were the direct ancestors of the *Lo P'an*.

(a) The layout of signs on a divining board in the National Museum of History, Pekin, and authenticated as being from the Former Han dynasty, ca. second century BC. Note that the four cardinal points 子, 卯, 午, 酉 (Branches I. IV, VII, X) are aligned with lunar mansions 11, 4, 25, and 18 respectively). The Trigrams, however, do not appear on this early example of the instrument, but there are four 'Gates' at the diagonals: Heaven, Earth, Ghosts and Mankind. Stems 5 and 6, being the two stems associated with Earth and the Centre, are also inscribed on these paths.

(b) Key to the characters on the Han Dynasty Divining Board.
The figures 1 to 28 round the perimeter indicate the positions of the twenty-eight lunar mansions. Elsewhere, the figures 1 to 10 represent the Ten Stems, and roman numerals I to XII the Twelve Branches.

(c) Copy of a diagram from *The Yellow Emperor's Classic of Dwellings* reputedly by Wang Wei, of the fifth century.
This is an intriguing diagram from an early text on geomancy. The diagram is actually a table showing the auspices associated with certain directions. The similarities between this diagram and the Han divining plate are astonishing. As in the divining board, only twenty of the compass points are given, the four corners being omitted and replaced by three of the four 'gates.' The fourth direction, south-east, however, replaces the character for gate with the character for 'window', which presents an intriguing theory. The characters for 'corpse' and 'window' are similar: the latter character has an extra stroke which might have been added at some later date in error, to complement 'door' with 'window'. But it may be that its original meaning referred to a ritual association with the direction of travel when a corpse was being taken for burial.
Added to the four corner paths are indications of harmonious months and days; the diagram reveals for example, that the north-east direction is compatible with the eighth month, and days bearing the stems 1 and 6. Exceptionally, at the south-west path, the character for 'Dragon' appears, a word which has considerable *Feng Shui* application.
Radiating vertically and horizontally from each of the points of the compass plate are characters indicating the auspices for each direction. The names of some of these are virtually identical to the list on page 171.

Chinese Geomancy

(a)

(b)

Han Divining Board

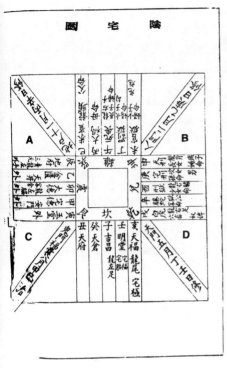 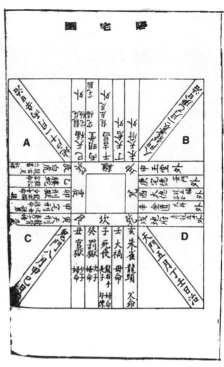

(c)   **Yin Dwelling**   **Yang Dwelling**   (d)

Key to Illustration.

**left hand illustration: Yin Dwelling;
right hand illustration: Yang Dwelling.**

A. Earth's Window
Tenth Month
Days 3 and 8
harmonious

B. Mankind's Gate
Second Month
Days 2 and 7
harmonious

C. Ghosts' Gate
Eighth Month
Days 1 and 6
harmonious

D. Heaven's Gate
Fifth Month
Days 4 and 9
harmonious

Commentary 14
Divining Sticks

Commentary to page 992

The idealised nineteenth-century portrait of Wu Wang of the Chou dynasty shows diviners consulting the stalks and the tortoise plastron (the undershell, rather than the carapace). A hundred years ago, diviners may have been expected to consult the *I Ching* in the correct manner by casting yarrow stalks. Today, however, evidence that the hexagrams are read by the formal method of counting out bundles of sticks is rare indeed. Most diviners consulting the hexagrams will use either three coins (an irregular method), the date of birth, or some other factor, such as counting the number of strokes in the characters formulating the question being put to the oracle. At the Lung Shan Temple in Taipei, diviners even used grains of rice to elicit the hexagram response.

In fact, both the illustration of the diviners on the left of the picture, and the narrative quoted by de Groot, though in some respects tallying with the virtually sacred ritual of manipulating the yarrow stalks, are much more likely to be a description of the widespread divination practice of *Ling Chi*.

There are usually two stages to the operation, and the procedure itself has many variations, though the principle and the end result remain the same. In general, a cylinder of numbered bamboo slips is shaken until one falls to the ground. The number of the slip is noted, a paper with the corresponding number is taken from another functionary, and finally the paper is taken to a diviner for interpretation. But there is often a secondary process known as the *Chiao Pai*, a form of divination of extreme antiquity. In this, two curved blocks of wood are thrown to the ground, and a yes-no response obtained. In Hong Kong, for example, the procedure is to consult the *Chiao Pai* in order to get a favourable response before moving on to the *Ling Chi*. At the Lung Shan Temple, however, the stalks were much larger, too big to be thrown, and there the petitioners first took a rod from a large vase-like receptacle, and then threw the *Chiao Pai* to ascertain whether the chosen rod was the correct one.

Wu Wang
[1st Ruler of Chou Dynasty]

Commentary 15
Talismans

When it is impracticable to remedy adverse *Feng Shui* in the manner deemed to be most efficacious, the final recourse is to the use of mystical charms and talismans, known as *Fu* 符 .

It is unusual for the geomancer not to take leave of his client without first handing over a sealed envelope containing a talisman. In the case of *Yang* dwellings, this might be placed under the floor boards, or perhaps attached to a roof beam, depending on the nature or purpose of the talisman; the geomancer would certainly advise on its purpose. In one case known to me, the manager of a commercial premises in mainland China was given a packet, which by its feel contained knotted string, and possibly some herbs, which he was asked to carry about his person at all times, in order to ensure the success of his business. This, however, was an exceptional circumstance, the manager having requested help in pursuing his own career.

Talismans may be of metal, wood, or other materials, peachwood again being the favoured medium. They are usually of mysterious designs, often incorporating the Eight Trigrams, and highly fanciful calligraphy representing the characters for spirits, demons, long life, happiness, and good fortune. If the *Feng Shui* manuals aver that a particular siting of a tomb will bring the evil spirits of the god of smallpox, for example, the talisman will be one which frightens away the smallpox demon. Talismans made by the geomancer for a particular client may be written in a special ink, and preferably with a pen made of peachwood, since this tree is regarded as sacred to the Queen Mother of the West, one of the more ancient and revered deities in the Taoist pantheon. Talismans are often associated with the Stem and Branch cycles, and may be prepared or burnt on the days which correspond to their purpose.

But printed paper talismans are universal. Tens, if not hundreds, of millions of paper talismans are printed annually, and bought daily by the sheaf, in every town and city throughout South-East Asia, to ensure the continuing favours of ancestors and supernatural agencies.

In the case of charms for *Yin* dwellings, their efficacy is rendered potent in the same way. Offering of paper clothes and 'hell money' are made to the dead, by being ceremoniously burnt. There may be special instructions regarding the time and manner of the burning, although all temples have sacrificial cauldrons or furnaces for burnt offerings.

符方東　　　符岳東　　　符年子

Talisman for the
Eastern Direction

Hostile
Eastern Direction
Talisman

Talisman for
Branch 1
or 'Rat' Years

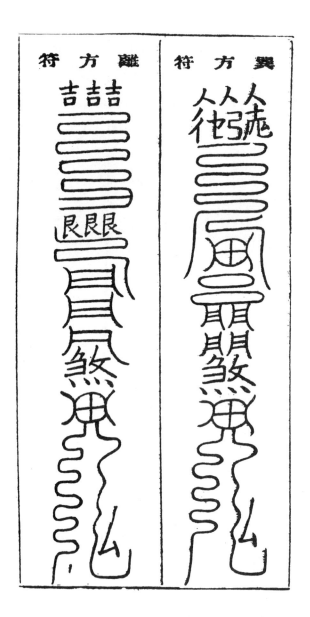

Talismans for the directions Li (South) and Sun (South-East)

Supplement
Examples of Feng Shui Charts

The following charts are actual examples of Feng Shui maps. They reveal the conventions by which hills, watercourses, obstacles and other significant details are indicated. One of the charts has been keyed for closer study.

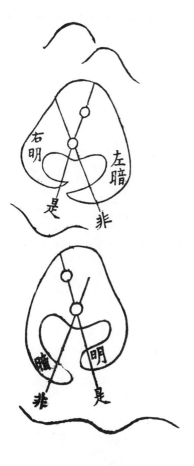

Left and Right Observations

(a) Right-hand side, bright
Left-hand side, dark.
Right observation line positive,
Left observation line negative

(b) Left-hand side, bright,
Right-hand side, dark
Right observation line negative
Left observation line positive

Diagram showing positive and negative alignments of a grave-site, from 'Appendix Clarifying the Burial Classics.' (*Imperial Encyclopaedia*, Section XVII, part 670.)

Feng Shui plans for grave-sites, taken from *Feng Shui Pao Tien*, A Treasury of *Feng Shui* Documents.

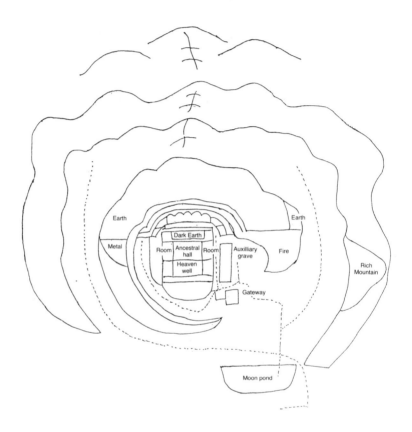

'Ken' Direction Site
(North East)

'Chia' Direction Site (East)

Earth
Depression
Approaching spur, wood
Earth
Room
Ancestral hall
Room
Auxilliary graves
Heaven well
Auxilliary graves
Bright hall
Pond

'Jen' Direction Site (North)

Ruined graveyard
Left and Right markers of 9 stars
Earth
Wood
Metal
Earth
Dark Earth
Wood upright Heaven well
Chief Ancestor well pound
Metal
Forecourt of Ancestors
Metal
Secondary court
Bright moon pond
Gateway

Diagrams of Water Dragons

Diagrams showing orientation of sites, and positions of Water Dragons, in order to ascertain their auspices, taken from *Feng Shui Ti Li Ju Men*, based on sources in the Water Dragon Classic and elsewhere. 156 permutations of orientation and water direction are catalogued, with twelve water locations for each branch orientation, as well as a dozen principal subdivisions.

The two contrasting orientations shown here are both south facing, but with the water located at different points of the compass. These particular orientations have been selected since they appear to be cases of prominence: they have been dignified by special titles, whereas most of the examples are unnamed.

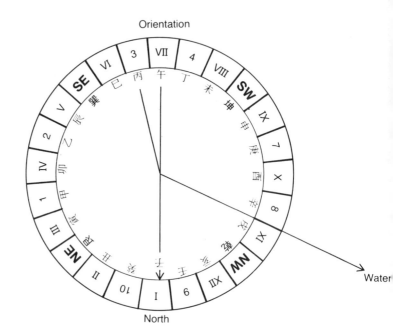

Link of Pearls

[Stem] 9 direction, [Stem] 3 facing; [Branch] I direction, [Branch] VII facing.
Water on the left, flowing to the right.
Water flows out from, that is to say, the water's mouth is in, the directions from [Stem] 8 to [Branch] XI.

This is called the Three Harmonies Link of Pearls. It brings riches and honour. Such a person will have abundance of glory, be honest, loyal and virtuous, while sons and daughters will be exalted in rank and have long life. Every house, those too of kindred, will achieve success in whatever undertaking is begun, and the favourable auspices will last for a long time thereafter.

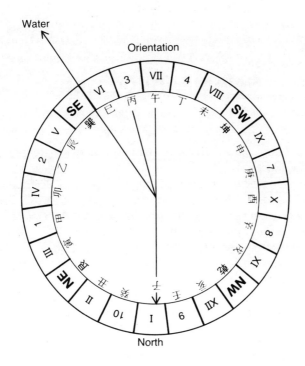

Yellow Fountain Curse

[Orientation as before.]

Water leaves through the directions [trigram] Sun and [Branch] VI.

All is destruction, the end of plans, loss of sons. It also shows infirmity in the legs, paralysis, consumption, vomiting blood, and disease, and accidents in childhood.

Hearing will be clear.

Sons will marry late, and take very young wives.

Select Bibliography

Edkins, J. *Feng Shui*. 'Chinese Recorder and Missionary Journal.' Foochow, March, 1872.

Eitel, E. J. *Feng Shui*, or the Rudiments of Natural Science in China. Trubner, London, 1873. Reprinted 1979, Pentacle Books, Bristol.

Feuchtwang, Stephan D. R. *An Anthropological Analysis of Chinese Geomancy*. Vithagna, Vientiane, 1974.

Kalinowsky, Marc. 'Les Instruments astrocalendriques des Han et la méthode Liu Jen.' *Bulletin de l'Ecole Française d'Extrême Orient*, Paris, 1983.

Loewe, M. *Ways to Paradise*. George Allen and Unwin, London, 1979.

Needham, J. *Science and Civilisation in China.*(In particular, Volume 2, History of Scientific Thought, and Volume 4 Tome I, Physics.) Cambridge University Press.

Savidge, Joyce. *This is Hong Kong – Temples*. Hong Kong Government, 1977.

Sherrill, W. A. and Chu, W. K. *An Anthology of I Ching*. Routledge Kegan Paul, London, 1977.

Walters, D. *Feng Shui*, Pagoda, London, (also Simon Shuster, New York) 1988.

Walters, D. *Chinese Astrology*. Aquarian Press, Wellingborough, 1986.

Chinese sources

Most of the original sources of *Feng Shui* theory were collated into the Imperial Encyclopaedia of 1726, *Ku Chin T'u Shu Chi Ch'eng*, of which there are now several reprints and editions; access to a copy of this monumental work is now generally available to researchers through the Chinese departments of most universities. The following standard classics on *Feng Shui* appear in section XVII, subsection *Kan Yü* (Geomancy). The numbers in brackets refer to the number of the *Chüan*, or volume number, in the original edition.

Ku Chin T'u Shu Chi Ch'eng, Section XVII, *Kan Yü* Geomancy.

[651]   *Huang Ti Chai Ching*
The Yellow Emperor Classic of Dwellings (5th century).

[652–654]   *Ch'ing Nang Hai Chio Ching*
Book of the Sea Angles of the Blue Bag. (The fourth book, Hsüeh Fa, concerns rules for finding a desirable site.)

[655]   *Ch'ing Wu Hsien Sheng Tsang Ching*
Venerable Master Blue Raven's Canon of Burial
[656–664]   *Kuan Shih Ti Li Chih Meng*
Geomantic Opinions of Kuan the Sage (3rd century?)
[665]   *Kuo P'o Ku Pen Tsang Ching*
The Canon of Burials of Kuo P'o (4th century)
[666]   *Yang Yün Sung Shih Erh Chang Fa*
The Twelve Rod Patterns of Yang Yün Sung (9th century)
[667]   *Liao Yü Shih Lu Tsang Fa*
The Sixteen Grave Patterns of Liao Yü.
[668]   *K'ung Shih Ch'ang Chi Wu Hsing Chuo Mo Cheng Pien Ming T'u*
The K'ung Shih Ch'ang Ch'i Five Star Method for identifying Dragon
   Veins Clearly Illustrated.
[669]   *Liu Chi Kan Yü*
Liu Ch'i's notes on Geomancy.
[670]   *Miu Hsi Yung Tsang Ching I*
Appendix Clarifying the Burial Classics
[671–674]   *Shui Lung Ching*
The Water Dragon Classic
[675–677]   *Yang Chai Shih Shu*
Ten Books on Dwellings for the Living
[678]   *Yang Chai Shih Shu Fu*
Talismans.

Twentieth century works in Chinese

There are probably more bookshops per head of population in Taipei than in any other capital city of the world, and most of them have several bookshelves packed tight with tomes on every aspect of geomancy, whether reprints of classic sources, or interpretations by modern writers. Add to this the books published in Hong Kong, Singapore, and China, and it soon becomes apparent that a bibliography of several dozen pages would be needed to index the Chinese books on *Feng Shui* currently available. The selection below is offered as a useful token list.

Feng Shui Mi Chi 風水秘笈
The Secret Portfolio of *Feng Shui*.
Hsi Pei Publishing, Tainan.

Feng Shui Pao Tien. Lin Hsien Ho. 風水寶典
A Treasury of *Feng Shui* Documents
Wen Lin Publishing, Taichung.

Feng Shui Ti Li Ju Men 風水地理入門
Introduction to *Feng Shui* and Geomancy.
Hsi Pei Publishing, Tainan.

Feng Shui Ti Li Mi Chüeh 風水地理秘訣
Mysterious Secrets of *Feng Shui* and Geomancy.
Hsi Pei Publishing, Tainan.

Lo P'an Shou Ts'e Kan Cheng-Hung. 羅盤手册
Handbook to the *Lo P'an*.
Ta Ch'ien Shih Publishing, Tainan.

Lo Ching T'ou Chiai 羅經透解
The *Lo P'an* Explained.
Wu Wang Kang, (Ming Dynasty), reprinted with
additional illustrations. Chan Wing Tai Book Co.,
Kowloon.

Plate 2.   Typical Chinese Grave
Showing two masonry walls, with a bank of earth between.

Plate 3   Dragon and Phoenix
The Phoenix is often preferred to the (Feng Shui) Tiger in grave ornamentation, as the latter animal is believed to devour the souls of the deceased.

Plate 4.   Setting up the Lo P'an
The red 'Earth Plate' can be clearly seen in this demonstration of the alignment of the Lo P'an.

Plate 5.   The Magnetic Inductor
A modern geomantic instrument for the detection of Feng Shui Currents.

Index

Abbreviations following Chinese expressions and proper names indicate: **b**–title of book; **n**–person's name; **p**–place name; **t**–technical term.